TRANSPORT **VG**

BRITISH RAILWAYS
LOCOMOTIVE
ALLOCATIONS
1948 - 1968

PART ONE :

Western Region (ex Great Western
Railway) Numbers 1 - 9799

Jim Grindlay

To my wife Elspeth, for her unwavering
support and encouragement

First Edition   *November 2006*
Reprinted   *January 2007*
2nd Reprint   *August 2007*
3rd Reprint   *December 2007*

Published by TRANSPORT PUBLISHING LTD,
31 Crown Street, Ayr, KA8 8AG
www.transportpublishing.com

Text printed in Scotland by TRANSPORT PUBLISHING LTD.,
31 Crown Street, Ayr, KA8 8AG
Tel +44 (0)1292 289770

Bookbinding & Sewing by Downie Allison Downie Bookbinders Ltd.,
Unit H, Purdon Street, Partick, Glasgow G11 6AF, Scotland
Tel. +44 (0)141 339 0333
www.dadbookbinders.com

ISBN 13   978 0 9544264 1 5

Grateful thanks are given to STEVE DAVIES for his assistance in illustrating this book.

BRITISH RAILWAYS LOCOMOTIVES 1948 - 1968

PART ONE : Western Region (ex G.W.R.)
Numbers 1 - 9799

Aimed at Railway Enthusiasts, Historians & Modellers, the purpose of this series of books is to list every locomotive acquired and built by British Railways, and to show where they were allocated.

Alongside each locomotive in Part One are the shed allocations for the years 1948, 1952, 1955, 1959, 1963, & December 1965. (Steam was abolished on the Western Region 31/12/65).

Details are also given of the thirteen 57xx Pannier Tanks which passed to London Transport, and also included is 3440 'City of Truro', which, uniquely amongst the Preserved locos working on B.R., was included in Capital Stock, being used on normal service trains.

JIM GRINDLAY
Ayr, Scotland

October 2006

Introduction to Part One

Whereas all other pre - group companies disappeared in 1923, and the other three of the 'big four' pre - nationalisation companies disappeared in 1948, the G.W.R. continued its separate identity until the end of steam in 1968 - an unbroken run of over 130 years!

At the Grouping it was business as usual. in 1923 the Great Western was a huge company which had already absorbed some small Welsh companies, and completed the process at Grouping. It was geographically well placed, and had excellent infrastructure and rolling stock.

Ever since the days of William Dean there had been a high degree of standardisation in locomotive and rolling stock design. This was perpetuated and increased by Churchward and Collett, and every locomotive design was related to every other - the family resemblance between an Edwardian 2-6-2T and a Hawksworth 0-6-0PT of nearly fifty years later was striking. Standard tenders, standard boilers, standard fittings, and standard wheel diameters all made for economies of scale, reduced maintenance costs and times out of service, and easier replacement of worn components. The 'Dukedogs' are an example of this ; two loco classes were made into one new one by combining the frames and wheels of one with the boilers of another. This was easily achieved because of the standardisation mentioned above. The absorbed locomotives from the various Welsh companies were very quickly 'Westernised' with standard G.W. fittings, not the least of which was fitting standard taper boilers to the majority of them. Even the R.O.D. 2-8-0s, which were originally a Great Central design, were given the indelible stamp of the Great Western in no time at all!

Come Nationalisation it was *still* business as usual. The Great Western locos were all fitted with brass or cast iron number plates on the cab sides, whereas the other three companies had painted numbers. Since the locos of three companies would have to be renumbered to create a new number series with no duplication, it was more cost effective to leave the cast metal plates on the ex - G.W.R. locos and to renumber the rest with transfers. New locos to G.W. design built after Nationalisation were still fitted with cast plates, and as late as 1959 two London area 57xx pannier tanks still had 'GREAT WESTERN' on the tank sides - eleven years after Nationalisation!

There is no doubt that the 'GREAT' in 'Great Western' is thoroughly deserved. The first 4-6-2 in Britain, the first loco recorded running at over 100mph, the excellent and pioneering 4-6-0s, the unique, but eminently sensible Pannier Tanks (much easier maintenance than more conventional saddle tanks or side tanks), and modern coaches and wagons, all made a railway company par excellence.

BRITISH RAILWAYS MOTIVE POWER DEPOT CODES
1948 - 1966

In the table below are the Motive Power Depot Codes for the years under review in this publication. There were several changes, both area and regional, made over the years, and the current code for a particular year is shown in the Locomotive Lists. This results in some locomotives which were allocated to the same depot for years on end having two, or even more, different shed codes!

The 1948 column shows the shedcodes in use by the four pre - nationalisation companies; it was not until 1950 that the L.M.S. system was adopted for *all* B.R. sheds. (1949 for Scottish Region).

Under the B.R. System, Shedcodes were allocated as follows:

1 - 29	LONDON MIDLAND REGION	30 - 49	EASTERN REGION
50 - 59	NORTH EASTERN REGION	60 - 69	SCOTTISH REGION
70 - 79	SOUTHERN REGION	80 - 89	WESTERN REGION

Where two companies shared a depot before Nationalisation, the B.R. shedcode is shown against both original codes on two lines, the second line being shown thus "

Sub Sheds & Stabling Points of Main Sheds *are shown in italics.*

Locomotive Shed	1948	1952	1955	1959	1963	1966	Locomotive Shed	1948	1952	1955	1959	1963	1966
Willesden	1A	1A	1A	1A	1A	1A	**Liverpool Edge Hill**	8A	8A	8A	8A	8A	8A
Camden	1B	1B	1B	1B	1B	1B	Warrington Dallam	8B	8B	8B	8B	8B	8B
Watford	1C	1C	1C	1C	1C	1C	Over and Wharton	8B					
Devons Road (Bow)	13B	1D	1D	1D	1D	-	Warrington Arpley	*8B*	*8B*	*8B*	*8B*	*8B*	
Bletchley	2B	1E	1E	1E	1E	1E	Speke Junction	8C	8C	8C	8C	8C	8C
Leighton Buzzard	*2B*	*1E*	*1E*	*1E*	-	-	Widnes	8D	8D	8D	8D	8D	8D
Newport Pagnell	*2B*	*1E*	*1E*	-	-	-	Widnes C.L.C.	*LIV*	*8D*	-	-	-	-
							Liverpool Brunswick	LIV	8E	8E	27F	-	-
Rugby	2A	2A	2A	2A	2A	1F	Warrington C.L.C.	*LIV*	*8E*	*8E*	*27F*	-	-
Market Harborough	*2A*	*2A*	*2A*	15F	*15C*	*15A*	Allerton	-	-	-	-	-	8J
Seaton	*2A*	*2A*	*2A*	*15F*	*15C*	-							
Nuneaton	2D	2B	2B	2B	2B	5E	**Longsight**	9A	9A	9A	9A	9A	9A
Warwick Milverton	2E	2C	2C	-	-	-	Stockport Edgeley	9B	9B	9B	9B	9B	9B
Coventry	2F	2D	2D	2D	-	-	Macclesfield	9C	9C	9C	9C	9C	-
Northampton	2C	2E	2E	2E	2E	1H	Buxton	9D	9D	9D	9D	9D	9L
							Trafford Park LMS	19G	9E	9E	9E	9E	9E
Bescot	3A	3A	3A	3A	21B	2F	Trafford Park LNER	TFD	"	"	"	"	"
Bushbury	3B	3B	3B	3B	21C	-	Heaton Mersey LMS	19D	9F	9F	9F	9F	9F
Walsall	3C	3C	3C	3C	21F	2G	Heaton Mersey LNER	STP	"	"	"	"	"
Aston	3D	3D	3D	3D	21D	-	Northwich	NTH	9G	9G	9G	8E	8E
Monument Lane	3E	3E	3E	3E	21E	2H							
							Springs Branch	10A	10A	10A	8F	8F	8F
Crewe North	5A	5A	5A	5A	5A	5A	Preston	10B	10B	10B	24K	-	-
Whitchurch	*5A*	*5A*	*5A*	*5A*	-	-	Patricroft	10C	10C	10C	26F	26F	9H
Crewe South	5B	5B	5B	5B	5B	5B	Bolton Plodder Lane	10D	10D	-	-	-	-
Crewe Gresty Lane	*CWR*	*5B*	*5B*	*5A*	*5B*	-	Sutton Oak	10E	10E	10E	8G	8G	8G
Stafford	5C	5C	5C	5C	5C	5C							
Coalport	*4A*	*5C*	-	-	-	-	**Carnforth**	11A	11A	11A	24L	24L	10A
Stoke	5D	5D	5D	5D	5D	5D	Barrow	11B	11B	11B	11A	12E	12C
Alsager	5E	5E	5E	5E	-	-	Lakeside	*11B*	-	-	-	-	-
Uttoxeter	5F	5F	5F	5F	5F	-	Coniston	*11B*	*11B*	11B	-	-	-
							Oxenholme	11C	11C	11C	11C	-	-
Chester LMS	6A	6A	6A	6A	6A	6A	Tebay	11D	11D	*11D*	11D	12H	12E
Mold Junction	6B	6B	6B	6B	6B	6B	Lancaster Green Ayre	20H	11E	11E	24J	24J	10J
Birkenhead LMS Jt	6C	6C	6C	6C	6C	8H							
Birkenhead GWR Jt	BHD	"	"	"	"	"	**Carlisle Kingmoor**	12A	68A	68A	12A	12A	12A
Chester (Northgate)	6D	6D	6D	6D	-	-	Carlisle Upperby	12B	12A	12A	12B	12B	12B
Wrexham	6E	6E	6E	6E	-	-	Carlisle Canal	CAR	68E	68E	12C	12C	-
Bidston	6F	6F	6F	6F	6F	-	Penrith	12C	12C	12C	*12B*	-	-
							Workington	12D	12D	12D	11B	12F	12D
Llandudno Jnct.	7A	6G	6G	6G	6G	6G	Moor Row	12E	12E	-	-	-	-
Bangor	7B	6H	6H	6H	6H	-							
Holyhead	7C	6J	6J	6J	6J	6J							
Rhyl	7D	6K	6K	6K	6K	-							
Denbigh	*7D*	*6K*	*6K*	-	-	-							

Locomotive Shed	1948	1952	1955	1959	1963	1966
Cricklewood	14A	14A	14A	14A	14A	-
Cricklewood East	-	-	-	-	-	14A
Cricklewood West	-	-	-	-	-	14B
Kentish Town	14B	14B	14B	14B	14B	-
St. Albans	14C	14C	14C	14C	-	-
Marylebone	-	-	-	-	14F	1D
Wellingborough	15A	15A	15A	15A	15A	15B
Kettering	15B	15B	15B	15B	15B	-
Leicester (Midland)	15C	15C	15C	15C	15C	15A
Bedford	15D	15D	15D	14E	14E	14C
Nottingham	16A	16A	16A	16A	16A	16D
Southwell	16A	16A	16A	-	-	-
Lincoln (Midland)	16A	16A	-	-	-	-
Kirkby	16C	16C	16C	16B	16B	16E
Mansfield	16D	16D	16D	16C	-	-
Derby	17A	17A	17A	17A	17A	16C
Burton	17B	17B	17B	17B	17B	16F
Overseal	17B	17B	17B	17B	17B	16F
Coalville	17C	17C	17C	15D	15D	15E
Rowsley	17D	17D	17D	17D	17C	-
Cromford	9D	17D	17D	17D	17C	16C
Middleton	9D	17D	17D	17D	17C	9L
Sheep Pasture	9D	17D	17D	17D	17C	16C
Toton	18A	18A	18A	18A	18A	16A
Westhouses	18B	18B	18B	18B	18B	16G
Hasland	18C	18C	18C	18C	18C	-
Clay Cross	18C	18C	18C	-	-	-
Staveley	18D	18D	18D	41E	41E	41E
Sheepbridge	18D	18D	18D	-	-	-
Grimesthorpe	19A	19A	19A	41B	-	-
Millhouses	19B	19B	19B	41C	-	-
Canklow	19C	19C	19C	41D	41D	41D
Leeds Holbeck	20A	20A	20A	55A	55A	55A
Stourton	20B	20B	20B	55B	55B	55B
Royston	20C	20C	20C	55D	55D	55D
Normanton	20D	20D	20D	55E	55E	55E
Manningham	20E	20E	20E	55F	55F	55F
Ilkley	20E	20E	20E	55A	52G	-
Ilkley (ex LNER)	ILK	20E	20E	-	-	-
Skipton	20F	20F	20F	24G	24G	10G
Keighley	20F	20F	20F	55F	55F	55F
Ingleton	20F	20G	20G	-	-	-
Hellifield	20G	20G	20G	24H	24H	-
Saltley	21A	21A	21A	21A	21A	2E
Bournville	21B	21B	21B	21B	-	-
Redditch	21B	21B	21B	85F	85D	85D
Bromsgrove	21C	21C	21C	85F	85D	85D
Stratford-on-Avon LMS	21D	21D	21A	-	-	-
Bristol Barrow Road	22A	22A	22A	82E	82E	-
Gloucester Barnwood	22B	22B	22B	85E	85C	-
Tewkesbury	22B	22B	22B	85E	-	-
Dursley	22B	22B	22B	85E	-	-
Accrington	24A	24A	24A	24A	24A	10E
Rose Grove	24B	24B	24B	24B	24B	10F
Lostock Hall	24C	24C	24C	24C	24C	10D
Lower Darwen	24D	24D	24D	24D	24D	-
Blackpool	24E	24E	24E	24E	24E	10B
Blackpool North	24E	24E	24E	-	-	-
Fleetwood	24F	24F	24F	24F	24F	-

Locomotive Shed	1948	1952	1955	1959	1963	1966
Wakefield	25A	25A	25A	56A	56A	56A
Huddersfield	25B	25B	25B	55G	55G	55G
Goole	25C	25C	25C	53E	50D	50D
Mirfield	25D	25D	25D	56D	56D	56D
Sowerby Bridge	25E	25E	25E	56E	56E	-
Low Moor	25F	25F	25F	56F	56F	56F
Farnley Junction	25G	25G	25G	55C	55C	55C
Newton Heath	26A	26A	26A	26A	26A	9D
Agecroft	26B	26B	26B	26B	26B	9J
Bolton	26C	26C	26C	26C	26C	9K
Bury	26D	26D	26D	26D	26D	-
Bacup	26E	26E	26E	-	-	-
Lees	26F	26F	26F	26E	26E	-
Belle Vue	19E	26G	26G	-	-	-
Bank Hall	23A	27A	27A	27A	27A	8K
Aintree	23B	27B	27B	27B	27B	8L
Southport	23C	27C	27C	27C	27C	-
Wigan (L& Y)	23D	27D	27D	27D	27D	-
Walton-on-the-Hill	WAL	27E	27E	27E	27E	-
Southport (C.L.C.)	LIV	27E	-	-	-	-
Stratford	STR	30A	30A	30A	30A	30A
Brentwood	STR	30A	30A	-	-	-
Chelmsford	STR	30A	30A	30A	-	-
Epping	STR	30A	30A	-	-	-
Spitalfields	STR	30A	-	-	-	-
Walthamstow	STR	30A	30A	30A	-	-
Palace Gates	STR	30A	30A	-	-	-
Enfield Town	STR	30A	30A	30A	-	-
Ware	STR	30A	30A	-	-	-
Hertford East	STR	30B	30B	30B	-	-
Buntingford	STR	30B	30B	30B	-	-
Bishops Stortford	STR	30C	30C	30C	-	-
Southend Victoria	STR	30D	30D	30A	-	-
Southminster	STR	30D	30D	-	-	-
Wickford	STR	30D	-	-	-	-
Colchester	COL	30E	30E	30E	-	-
Clacton	COL	30E	30E	30E	-	-
Walton-on-Naze	COL	30E	30E	30E	-	-
Kelvedon	COL	30E	30E	-	-	-
Maldon	COL	30E	30E	30E	-	-
Braintree	COL	30E	30E	30E	-	-
Parkeston	PKS	30F	30F	30F	30F	30F
Cambridge	CAM	31A	31A	31A	31A	31A
Ely	CAM	31A	31A	31A	31A	31A
Huntingdon East	CAM	31A	31A	31A	-	-
Saffron Walden	CAM	31A	31A	31A	-	-
Thaxted	CAM	31A	31A			
March	MAR	31B	31B	31B	31B	31B
Kings Lynn	KL	31C	31C	31C	-	-
Wisbech	KL	31C	31C	31B	-	-
Hunstanton	KL	31C	31C	31C	-	-
South Lynn	SL	31D	31D	31D	-	-
Bury St. Edmunds	BSE	31E	31E	31E	-	-
Sudbury	BSE	31E	31E	31E	-	-
Norwich	NOR	32A	32A	32A	32A	32A
Cromer	NOR	32A	32A	32A	32A	32A
Wells-on-Sea	NOR	32A	32A	-	-	-
Dereham	NOR	32A	32A	32A	-	-
Swaffham	NOR	32A	32A	-	-	-
Wymondham	NOR	32A	32A	32A	-	-
Ipswich	IPS	32B	32B	32B	32B	32B

Locomotive Shed	1948	1952	1955	1959	1963	1966
Ipswich	IPS	32B	32B	32B	32B	32B
Laxfield	IPS	32B	-	-	-	-
Felixstowe Beach	IPS	32B	32B	32B	-	-
Aldeburgh	IPS	32B	32B	-	-	-
Framlingham	IPS	32B	-	-	-	-
Stowmarket	IPS	32B	32B	32B	-	-
Lowestoft	LOW	32C	32C	32C	32C	32C
Yarmouth (South Town)	YAR	32D	32D	32D	32D	32D
Yarmouth (Vauxhall)	YAR	32E	32E	32E	-	-
Yarmouth (Beach)	YB	32F	32F	-	-	-
Melton Constable	MC	32G	32G	32G	-	-
Norwich City	MC	32G	32G	32G	-	-
Cromer Beach	MC	32G	32G	-	-	-
Plaistow	13A	33A	33A	33A	-	-
Upminster	13E	33A	33A	-	-	-
Tilbury	13C	33B	33B	33B	33B	-
Shoeburyness	13D	33C	33C	33C	33C	-
Kings Cross	KX	34A	34A	34A	34A	-
Hornsey	HSY	34B	34B	34B	34B	34B
Hatfield	HAT	34C	34C	34C	-	
Hitchin	HIT	34D	34D	34D	34D	34D
Neasden	NEA	34E	34E	14D	14F	-
Aylesbury	NEA	34E	34E	14D	-	-
Chesham	NEA	34E	34E	14D	-	-
Finsbury Park	-	-	-	-	34G	34G
New England	NWE	35A	35A	34E	34E	34E
Spalding	NWE	35A	35A	-	-	-
Bourne	NWE	35A	35A	-	-	-
Stamford	NWE	35A	35A	-	-	-
Grantham	GRA	35B	35B	34F	34F	-
Peterborough Spital	16B	35C	35C	31F	-	-
Doncaster	DON	36A	36A	36A	36A	36A
Mexborough	MEX	36B	36B	41F	41F	-
Frodingham	FRO	36C	36C	36C	36C	36C
Barnsley	BRN	36D	36D	-	-	-
Retford	RET	36E	36E	36E	36E	-
Newark	GRA	36E	36E	36E	-	-
Ardsley	ARD	37A	37A	56B	56B	56B
Copley Hill	COP	37B	37B	56C	56C	-
Bradford	BFD	37C	37C	56G	56G	56G
Colwick	CLK	38A	38A	40E	40E	16B
Derby Friargate	CLK	38A	38A	17A	-	-
Annesley	ANN	38B	38B	16D	16D	-
Leicester (ex G.C.)	LEI	38C	38C	15E	15E	-
Leicester (ex G.N.)	LEI	38C	38C	-	-	-
Staveley (Ex G.C.)	STV	38D	38D	41H	41H	-
Woodford Halse	WFD	38E	38E	-	-	-
Gorton	GOR	39A	39A	9G	9G	-
Dinting	GOR	39A	39A	9G	9G	-
Hayfield	GOR	39A	39A	-	-	-
Macclesfield	GOR	39A	39A	9C	-	-
Sheffield Darnall	SHF	39B	39B	41A	41A	-
Lincoln	LIN	40A	40A	40A	40A	40A
Immingham	IMM	40B	40B	40B	40B	40B
Louth	LTH	40C	40C	-	-	-
Tuxford	TUX	40D	40D	41K	-	-
Langwith Junction	LNG	40E	40E	41J	41J	41J
Boston	BOS	40F	40F	40F	40F	40F

Locomotive Shed	1948	1952	1955	1959	1963	1966
Sheffield Tinsley	-	-	-	-	-	41A
Shirebrook West	-	-	-	-	-	41A
York	YK	50A	50A	50A	50A	50A
Leeds (Neville Hill)	NEV	50B	50B	50B	55H	55H
Selby	SEL	50C	50C	50C	-	-
Starbeck	SBK	50D	50D	50D	-	-
Scarborough	SCA	50E	50E	50E	50E	-
Malton	MAL	50F	50F	50F	50F	-
Pickering	MAL	50F	50F	50F	-	-
Whitby	WBY	50G	50G	50G	-	-
Darlington	DAR	51A	51A	51A	51A	51A
Middleton-in-Teesdale	DAR	51A	51A	51A	-	-
Newport	NPT	51B	51B	-	-	-
West Hartlepool	WHL	51C	51C	51C	51C	51C
Middlesbrough	MID	51D	51D	-	-	-
Guisborough	MID	51D	51D	-	-	-
Stockton	SKN	51E	51E	51E	-	-
West Aukland	AUK	51F	51F	51F	51F	-
Wearhead	AUK	51F	51F	-	-	-
Haverton Hill	HAV	51G	51G	51G	-	-
Kirkby Stephen	KBY	51H	51H	-	-	-
Northallerton	NLN	51J	51J	51J	51J	-
Leyburn	NLN	51J	51J	-	-	-
Saltburn	SAL	51K	51K	-	-	-
Thornaby	-	-	-	51L	51L	51L
Gateshead	GHD	52A	52A	52A	52A	52A
Bowes Bridge	GHD	52A	52A	52A	52A	52A
Heaton	HTN	52B	52B	52B	52B	52B
Blaydon	BLA	52C	52C	52C	52C	52C
Hexham	BLA	52C	52C	52C	-	-
Alston	BLA	52C	52C	52C	52C	52C
Reedsmouth	BLA	52C	52C	-	-	-
Tweedmouth	TWD	52D	52D	52D	52D	52D
Alnmouth	TWD	52D	52D	52D	52D	52D
Percy Main	PMN	52E	52E	52E	52E	52E
North Blyth	NBH	52F	52F	52F	52F	52F
South Blyth	NBH	52F	52F	52F	52F	52F
Rothbury	NBH	52F	52F	-	-	-
Hull (Dairycotes)	HLD	53A	53A	53A	50B	50B
Hull (Botanic Gardens)	HLB	53B	53B	53B	50C	50C
Hull (Springhead)	HLS	53C	53C	53C	-	-
Alexandra Dock	HLS	53C	53C	53C	50B	-
Bridlington	BRI	53D	53D	53D	-	-
Sunderland	SUN	54A	54A	52G	52G	52G
Durham	SUN	54A	54A	52G	-	-
Tyne Dock	TDK	54B	54B	52H	52H	52H
Pelton Level	TDK	54B	54B	52H	52H	-
Borough Gardens	BOR	54C	54C	52J	-	-
Consett	CON	54D	54D	52K	52K	52K
Inverness	32A	60A	60A	60A	60A	60A
Dingwall	32A	60A	60A	60A	60A	-
Fortrose	32A	60A	60A	-	-	-
Kyle of Lochalsh	32A	60A	60A	60A	60A	60A
Aviemore	32B	60B	60B	60B	60B	60B
Boat of Garten	KEI	60B	60B	60B	60B	-
Helmsdale	32A	60C	60C	60C	60C	-
Dornoch	32A	60C	60C	-	-	-
Tain	32A	60C	60C	60C	60C	-
Wick	32A	60D	60D	60D	60D	60D
Thurso	32A	60D	60D	60D	60D	60D
Forres	32C	60E	60E	60A	60A	60A

Locomotive Shed	1948	1952	1955	1959	1963	1966
Kittybrewster	KIT	61A	61A	61A	61A	61A
Ballater	KIT	61A	61A	61A	61A	61A
Fraserburgh	KIT	61A	61A	61A	61A	61A
Peterhead	KIT	61A	61A	61G	61A	61A
Inverurie	-	-	-	61A	61A	61A
Ferryhill L.M.S	29B	61B	61B	61B	61B	61B
Ferryhill L.N.E.R	ABD	"	"	"	"	"
Keith	KEI	61C	61C	61C	61C	61C
Banff	KEI	61C	61C	61C	61C	-
Elgin	KEI	61C	61C	61C	61C	61C
Thornton Jnct.	THJ	62A	62A	62A	62A	62A
Anstruther	THJ	62A	62A	62A	62A	62A
Burntisland	THJ	62A	62A	62A	62A	62A
Ladybank	THJ	62A	62A	62A	62A	62A
Methil	THJ	62A	62A	62A	62A	62A
Kirkcaldy	-	-	62A	62A	62A	62A
Dundee	DEE	62B	62B	62B	62B	62B
Dundee West	29C	62B	62B	62B	-	-
Arbroath	29D	62B	62B	62B	62B	-
Montrose	DEE	62B	62B	62B	62B	62B
St. Andrews	DEE	62B	62B	62B	62B	62B
Dunfermline Upper	DFU	62C	62C	62C	62C	62C
Alloa	STG	62C	62C	62C	62C	62C
Kelty	DFU	62C	62C	62C	62C	-
Perth LMS	29A	63A	63A	63A	63A	63A
Perth LNER	PTH	63A	63A	63A	63A	63A
Aberfeldy	29A	63A	63A	63A	63A	63A
Blair Atholl	29A	63A	63A	63A	63A	63A
Crieff	29A	63A	63A	63A	63A	63A
Stirling	31B	63B	63B	63B	65J	65J
Killin	29D	63B	63B	63B	65J	-
Stirling Shore Road	STG	63B	63B	-	-	-
Forfar	29D	63C	63C	63C	63A	-
Brechin	29D	63C	63C	-	-	-
Fort William	FW	63D	63D	65J	63B	63B
Mallaig	FW	63D	63D	65J	63B	63B
Oban	31C	63E	63E	63D	63C	63C
Ballachulish	31C	63E	63E	63D	63C	63C
St. Margarets	STM	64A	64A	64A	64A	64A
Dunbar	STM	64A	64A	64A	64A	-
Galashiels	STM	64A	64A	64A	64A	64A
Granton	-	-	-	-	64A	64A
Hardengreen	STM	64A	64A	64A	64A	-
Longniddry	STM	64A	64A	64A	64A	-
North Berwick	STM	64A	64A	64A	64A	64A
Peebles	STM	64A	64A	-	-	-
Seafield	STM	64A	64A	64A	64A	-
South Leith	-	-	-	64A	64A	64A
Haymarket	HAY	64B	64B	64B	64B	64B
Dalry Road	28B	64C	64C	64C	64C	64C
Carstairs	28C	64D	64D	64D	66E	66E
Polmont	POL	64E	64E	64E	65K	-
Bathgate	BGT	64F	64F	64F	64F	64F
Hawick	HAW	64G	64G	64G	64G	64G
Kelso	HAW	64G	64G	-	-	-
Riccarton	HAW	64G	64G	64G	-	-
St. Boswells	HAW	64G	64G	64G	-	-
Leith Central	-	-	-	64H	64H	64H
Eastfield	EFD	65A	65A	65A	65A	65A
St. Rollox	31A	65B	65B	65B	65B	65B
Parkhead	PKD	65C	65C	65C	65C	-
Dawsholm	31E	65D	65D	65D	65D	-

Locomotive Shed	1948	1952	1955	1959	1963	1966
Dumbarton	31E	65D	65D	65D	65D	65D
Kipps	KPS	65E	65E	65E	65E	65E
Grangemouth	31D	65F	65F	65F	65F	65F
Yoker	31E	65G	65G	65G	65G	-
Helensburgh	PKD	65H	65H	65H	65H	-
Arrochar	EFD	65H	65H	65A	65A	-
Balloch	EFD	65I	65I	65I	65I	-
Polmadie	27A	66A	66A	66A	66A	66A
Motherwell	28A	66B	66B	66B	66B	66B
Morningside	BGT	66B	-	-	-	-
Hamilton	27C	66C	66C	66C	66C	66C
Greenock Ladyburn	27B	66D	66D	66D	66D	66D
Greenock Princes Pier	27B	66D	66D	-	-	-
Corkerhill	30A	67A	67A	67A	67A	67A
Hurlford	30B	67B	67B	67B	67B	67B
Beith	30B	67B	67B	67B	67B	-
Muirkirk	30B	67B	67B	67B	67B	-
Ayr	30D	67C	67C	67C	67C	67C
Ardrossan	30C	67D	67D	67D	67D	-
Carlisle Kingmoor	12A	68A	68A	12A	12A	12A
Dumfries	12G	68B	68B	68B	67E	67E
Kircudbright	12G	68B	68B	-	-	-
Stranraer	12H	68C	68C	68C	67F	67F
Newton Stewart	12H	68C	68C	68C	-	-
Beattock	12F	68D	68D	68D	66F	66F
Carlisle Canal	CAR	68E	68E	12C	-	-
Nine Elms	9E	70A	70A	70A	70A	70A
Feltham	FEL	70B	70B	70B	70B	70B
Guildford	GFD	70C	70C	70C	70C	70C
Bordon	GFD	70C	-	-	-	-
Basingstoke	BAS	70D	70D	70D	70D	70D
Reading	RDG	70E	70E	70E	70C	70C
Eastleigh	ELH	71A	71A	71A	71A	70D
Winchester (SR)	ELH	71A	71A	71A	71A	-
Winchester (WR)	WIN	71A	71A	-	-	-
Lymington	LYM	71A	71A	71A	-	-
Andover Junction	AND	71A	71A	71A	71A	-
Bournemouth	BM	71B	71B	71B	71B	70F
Swanage	BM	71B	71B	-	-	-
Hamworthy Jnct.	BM	71B	-	-	-	-
Branksome	22C	71B	71B	71B	71B	70F
Dorchester	DOR	71C	71C	71B	71B	-
Fratton	FRA	71D	70F	70F	-	-
Gosport	FRA	71D	-	-	-	-
Midhurst	FRA	71D	-	-	-	-
Newport (I.O.W.)	NPT	71E	70G	-	-	-
Ryde (I.O.W.)	RYD	71F	70H	70H	70H	70H
Bath (S. & D.)	22C	71G	71G	82F	82F	82F
Radstock	22C	71G	71G	82F	82F	82F
Templecombe	22D	71H	71H	82G	82G	83G
Southampton Docks	SOT	71I	71I	71I	71I	70I
Highbridge	22E	71J	71J	82F	82F	82F
Exmouth Jnct.	EXJ	72A	72A	72A	72A	83D
Seaton	EXJ	72A	72A	72A	72A	-
Lyme Regis	EXJ	72A	72A	72A	72A	-
Exmouth	EXJ	72A	72A	72A	72A	-
Okehampton	EXJ	72A	72A	72A	72A	83D
Bude	EXJ	72A	72A	72A	72A	83D
Salisbury	SAL	72B	72B	72B	70E	70E

Locomotive Shed	1948	1952	1955	1959	1963	1966
Yeovil Town	YEO	72C	72C	72C	72C	83E
Plymouth	PLY	72D	72D	83H	83H	-
Callington	PLY	72D	72D	72A	72A	-
Barnstaple Jnct.	BPL	72E	72E	72E	72E	-
Torrington	BPL	72E	72E	72E	-	-
Ilfracombe	BPL	72E	72E	72E	72E	-
Wadebridge	WAD	72F	72F	72F	72F	84E
Stewarts Lane	BAT	73A	73A	73A	75D	75D
Bricklayers Arms	BA	73B	73B	73B	-	-
Hither Green	HIT	73C	73C	73C	73C	73C
Gillingham (Kent)	GIL	73D	73D	73D	-	-
Faversham	FAV	73E	73E	73E	73D	-
Ashford (Kent)	AFD	74A	74A	73F	73F	73F
Canterbury West	AFD	74A	74A	-	-	-
Ramsgate	RAM	74B	74B	73G	-	-
Dover	DOV	74C	74C	73H	-	-
Folkestone Jnct.	DOV	74C	74C	73H	-	-
Tonbridge	TON	74D	74D	73J	-	-
St. Leonards	STL	74E	74E	73D	73D	73D
Brighton	BTN	75A	75A	75A	75A	75A
Newhaven	BTN	75A	75A	75A	-	-
Redhill	RED	75B	75B	75B	75B	-
Norwood Junction	NOR	75C	75C	75C	75C	-
Selhurst	-	-	-	-	-	75C
Horsham	HOR	75D	75D	75D	75E	-
Three Bridges	3B	75E	75E	75E	75E	-
Tunbridge Wells West	TWW	75F	75F	75F	75F	-
Eastbourne	EBN	75G	-	-	-	-
Old Oak Common	PDN	81A	81A	81A	81A	81A
Slough	SLO	81B	81B	81B	81B	-
Aylesbury	SLO	81B	-	-	-	-
Marlow	SLO	81B	81B	81B	-	-
Watlington	SLO	81B	81B	-	-	-
Southall	SHL	81C	81C	81C	81C	81C
Staines	SHL	81C	-	-	-	-
Reading	RDG	81D	81D	81D	81D	81D
Henley-on-Thames	RDG	81D	81D	81D	-	-
Didcot	DID	81E	81E	81E	81E	81E
Newbury	DID	81E	-	-	-	-
Wallingford	DID	81E	81E	-	-	-
Oxford	OXF	81F	81F	81F	81F	81F
Abingdon	OXF	81F	-	-	-	-
Fairford	OXF	81F	81F	81F	-	-
Bristol Bath Road	BRD	82A	82A	82A	82A	82A
Bath	BRD	82A	82A	82A	-	-
Wells	BRD	82A	82A	82A	-	-
Weston-super-Mare	BRD	82A	82A	82A	-	-
Yatton	BRD	82A	82A	82A	-	-
St. Philip's Marsh	SPM	82B	82B	82B	82B	-
Swindon	SDN	82C	82C	82C	82C	-
Andover Junction	SDN	82C	82C	82C	-	-
Chippenham	SDN	82C	82C	82C	82C	-
Westbury	WES	82D	82D	82D	82D	-
Salisbury	SAL	-	-	-	-	-
Frome	WES	82D	82D	82D	-	-
Yeovil Pen Mill	YEO	82E	82E	71H	-	-
Weymouth	WEY	82F	82F	71G	71G	70G
Bridport	WEY	82F	82F	71G	-	-
Newton Abbot	NA	83A	83A	83A	83A	83A

Locomotive Shed	1948	1952	1955	1959	1963	1966
Ashburton	NA	83A	83A	-	-	-
Kingsbridge	NA	83A	83A	83A	-	-
Taunton	TN	83B	83B	83B	83B	83B
Bridgwater	TN	83B	83B	83B	-	-
Minehead	TN	83B	83B	-	-	-
Exeter	EXE	83C	83C	83C	83C	-
Tiverton Junction	EXE	83C	83C	83C	83C	-
Plymouth Laira	LA	83D	83D	83D	83D	84A
Princetown	LA	83D	83D	-	-	-
Launceston	LA	83D	83D	83D	83D	-
St. Blazey	SBZ	83E	83E	83E	83E	84B
Bodmin	SBZ	83E	83E	83E	-	-
Moorswater	SBZ	83E	83E	83E	-	-
Truro	TR	83F	83F	83F	83F	84C
Penzance	PZ	83G	83G	83G	83G	84D
Helston	PZ	83G	83G	83G	-	-
St. Ives	PZ	83G	83G	83G	-	-
Wolverhampton	SRD	84A	84A	84A	84A	-
Oxley	OXY	84B	84B	84B	84B	2B
Banbury	BAN	84C	84C	84C	84C	2D
Leamington Spa	LMTN	84D	84D	84D	84D	-
Tyseley	TYS	84E	84E	84E	84E	2A
Stratford-on-Avon	21D	84E	84E	84E	84E	2A
Stourbridge	STB	84F	84F	84F	84F	-
Shrewsbury LMS	4A	84G	84G	84G	89A	6D
Shrewsbury GW	SALOP	"	"	"	"	"
Clee Hill	4A	84G	84G	84G		
Cravens Arms	4A	84G	84G	84G	86C	-
Knighton	4A	84G	84G	84G		
Builth Road	4A	84G	84G	84G	89A	6D
Wellington	WLN	84H	84H	84H	84H	-
Croes Newydd	CNYD	84J	84J	84J	89B	6C
Bala	CNYD	84J	84J	84J	89B	-
Trawsfynydd	CNYD	84J	84J	84J	-	-
Penmaenpool	CNYD	84J	84J	84J	89B	-
Chester G.W.R.	CHR	84K	84K	6E	-	-
Worcester	WOS	85A	85A	85A	85A	85A
Honeybourne	-	-	-	-	85A	85A
Evesham	WOS	85A	85A	85A	-	-
Kingham	WOS	85A	85A	85A	-	-
Gloucester	GLO	85B	85B	85B	85B	85B
Cheltenham	CHEL	85B	85B	85B	85B	-
Brimscombe	CHEL	85B	85B	85B	-	-
Cirencester	CHEL	85B	85B	85B	-	-
Lydney	LYD	85B	85B	85B	85B	-
Tetbury	LYD	85B	85B	85B	-	-
Hereford	HFD	85C	85C	85C	86C	-
Leominster	HFD	85C	85C	85C	-	-
Ross	HFD	85C	85C	85C	-	-
Kidderminster	KDR	85D	85D	85D	84G	-
Ebbw Junction	NPT	86A	86A	86A	86A	86B
Newport Pill	PILL	86B	86B	86B	86B	-
Cardiff (Canton)	CDF	86C	86C	86C	86A	86A
Llantrisant	LTS	86D	86D	86D	88G	-
Severn Tunnel Jnct.	STJ	86E	86E	86E	86E	86E
Tondu	TDU	86F	86F	86F	88H	-
Pontypool Road	PPRD	86G	86G	86G	86G	-
Branches Fork	PPRD	86G				
Aberbeeg	ABEEG	86H	86H	86H	86F	-
Aberdare	ABDR	86J	86J	86J	88J	-
Abergavenny	4D	86K	86K	-	-	-
Tredegar	4E	86K	86K	86K	-	-

Locomotive Shed	1948	1952	1955	1959	1963	1966
Neath	NEA	87A	87A	87A	87A	87A
Margam	-	-	-	-	-	87B
Glyn Neath	NEA	87A	87A	87A	87A	-
Neath (N. & B.)	NEA	87A	87A	87A	87A	-
Duffryn Yard	DYD	87B	87B	87B	87B	-
Danygraig	DG	87C	87C	87C	87C	-
Swansea East Dock	SED	87D	87D	87D	87D	87E
Landore	LDR	87E	87E	87E	87E	87F
Llanelly	LLY	87F	87F	87F	87F	-
Burry Port	LLY	87F	87F	87F	-	-
Pantyfynnon	LLY	87F	87F	87F	87F	-
Carmarthen	CARM	87G	87G	87G	87G	-
Newcastle Emlyn	CARM	87G	-	-	-	-
Neyland	NEY	87H	87H	87H	87H	-
Cardigan	WTD	87H	87H	87H	-	-
Milford Haven	NEY	87H	87H	87H	-	-
Pembroke Dock	WTD	87H	87H	87H	87H	87H
Whitland	WTD	87H	87H	87H	87H	-
Goodwick	FGD	87J	87J	87J	87J	-
Swansea Victoria	4B	87K	87K	87K	-	-
Llandovery	4B	87K	87K	87K	87F	-
Upper Bank	4C	87K	87K	87K	-	-
Gurnos	4C	87K	87K	87K	-	-
Cardiff Cathays	CHYS	88A	88A	88A	88M	-
Radyr	RYR	88A	88A	88A	88B	-
Cardiff East Dock	CED	88B	88B	88B	88L	-
Barry	BRY	88C	88C	88C	88C	-
Merthyr	MTHR	88D	88D	88D	88D	-
Cae Harris	CH	88D	88D	88D	88D	-
Dowlais Central	DLS	88D	88D	88D	88D	-
Rhymney	RHY	88D	88D	88D	88D	-
Abercynon	AYN	88E	88E	88E	88E	-
Treherbert	THT	88F	88F	88F	88F	-
Ferndale	FDL	88F	88F	88F	88F	-

Locomotive Shed	1948	1952	1955	1959	1963	1966
Oswestry	OSW	89A	89A	89A	89D	-
Llanfyllin	OSW	89A	-	-	-	-
Llanidloes	OSW	89A	89A	89A	89D	-
Moat Lane	OSW	89A	89A	89A	89D	-
Welshpool (W & L)	OSW	89A	89A	-	-	-
Brecon	BCN	89B	89B	89B	-	-
Builth Wells	BCN	89B	89B	-	-	-
Machynlleth	MCH	89C	89C	89C	89C	6F
Aberayron	MCH	89C	89C	89C	-	-
Aberystwyth	ABH	89C	89C	89C	89C	-
Aberystwyth (V of R)	-	-	-	89C	89C	6F
Portmadoc	MCH	89C	89C	89C	89C	6F
Pwllheli	MCH	89C	89C	89C	89C	6F
Western A.C. Lines					ACL	ACL
Western Lines						WL
Midland Lines						ML
London (W) Division						D01
Birmingham Division						D02
Stoke Division						D03
London (M) Division						D14
Leicester Division						D15
Nottingham Division						D16
Crewe Works	CW	CW	CW	CW	CW	CW
Derby Works	DW	DW	DW	DW	DW	DW
Horwich Works	HW	HW	HW	HW	HW	HW
Wolverton Works	WW	WW	WW	WW	WW	WW
St Rollox Works	SRW	SRW	SRW	SRW	SRW	SRW
C.M.E., Crewe		CMEC	CMEC	CMEC	CMEC	CMEC
Rugby Testing Stn.		RTS	RTS	RTS	RTS	RTS

Notes on Using this Book :

1) Locomotives which carried their allocated B. R. Number are shown in bold type :- **67890**. Locomotives which *never* carried their allocated B. R. Number are shown in italics :- *67890*.

2) The building or acquisition date of locos in to stock after 1/1/48, is shown in the '1948' locoshed column in bold italics :- **06/51**

3) *Final* withdrawal dates are also shown in bold italics :- **09/65**

4) Allocation dates shown in this book are as follows:- January 1st 1948, August 1st 1952, January 1st 1955, January 1st 1959, March 1st 1963 and December 1st 1965. (Steam ended on the Western Region on 31st December 1965, hence the earlier date in this volume)

Publishers Note :

Every effort has been made to be 100% accurate, but if there are mistakes, then please let us know, so that we can get them altered for our next print run.

During the research which has gone in to these publications, the writer has obtained information from many different sources including British Railways, the Public Records Office at Kew, the National Library of Scotland, the British Library, the National Railway Museum, the Railway Correspondence and Travel Society, the Stephenson Locomotive Society, and countless professional railwaymen and enthusiasts throughout the length and breadth of the country.

However, the story is not complete. We would like details of all the locomotives which survived into British Railways and never *became* B.R. capital stock, but were used for other duties such as internal shunters, stationery boilers, C.M.E. test locos (like **10897** at Uttoxeter, for instance), generators, either mobile of fixed, etc.. If you have any further information, please email us at

enquiries@transportpublishing.com, or write to :

TRANSPORT PUBLISHING LTD., 31 CROWN STREET, AYR, SCOTLAND, KA8 8AG

Peckett — Ystalyfera — 0-4-0ST

Built by Peckett in 1900 for Ystalyfera Tin Works, purchased by B.R. in 1948, and became B.R. number 1. Both this loco, which was very small, and the highest numbered B.R. loco, 92250, which was massive, worked on the Western Region, but No.1 was scrapped long before 92250 was built.

Loco Weight: 23t 0c *Driving Wheels:* 3' 2" *Cylinders:* (O) 14½" x 22" *Valve Gear:* Stephenson (Slide Valves)

Number	1948	1952	1955	1959	1963	1965	w/dwn	
1	07/48	87C	-	-	-	-	01/54	TOTAL 1

2'3" Gauge — Corris — 0-4-2ST

Built 1878 by Falcon Engine & Car Co. for Corris Railway as 0-4-0ST, rebuilt 1901 as 0-4-2ST.

Loco Weight: 9t 0c *Driving Wheels:* 2' 6" *Cylinders:* (O) 7" x 12" *Valve Gear:* Stephenson (Slide Valves)

Number	1948	w/dwn	
3	MCH	10/48	TOTAL 1

2'3" Gauge — Corris — 0-4-2ST

Built 1921 by Kerr Stuart for Corris Railway. Both this Loco & Number 3 (above), were withdrawn in 1948, and sold to the Tal-y-Llyn Railway early in 1951.

Loco Weight: 8t 0c *Driving Wheels:* 2' 0" *Cylinders:* (O) 7" x 12" *Valve Gear:* Stephenson (Slide Valves)

Number	1948	w/dwn	
4	MCH	10/48	TOTAL 1

A1X — Weston, Cleveland & Portishead — 0-6-0T

Originally built for London, Brighton & South Coast Railway (Class A1X), and purchased by Weston, Cleveland & Portishead Railway from the Southern Railway in 1925 and 1937 respectively. Acquired by G.W.R. in 1940.

Loco Weight: 28t 5c *Driving Wheels:* 4' 0" *Cylinders:* (I) 12" x 20" *Valve Gear:* Stephenson (Slide Valves)

Number & Name	1948	1952	w/dwn	Number	1948	1952	w/dwn
5 Portishead	SPM	82C	03/54	6	SPM	-	01/48

TOTAL 2

1'11½" Gauge — Vale of Rheidol — 2-6-2T

Originally built for Vale of Rheidol Railway in 1902 by Davies & Metcalfe (7 & 8 built by G.W.R. in 1923. These were the only *BRITISH RAILWAYS* owned steam locomotives to survive after the last standard gauge steam locomotives were withdrawn in August 1968, and later were the only B.R. steam locos to be painted in Rail Blue with the 'Double Arrow' emblem. All three still run on the V of R today*, albeit not in British railways ownership. (*As at October 2006)

Loco Weight: 25t 0c *Driving Wheels:* 2' 6" *Cylinders:* (O) 11" x 17" (7 & 8 are 11½" x 17")
Valve Gear: Stephenson (Slide Valves)

Number & Name	1948	1952	1948	1952	1955	1959	1963	1965	Notes
7 Owain Glyndŵr	ABH	89C	89C	89C	89C	89C	89C	6F	
8 Llywelyn	ABH	89C	89C	89C	89C	89C	89C	6F	
9 Prince of Wales	ABH	89C	89C	89C	89C	89C	89C	6F	Renumbered from *1213 03/49*

TOTAL 3

Brecon & Merthyr Railway — 0-6-2T

Number	1948	1952	1955	w/dwn
11	PILL	-	-	01/49

Continued with Number 332. For Class Notes see Number 422

Taff Vale Class O4 0-6-2T No. 219 stands forlornly in Swindon Works Yard. This photo shows the heavy rebuilding that many absorbed engines were subjected to by the Great Western. Built 1910, scrapped 1951.

photo courtesy Steve Davies

Ex Cambrian 0-6-0 No. 849 trundles through Dovey Junction with a freight train. Withdrawn in September 1954 after thirty six years service.

photo courtesy Steve Davies

Cleobury, Mortimer & Ditton Priors Railway — 0-6-0PT

1905 design by Manning Wardle for CMDPR. Reboilered & fitted with pannier tanks by G.W.R.

Loco Weight : 39t 18c *Driving Wheels :* 3' 6" *Cylinders :* (O) 16" x 22" *Valve Gear :* Stephenson (Slide Valves)

Number	1948	1952	1955	1959	1963	1965	w/dwn	Number	1948	1952	1955	1959	1963	1965	w/dwn
28	KDR	85D	-	-	-	-	11/53	29	KDR	85D	-	-	-	-	01/54

TOTAL 2

Classes M, R & R1 — Rhymney — 0-6-2T

* Class R Introduced 1907 by Hurry Riches for Rhymney Railway. ‡ Class R1 was a 1921 development of Class R.   † Rebuilt by G.W.R. with superheated standard taper boiler. ** Class M Jenkins design introduced 1904.

* *Loco Weight :* 66t 19c ‡ *Loco Weight :* 62t 10c † *Loco Weight :* 66t 0c ** *Loco Weight :* 63t 0c

Driving Wheels : 4' 6" *Cylinders :* (I) 18½" x 26" *Valve Gear :* Stephenson (Slide Valves)

Number	1948	1952	1955	1959	1963	1965	w/dwn	Number	1948	1952	1955	1959	1963	1965	w/dwn
30 *	RYR	-	-	-	-	-	05/49	39 ‡†	RHY	88B	88B	-	-	-	08/55
31 *†	CED	-	-	-	-	-	02/51	40 ‡†	RYR	88B	-	-	-	-	10/53
32 *	RYR	-	-	-	-	-	02/50	41 ‡	RYR	88B	88B	-	-	-	05/56
33 **	CED	-	-	-	-	-	02/51	42 ‡	RYR	88A	88B	-	-	-	09/57
34 *†	RYR	-	-	-	-	-	11/49	43 ‡	RYR	88A	88A	-	-	-	02/57
35 ‡	RYR	88B	88B	-	-	-	11/56	44 ‡†	RYR	88A	88A	-	-	-	07/56
36 ‡	CED	88B	88B	-	-	-	10/57	46 *	RYR	-	-	-	-	-	07/50
37 ‡	CED	88B	88B	-	-	-	09/56	47 **†	CED	-	-	-	-	-	04/49
38 ‡	RYR	88B	88B	-	-	-	10/57	51 **	CED	-	-	-	-	-	10/48

TOTAL 18

Classes A & A1 — Rhymney — 0-6-2T

* Class A Introduced 1910 by Hurry Riches for Rhymney Railway. ‡ Class A1 was a 1914 development of Class A.   † Rebuilt by G.W.R. with superheated standard taper boiler

* ‡ *Loco Weight :* 64t 3c *Driving Wheels :* 4' 4½" *Cylinders :* (I) 18" x 26" *Valve Gear :* Stephenson (Slide Valves)

† *Loco Weight :* 63t 0c *Driving Wheels :* 4' 4½" *Cylinders :* (I) 18½" x 26" *Valve Gear :* Stephenson (Slide Valves)

Number	1948	1952	1955	1959	1963	1965	w/dwn	Number	1948	1952	1955	1959	1963	1965	w/dwn
52 * †	CED	-	-	-	-	-	11/49	64 ‡	RYR	-	-	-	-	-	05/50
53 *	CED	-	-	-	-	-	06/49	65 ‡ †	ABDR	86J	-	-	-	-	01/54
54 *	CED	-	-	-	-	-	04/48	66 ‡ †	CED	88A	88B	-	-	-	07/55
55 * †	CED	88B	-	-	-	-	02/53	67 ‡	RHY	88B	-	-	-	-	09/52
56 * †	RYR	88A	-	-	-	-	09/53	68 ‡	CED	88B	-	-	-	-	06/54
57 *	BRY	-	-	-	-	-	04/52	69 ‡ †	DYD	87B	87B	-	-	-	07/55
58 * †	BRY	88A	-	-	-	-	09/54	70 ‡ †	DYD	87B	87B	-	-	-	07/55
59 * †	BRY	88B	88B	-	-	-	07/55	71 * †	DG	-	-	-	-	-	12/48
60 * †	DG	-	-	-	-	-	03/51	72 *	CED	-	-	-	-	-	02/52
61 *	CED	-	-	-	-	-	02/50	73 *	CED	88A	-	-	-	-	06/52
62 * †	PILL	-	-	-	-	-	12/48	74 * †	CED	-	-	-	-	-	01/51
63 ‡ †	BRY	88B	-	-	-	-	09/52	75 * †	NEA	87A	-	-	-	-	10/53

TOTAL 24

Classes P & AP — Rhymney — 0-6-2T

Class P Introduced 1909 by Hurry Riches for Rhymney Railway. * Class AP was a 1921 superheated development of Class P.   Both classes were rebuilt by G.W.R.

Loco Weight : 58t 19c *Driving Wheels :* 5' 0" *Cylinders :* (I) 18" x 26" *Valve Gear :* Stephenson (Slide Valves)

* *Loco Weight :* 63t 0c *Driving Wheels :* 5' 0" *Cylinders :* (I) 18½" x 26" *Valve Gear :* Stephenson (Slide Valves)

Number	1948	1952	1955	1959	1963	1965	w/dwn	Number	1948	1952	1955	1959	1963	1965	w/dwn
76	RHY	-	-	-	-	-	11/50	78 *	RHY	88D	-	-	-	-	07/55
77	RHY	88D	-	-	-	-	11/53	79 *	RHY	88D	-	-	-	-	07/55

Number	1948	1952	1955	1959	1963	1965	w/dwn	Number	1948	1952	1955	1959	1963	1965	w/dwn
80 *	RHY	88D	-	-	-	-	01/54	82	RHY	88D	-	-	-	-	05/54
81 *	RHY	88D	-	-	-	-	05/54	83	CH	88D	-	-	-	-	05/55

TOTAL 8

Class S1 Rhymney Railway 0-6-0T

Hurry Riches designed class for Rhymney Railway, introduced 1920.
Number 91 (605), had (I) 18½" x 26" cylinders.

Loco Weight : 56t 8c *Driving Wheels :* 4' 4½" *Cylinders :* (I) 18" x 26" *Valve Gear :* Stephenson (Slide Valves)

Number	1948	1952	1955	1959	w/dwn	Notes
90	CED	88B	-	-	05/54	
91	CED	88B	-	-	06/54	Renumbered from *605, 03/48*
92	CED	88B	-	-	06/54	

TOTAL 3

Class S Rhymney Railway 0-6-0T

Hurry Riches designed class for Rhymney Railway, introduced 1908. Rebuilt by G.W.R. with taper boilers from 1930.

Loco Weight : 54t 8c *Driving Wheels :* 4' 4½" *Cylinders :* (I) 18" x 26" *Valve Gear :* Stephenson (Slide Valves)

Number	1948	1952	1955	1959	w/dwn	Notes
93	CED	88B	-	-	05/54	
94	CED	88B	-	-	03/54	
95	CED	88B	-	-	09/53	Renumbered from *610, 09/48*
96	CED	88B	-	-	04/54	Renumbered from *611, 12/49*

TOTAL 4

4073 'Castle' 4-6-0

Collett development of 'Star' Class, introduced in 1923. 111 was rebuilt from 4-6-2, and others numbered below 4073 were rebuilt form 'Star' Class.
Construction continued for almost thirty years, into B.R. days; the first rebuilds being scrapped as the last of the class were being built! Some locos were fitted with double chimneys (DC) from 1956 onward.
4082 Windsor Castle & 7013 Bristol Castle exchanged identities in February 1952 for the funeral of H.M. King George VI, as it was desired to use Windsor Castle as the train engine, but 4082 was in works.

Loco Weight : 79t 17c *Driving Wheels :* 6' 8½" *Cylinders :* (4) 16" x 26" *Valve Gear :* Walschaerts (piston valves)

Number & Name		1948	1952	1955	1959	1963	1965	w/dwn	Notes
100	A1 Lloyds	PDN	-	-	-	-	-	03/50	
111	Viscount Churchill	PDN	83D	-	-	-	-	06/53	

Continued with Number 4000

Cardiff Railway 0-6-2T

Ree design for Cardiff Railway, introduced 1908.
Rebuilt by G.W.R. with taper boiler during 1928.

Loco Weight : 66t 12c *Driving Wheels :* 4' 6½" *Cylinders :* (I) 17" x 26" *Valve Gear :* Stephenson (Slide Valves)

Number	1948	1952	1955	1959	w/dwn
155	CED	88B	-	-	09/53

TOTAL 1

Port Talbot Railway 0-6-2T

1898 design for Port Talbot Railway.
Rebuilt by G.W.R. with superheated taper boiler during 1925.

Loco Weight : 56t 0c *Driving Wheels :* 4' 6" *Cylinders :* (I) 18" x 26" *Valve Gear :* Stephenson (Slide Valves)

Number	1948	1952	1955	1959	w/dwn
184	DYD	-	-	-	10/48

TOTAL 1

Barclay   Alexandra Docks & Railway Company   0-6-2ST

Andrew Barclay design for Alexandra Docks & Railway Company dating from 1908.
Rebuilt by G.W.R. in 1924.

Loco Weight: 52t 13c   *Driving Wheels:* 4' 3"   *Cylinders:* (O) 18" x 26"   *Valve Gear:* Stephenson (Slide Valves)

Number	1948	1952	1955	1959	w/dwn
190	PILL	-	-	-	04/48

TOTAL 1

Class H   Taff Vale   0-6-0T

Introduced in 1884 for Taff Vale Railway. Steeply tapered boiler design for use on Pwllyrhebog Colliery incline.

Loco Weight: 44t 15c   *Driving Wheels:* 5' 3"   *Cylinders:* (I) 17½" x 26"   *Valve Gear:* Stephenson (Slide Valves)

Number	1948	1952	1955	1959	w/dwn	Notes
193	THT	-	-	-	02/52	Renumbered from 792, 06/48
194	THT	88F	-	-	11/53	Renumbered from 793, 09/48
195	THT	-	-	-	11/51	Renumbered from 794, 02/49

TOTAL 3

Class B   Barry Railway   0-6-2T

Barry Railway Class B, introduced in 1888, and built by Sharp, Stewart. Rebuilt with new boiler by Great Western Railway in 1924

Loco Weight: 50t 2c   *Driving Wheels:* 4' 3"   *Cylinders:* (I) 18" x 26"   *Valve Gear:* Stephenson (Slide Valves)

Number	1948	1952	1955	1959	1963	1965	w/dwn	Number	1948	1952	1955	1959	1963	1965	w/dwn
198	RYR	-	-	-	-	-	01/48	213	BRY-	-	-	-	-	-	01/49
212	CED	-	-	-	-	-	07/48	231	BRY	-	-	-	-	-	11/49

TOTAL 4

Class O4   Taff Vale   0-6-2T

Introduced in 1907 by Hurry Riches for Taff Vale Railway.
Rebuilt from 1924 by G.W.R. with superheated taper boiler.

Loco Weight: 61t 0c   *Driving Wheels:* 4' 6½"   *Cylinders:* (I) 17½" x 26"   *Valve Gear:* Stephenson (Slide Valves)

Number	1948	1952	1955	1959	1963	1965	w/dwn	Notes
200	CDF	-	-	-	-		07/48	
203	CDF	-	-	-	-		01/52	Renumbered from 310, 12/48
204	ABDR	86J	-	-	-		07/55	
205	CDF	86C	-	-	-		07/54	
207	FDL	88F	-	-	-		11/52	
208	CDF	86C	-	-	-		07/55	Renumbered from 317, 09/48
209	CDF	86C	-	-	-		08/52	
210	CED	88B	-	-	-		03/55	
211	CH	88B	-	-	-		05/55	Renumbered from 320, 05/48
215	FDL	88F	-	-	-		07/55	Renumbered from 321, 04/48
216	FDL	88F	-	-	-		01/55	Renumbered from 324, 03/48
217	MTHR	88F	-	-	-		09/52	Renumbered from 333, 04/49
218	FDL	88F	-	-	-		12/52	Renumbered from 409, 01/50
219	AYN	-	-	-	-		06/51	Renumbered from 414, 05/48
220	CDF	-	-	-	-		04/51	Renumbered from 420, 11/48

Number	1948	1952	1955	1959	1963	1965	w/dwn	Number	1948	1952	1955	1959	1963	1965	w/dwn
236	AYN	88F	-	-	-	-	01/53	283	FDL	-	-	-	-	-	03/49
278	FDL	-	-	-	-	-	05/51	284	ABDR	86J	-	-	-	-	11/52
279	FDL	88F	-	-	-	-	05/54	285	CED	88F	-	-	-	-	08/53
280	CDF	-	-	-	-	-	05/49	286	BRY	-	-	-	-	-	10/50
281	AYN	-	-	-	-	-	08/50	287	AYN	-	-	-	-	-	12/49
282	ABDR	86C	-	-	-	-	06/54	288	AYN	-	-	-	-	-	03/50

Number	1948	1952	1955	1959	1963	1965	w/dwn	Number	1948	1952	1955	1959	1963	1965	w/dwn
289	SED	-	-	-	-	-	08/49	296	DYD	-	-	-	-	-	09/49
290	THT	88F	-	-	-	-	07/55	297	CED	-	-	-	-	-	12/49
291	DYD	-	-	-	-	-	01/50	298	FDL	-	-	-	-	-	07/48
292	RHY	-	-	-	-	-	04/52	299	FDL	-	-	-	-	-	06/51
293	RYR	-	-	-	-	-	07/51	301	CHYS	-	-	-	-	-	12/48
294	DYD	-	-	-	-	-	07/50	302	THT	-	-	-	-	-	04/48
295	AYN	-	-	-	-	-	06/51	314	ABDR	-	-	-	-	-	12/49

TOTAL 41

Class B1   Barry Railway   0-6-2T

Hosgood design for Barry Railway, introduced 1890. * Rebuilt by G.W.R. from 1924 with new boiler.

Loco Weight : 55t 3c *Driving Wheels :* 4' 3" *Cylinders :* (I) 17½" x 26" *Valve Gear :* Stephenson (Slide Valves)
* Loco Weight : 53t 9c *Driving Wheels :* 4' 3" *Cylinders :* (I) 17½" x 26" *Valve Gear :* Stephenson (Slide Valves)

Number	1948	1952	1955	1959	1963	1965	w/dwn	Number	1948	1952	1955	1959	1963	1965	w/dwn
238	CDF	-	-	-	-	-	06/48	267 *	BRY	-	-	-	-	-	04/51
240 *	RYR	-	-	-	-	-	04/51	268 *	BRY	-	-	-	-	-	04/48
246	RYR	-	-	-	-	-	01/49	269 *	CED	-	-	-	-	-	10/49
248 *	BRY	-	-	-	-	-	07/48	270 *	BRY	-	-	-	-	-	05/51
258	RYR	-	-	-	-	-	11/49	271 *	BRY	-	-	-	-	-	05/51
259	CED	-	-	-	-	-	08/48	272 *	BRY	-	-	-	-	-	03/50
261 *	BRY	-	-	-	-	-	08/48	274 *	BRY	-	-	-	-	-	04/51
262 *	BRY	-	-	-	-	-	03/50	275 *	BRY	-	-	-	-	-	04/48
263 *	BRY	-	-	-	-	-	04/51	276 *	BRY	-	-	-	-	-	04/51
265 *	BRY	-	-	-	-	-	11/49	277 *	BRY	-	-	-	-	-	04/49

TOTAL 20

Class A   Taff Vale   0-6-2T

Cameron design, introduced in 1914.   * Rebuilt from 1924 with rebuilt superheated taper boiler.

Loco Weight : 65t 14c *Driving Wheels :* 4' 3" *Cylinders :* (I) 18½" x 26" *Valve Gear :* Stephenson (Slide Valves)
* Loco Weight : 65t 14c *Driving Wheels :* 4' 3" *Cylinders :* (I) 17½" x 20" *Valve Gear :* Stephenson (Slide Valves)

Number	1948	1952	1955	1959	1963	1965	w/dwn	Notes
303 *	THT	88F	88C	-	-	-	05/56	
304 *	AYN	88E	88E	-	-	-	08/57	Renumbered from *402, 03/48*
305 *	CHYS	88A	88A	-	-	-	05/57	
306 *	BRY	88C	88C	-	-	-	04/56	Renumbered from *404, 07/49*
307	CHYS	88A	88A	-	-	-	03/56	Renumbered from *406, 07/49*
308	SED	87D	88B	-	-	-	12/55	Renumbered from *408, 12/48*
309	SED	87D	-	-	-	-	02/53	Renumbered from *438, 06/49*
312 *	BRY	88C	88C	-	-	-	06/56	Renumbered from *439, 09/49*
316 *	BRY	88D	88E	-	-	-	07/56	Renumbered from *440, 06/50*

Number	1948	1952	1955	1959	1963	1965	w/dwn	Number	1948	1952	1955	1959	1963	1965	w/dwn
322	BRY	88E	-	-	-	-	09/54	357 *	CDF	86J	88C	-	-	-	01/56
335	CDF	86C	-	-	-	-	03/54	360	CHYS	88A	88A	-	-	-	02/55
337	AYN	88E	-	-	-	-	02/53	361	BRY	88C	88C	-	-	-	01/57
343 *	CHYS	88A	88A	-	-	-	10/55	362 *	ABDR	86J	88A	-	-	-	05/56
344	CHYS	88A	-	-	-	-	11/52	364 *	CHYS	88A	88A	-	-	-	03/57
345 *	BRY	88A	88A	-	-	-	08/55	365 *	THT	88F	88F	-	-	-	10/55
346 *	CHYS	88A	88A	-	-	-	10/55	366	THT	88F	88F	-	-	-	10/55
347 *	CHYS	88A	88A	-	-	-	12/56	367 *	CHYS	88A	88A	-	-	-	03/56
348 *	CHYS	88A	88A	-	-	-	05/56	368 *	THT	88F	88F	-	-	-	10/56
349	PPRD	86C	88C	-	-	-	03/57	370	RHY	88D	88E	-	-	-	08/57
351 *	AYN	88E	88E	-	-	-	07/56	371	CHYS	86J	88B	-	-	-	01/55
352	THT	88F	88F	-	-	-	03/55	372	BRY	88C	88C	-	-	-	02/55
356 *	AYN	88E	88E	-	-	-	01/55	373 *	THT	88C	88C	-	-	-	08/57

No.	1948	1952	1955	1959	1963	1965	w/dwn	No.	1948	1952	1955	1959	1963	1965	w/dwn
374 *	ABDR	86J	88B	-	-	-	08/55	386 *	BRY	88E	88E	-	-	-	04/56
375 *	RHY	88C	-	-	-	-	11/54	387	BRY	88C	88C	-	-	-	11/56
376 *	CHYS	88A	88C	-	-	-	01/57	388 *	BRY	88C	88C	-	-	-	10/56
377 *	BRY	88A	88F	-	-	-	05/56	389 *	BRY	88C	88C	-	-	-	01/56
378 *	THT	88F	88B	-	-	-	12/56	390 *	CHYS	88A	88C	-	-	-	08/57
379 *	BRY	88D	88E	-	-	-	02/56	391 *	CHYS	88A	88A	-	-	-	09/56
380 *	AYN	88E	88E	-	-	-	10/56	393 *	CHYS	88D	88C	-	-	-	05/57
381 *	CDF	86C	88F	-	-	-	08/57	394 *	BRY	88C	88C	-	-	-	07/56
382 *	BRY	88C	88C	-	-	-	04/56	397 *	AYN	88E	88E	-	-	-	04/57
383 *	CHYS	88A	88A	-	-	-	08/57	398 *	RHY	88D	88E	-	-	-	08/57
384 *	CHYS	88A	88F	-	-	-	02/56	399 *	THT	88F	88E	-	-	-	09/56
385 *	PPRD	86J	88F	-	-	-	04/57								TOTAL 58

Brecon & Merthyr Railway   0-6-2T

Continued from Number 11.

Number	1948	1952	w/dwn
332	STJ	-	12/49

Continued with Number 422. For Class Notes see Number 422

Llanelly & Mynydd Mawr Railway   0-6-0ST

Hudswell Clarke design introduced in 1917 for Llanelly & Mynydd Mawr Railway. Later reboilered by G.W.R.

Loco Weight: 34t 9c *Driving Wheels:* 3' 7½" *Cylinders:* (O) 15" x 22" *Valve Gear:* Stephenson (Slide Valves)

Number & Name	1948	1952	1955	1959	w/dwn
359 Hilda	DG	87C	-	-	01/54

TOTAL 1

Class O3   Taff Vale   0-6-2T

Introduced in 1902 by Hurry Riches, rebuilt & reboilered in 1930 by G.W.R.

Loco Weight: 63t 0c *Driving Wheels:* 4' 6½" *Cylinders:* (I) 17½" x 26" *Valve Gear:* Stephenson (Slide Valves)

Number	1948	1952	1955	1959	1963	1965	w/dwn	Number	1948	1952	1955	1959	1963	1965	w/dwn
410	CDF	-	-	-	-	-	03/48	411	CDF	-	-	-	-	-	02/48

TOTAL 2

Brecon & Merthyr Railway   0-6-2T

1909 design by Dunbar for Brecon & Merthyr, built by Robert Stephenson. * Rebuilt by G.W.R.

Loco Weight: 66t 19c *62t 10c *Driving Wheels:* 4' 6" *Cylinders:* (I) 18½" x 24" *Valve Gear:* Stephenson (Slide Valves)

Continued from Number 332.

Number	1948	1952	1955	1959	1963	1965	w/dwn	Number	1948	1952	1955	1959	1963	1965	w/dwn
422 *	STJ	-	-	-	-	-	06/50	428	DYD	-	-	-	-	-	08/50
425	PILL	-	-	-	-	-	03/51	504	PILL	-	-	-	-	-	01/48
426 *	PILL	-	-	-	-	-	03/50								TOTAL 7

Brecon & Merthyr Railway   0-6-2T

Introduced 1915 by Dunbar for Brecon & Merthyr Railway. Reboilered with taper boiler by G.W.R. from 1926.   * Reboilered by G.W.R. with ex - Rhymney Railway boiler.

Loco Weight: 59t 5c *Driving Wheels:* 5' 0" *Cylinders:* (I) 18" x 26" *Valve Gear:* Stephenson (Slide Valves)

Number	1948	1952	1955	1959	1963	1965	w/dwn	Notes
431	NPT	86A	-	-	-	-	10/53	Renumbered from 1372, 07/49
432	NPT	86A	-	-	-	-	05/53	Renumbered from 1373, 11/48
433	RYR	-	-	-	-	-	02/51	
434	CHYS	88A	-	-	-	-	09/53	Renumbered from 1375, 04/49
435	NPT	86A	-	-	-	-	01/54	Renumbered from 1668, 04/50
436 *	NPT	86A	-	-	-	-	01/54	Renumbered from 1670, 10/49

    TOTAL 6

'County' 4-6-0 No. 1000 'County of Middlesex' at Old Oak Common in the early 1960s, with recently built London high rise flats in the background.

Photo courtesy Steve Davies

Hawksworth 16xx Pannier Tank No. 1649 (with 82B shedplate) stands next to ex - Caledonian 0-6-0 No. 57575 at Inverness M.P.D., shortly after being transferred (along with 1646) to the Scottish Region.

Transport Publishing Ltd. Collection

Alexandra Docks & Railway Co. 0-6-0T

Ex R.O.D. design from 1917 (built by Hudswell Clark), purchased by A.D. & R. Co., 1919.

Loco Weight : 50t 0c *Driving Wheels :* 4' 0" *Cylinders :* (O) 17" x 24" *Valve Gear :* Stephenson (Slide Valves)

Number	1948	1952	1955	1959	1963	1965	w/dwn	Number	1948	1952	1955	1959	1963	1965	w/dwn
666	PILL	86B	86B	-	-	-	04/55	667	PILL	86B	-	-	-	-	11/54

TOTAL 2

Alexandra Docks & Railway Co. 0-6-0ST

Introduced 1886, Peckett 'off the shelf ' design.

Loco Weight : 26t 17c *Driving Wheels :* 3' 6" *Cylinders :* (O) 14" x 20" *Valve Gear :* Stephenson (Slide Valves)

Number	1948	1952	1955	1959	1963	1965	w/dwn
680	OSW	-	-	-	-	-	12/48

TOTAL 1

Cardiff Railway 0-6-0PT

Hudswell Clarke design introduced in 1920. Later Reboilered & fitted with pannier tanks by G.W.R.

Loco Weight : 45t 6c *Driving Wheels :* 4' 1½" *Cylinders :* (I) 18" x 24" *Valve Gear :* Stephenson (Slide Valves)

Number	1948	1952	1955	1959	1963	1965	w/dwn	Number	1948	1952	1955	1959	1963	1965	w/dwn
681	CED	88B	88B	-	-	-	02/55	683	CED	88B	-	-	-	-	12/54
682	CED	88B	-	-	-	-	10/53	684	CED	88B	-	-	-	-	05/54

TOTAL 4

Class E Barry Railway 0-6-0T

Hudswell Clarke design introduced in 1889

Loco Weight : 33t 7c *Driving Wheels :* 3' 6½" *Cylinders :* (I) 14" x 20" *Valve Gear :* Stephenson (Slide Valves)

Number	1948	1952	1955	1959	1963	1965	w/dwn	Number	1948	1952	1955	1959	1963	1965	w/dwn
783	BRY	-	-	-	-	-	08/48	784	BRY	-	-	-	-	-	08/49

TOTAL 2

Llanelly & Mynydd Mawr Railway 0-6-0T

Hudswell Clarke design introduced in 1911. Later reboilered by G.W.R.

Loco Weight : 40t 12c *Driving Wheels :* 4' 0" *Cylinders :* (I) 16" x 24" *Valve Gear :* Stephenson (Slide Valves)

Number	1948	1952	1955	1959	1963	1965	w/dwn
803	DG	-	-	-	-	-	03/51

TOTAL 1

2'6" Gauge Welshpool & Llanfair 0-6-0T

Built in 1902 by Beyer Peacock for the 2' 6" Welshpool & Llanfair Rly., as Nos. **1** & **2** respectively.

Loco Weight : 19t 18c *Driving Wheels :* 2' 9" *Cylinders :* (O) 11½" x 16" *Valve Gear :* Walschaerts (Slide Valves)

Number & Name	1948	1952	1955	1959	w/dwn	Notes
822 The Earl	OSW	89A	89A	89A	08/61	Both locos were taken over by the Welshpool &
823 Countess	OSW	89A	89A	89A	06/62	Llanfair Preservation Society in 1963.

TOTAL 2

'89' Class Cambrian 0-6-0

Jones design introduced in 1903, reboilered by G.W.R. from 1924

Loco Weight : 38t 17c *Driving Wheels :* 5' 1½" *Cylinders :* (I) 18" x 26" *Valve Gear :* Stephenson (Slide Valves)

Number	1948	1952	1955	1959	1963	1965	w/dwn	Number	1948	1952	1955	1959	1963	1965	w/dwn
844	OSW	89A	-	-	-	-	08/54	892	OSW	89C	-	-	-	-	04/53
849	OSW	89A	-	-	-	-	09/54	893	OSW	89A	-	-	-	-	02/53
855	OSW	89A	-	-	-	-	09/54	894	MCH	89C	-	-	-	-	04/53
864	MCH	89C	-	-	-	-	11/52	895	OSW	89A	-	-	-	-	09/54
873	OSW	89A	-	-	-	-	03/54	896	OSW	89A	-	-	-	-	04/53
887	OSW	89A	-	-	-	-	11/52								

TOTAL 11

1854   Dean G.W.R.   0-6-0PT

Dean design from 1890 using parts from older engines. All originally built as saddle tanks, but
Were rebuilt as pannier tanks from 1909 onwards.

Loco Weight: 46t 13c   *Driving Wheels:* 4' 7½"   *Cylinders:* (I) 17" x 24"   *Valve Gear:* Stephenson (Slide Valves)

Number	1948	1952	1955	1959	1963	1965	w/dwn	Number	1948	1952	1955	1959	1963	1965	w/dwn
906	NEA	-	-	-	-	-	04/48	907	DID	-	-	-	-	-	03/51

Continued with Number 1705

1901   Dean / Armstrong G.W.R.   0-6-0PT, 0-6-0ST *

Originally introduced in 1874, the majority of these saddle tanks were rebuilt from 1910 with pannier
tanks. (Locos still fitted with original saddle tanks marked thus *)
Loco Weight: 36t 3c   *Driving Wheels:* 4' 1½"   *Cylinders:* (I) 16" x 24"   *Valve Gear:* Stephenson (Slide Valves)

Number	1948	1952	1955	1959	1963	1965	w/dwn
992	SDN	-	-	-	-	-	02/51

Continued with Number 1903

1000   'County'   4-6-0

Introduced by Hawksworth in 1945 for G.W.R. After 1955, all were fitted with double chimneys.

Loco Weight: 76t 17c   *Driving Wheels:* 6' 3"   *Cylinders:* (O) 18½" x 30"   *Valve Gear:* Stephenson (piston valves)

Number & Name	1948	1952	1955	1959	1963	1965	w/dwn	Notes
1000 County of Middlesex	PDN	83D	82A	82A	82B	-	07/64	
1001 County of Bucks	NA	87H	87H	87H	87H	-	05/63	
1002 County of Berks	BRD	82A	83G	83G	89A	-	09/63	
1003 County of Wilts	PDN	84G	84G	84G	-	-	10/62	
1004 County of Somerset	LA	84G	82C	82C	-	-	09/62	
1005 County of Devon	BRD	82A	82A	82A	82B	-	06/63	
1006 County of Cornwall	LA	83D	83G	83G	82C	-	09/63	
1007 County of Brecknock	BRD	82A	83F	83F	-	-	10/62	
1008 County of Cardigan	PDN	81A	84K	83D	89A	-	10/63	
1009 County of Carmarthen	LA	87H	87H	82A	-	-	02/63	
1010 County of Caernarvon	PDN	83D	83D	83D	82C	-	07/64	
1011 County of Chester	BRD	82A	82A	82A	82B	-	11/64	
1012 County of Denbigh	PDN	83D	83D	82C	82C	-	04/64	
1013 County of Dorset	BRD	84G	84G	84G	89A	-	07/64	
1014 County of Glamorgan	BRD	82A	82A	82A	87H	-	04/64	
1015 County of Gloucester	PDN	83D	83D	83D	-	-	12/62	
1016 County of Hants	SRD	84A	84G	84G	89A	-	09/63	
1017 County of Hereford	SRD	84G	84G	84G	-	-	12/62	
1018 County of Leicester	NA	84G	83G	83G	-	-	09/62	
1019 County of Merioneth	PZ	84G	82C	82C	-	-	02/63	
1020 County of Monmouth	EXE	87H	87H	87H	82B	-	02/64	
1021 County of Montgomery	PDN	83D	83D	83D	82B	-	11/63	
1022 County of Northampton	PZ	84K	84K	84G	-	-	10/62	
1023 County of Oxford	TR	83F	83F	83F	89A	-	03/63	
1024 County of Pembroke	SRD	83D	84K	82A	82B	-	04/64	
1025 County of Radnor	SRD	84G	84G	84G	-	-	02/63	
1026 County of Salop	PDN	81A	84K	84G	-	-	09/62	
1027 County of Stafford	WES	87H	87H	87H	87H	-	10/63	
1028 County of Warwick	BRD	82A	82A	82A	82B	-	12/63	
1029 County of Worcester	SRD	84A	87H	87H	-	-	12/62	

TOTAL 30

1101   Avonside for G.W.R.   0-4-0T

1926 design by Avonside Engine Co. for G.W.R.
Loco Weight : 38t 4c   *Driving Wheels :* 3' 9½"   *Cylinders :* (O) 16" x 24"   *Valve Gear :* Walschaerts (Piston Valves)

Number	1948	1952	1955	1959	1963	1965	w/dwn	Number	1948	1952	1955	1959	1963	1965	w/dwn
1101	DG	87C	87C	87C	-	-	11/59	1104	DG	87C	87C	87C	-	-	01/60
1102	DG	87C	87C	87C	-	-	01/60	1105	DG	87C	87C	87C	-	-	01/60
1103	DG	87C	87C	87C	-	-	01/60	1106	DG	87C	87C	87C	-	-	01/60

TOTAL 6

Barclay   Swansea Harbour Trust   0-4-0ST

Barclay design for Swansea Harbour Trust, introduced 1905
Loco Weight : 28t 0c   *Driving Wheels :* 3' 5"   *Cylinders :* (O) 14" x 22"   *Valve Gear :* Stephenson (Slide Valves)

Number	1948	1952	1955	1959	1963	1965	w/dwn	Notes
1140	SED	87D	87D	-	-	-	05/58	Renumbered from *701*, *06/48*

TOTAL 1

Peckett   Swansea Harbour Trust   0-4-0ST

Peckett design for Swansea Harbour Trust, introduced 1906
Loco Weight : 33t 10c   *Driving Wheels :* 3' 7"   *Cylinders :* (O) 15" x 21"   *Valve Gear :* Stephenson (Slide Valves)

Number	1948	1952	1955	1959	1963	1965	w/dwn	Notes
1141	DG	87C	-	-	-	-	06/52	Renumbered from *929*, *03/48*
1143	DG	87C	87C	87C	-	-	11/60	Renumbered from *968*, *02/49*
1145	DG	87C	87C	87C	-	-	07/59	Renumbered from *1098*, *01/50*

TOTAL 3

Hudswell Clarke   Swansea Harbour Trust   0-4-0ST

Hudswell Clark design for Swansea Harbour Trust, introduced 1911
Loco Weight : 28t 15c   *Driving Wheels :* 3' 4"   *Cylinders :* (O) 15" x 22"   *Valve Gear :* Stephenson (Slide Valves)

Number	1948	1952	1955	1959	1963	1965	w/dwn	Notes
1142	DG	87C	87C	84G	-	-	11/59	Renumbered from *943*, *11/48*

TOTAL 1

Hawthorn Leslie   Swansea Harbour Trust   0-4-0ST

Hawthorn Leslie design for Swansea Harbour Trust, introduced 1909
Loco Weight : 26t 17c   *Driving Wheels :* 3' 6"   *Cylinders :* (O) 14" x 22"   *Valve Gear :* Stephenson (Slide Valves)

Number	1948	1952	1955	1959	1963	1965	w/dwn	Notes
1144	SED	87D	87D	87D	-	-	01/60	Renumbered from *974*, *09/48*

TOTAL 1

Peckett   Swansea Harbour Trust   0-6-0ST

Peckett design for Swansea Harbour Trust, introduced 1912
Loco Weight : 38t 10c   *Driving Wheels :* 3' 10"   *Cylinders :* (I) 16" x 22"   *Valve Gear :* Stephenson (Slide Valves)

Number	1948	1952	1955	1959	1963	1965	w/dwn	Notes
1146	DG	-	-	-	-	-	01/51	Renumbered from *1085*, *02/49*
1147	DG	-	-	-	-	-	04/51	Renumbered from *1086*, *03/49*

TOTAL 2

Peckett   Powlesland & Mason   0-4-0ST

Peckett design for Powlesland & Mason, introduced 1907
Loco Weight : 33t 10c   *Driving Wheels :* 3' 7"   *Cylinders :* (O) 15" x 21"   *Valve Gear :* Stephenson (Slide Valves)

Number	1948	1952	1955	1959	1963	1965	w/dwn	Notes
1150	SED	87D	-	-	-	-	11/52	Renumbered from *696*, *12/51*
1151	DG	87C	87C	87C	87C	-	08/63	Renumbered from *779*, *10/50*
1152	SED	87D	87D	87K	-	-	12/61	Renumbered from *935*, *06/49*

       TOTAL 3

Hawthorn Leslie   Powlesland & Mason   0-4-0ST

Introduced 1903. Later reboilered by G.W.R.
Loco Weight: 26t 13c *Driving Wheels:* 3' 6" *Cylinders:* (O) 14" x 20" *Valve Gear:* Stephenson (Slide Valves)

Number	1948	1952	1955	1959	1963	1965	w/dwn	Notes
1153	DG	87C	87K	-	-	-	10/55	Renumbered from *942, 11/49*

TOTAL 1

Cambrian   2-4-0T

1866 design by Sharp, Stewart for Cambrian Railways.
Loco Weight: 33t 3c *Driving Wheels:* 4' 6" *Cylinders:* (I) 14" x 20" *Valve Gear:* Stephenson (Slide Valves)

Number	1948	1952	1955	1959	1963	1965	w/dwn	Number	1948	1952	1955	1959	1963	1965	w/dwn
1196	OSW	-	-	-	-	-	04/48	1197	OSW	-	-	-	-	-	04/48

TOTAL 2

Alexandra Docks & Railway Co.   2-6-2T

Introduced 1920 by Hawthorn Leslie
Loco Weight: 65t 0c *Driving Wheels:* 4' 7" *Cylinders:* (O) 19" x 26" *Valve Gear:* Stephenson (Slide Valves)

Number	1948	1952	1955	1959	1963	1965	w/dwn	Number	1948	1952	1955	1959	1963	1965	w/dwn
1205	LTS	86C	86C	-	-	-	01/56	1206	HFD	-	-	-	-	-	01/51

TOTAL 2

Barclay   Liskaerd & Looe Railway   2-4-0T

Barclay design of 1902, later rebuilt with G.W.R. boiler during 1929.
Loco Weight: 32t 0c *Driving Wheels:* 4' 0" *Cylinders:* (I) 14½" x 22" *Valve Gear:* Stephenson (Slide Valves)

Number & Name		1948	1952	1955	1959	1963	1965	w/dwn
1308	Lady Margaret	OSW	-	-	-	-	-	05/48

TOTAL 1

Fox Walker   Whitland & Cardigan Railway   0-6-0ST

Introduced in 1877, and rebuilt by G.W.R. in 1927.
Loco Weight: 31t 0c *Driving Wheels:* 4' 0" *Cylinders:* (I) 16½" x 24" *Valve Gear:* Stephenson (Slide Valves)

Number	1948	1952	1955	1959	1963	1965	w/dwn
1331	OSW	-	-	-	-	-	01/50

TOTAL 1

Dübs   Midland & South Western Junction Railway   2-4-0

Introduced in 1894 by Dübs for the Midland and South Western Junction Railway, subsequently reboilered by the Great Western Railway.

Loco Weight: 35t 5c *Driving Wheels:* 5' 6" *Cylinders:* (I) 17" x 24" *Valve Gear:* Stephenson (Slide Valves)

Number	1948	1952	1955	1959	1963	1965	w/dwn	Number	1948	1952	1955	1959	1963	1965	w/dwn
1334	DID	81E	-	-	-	-	09/52	1336	RDG	81D	-	-	-	-	03/54
1335	RDG	81D	-	-	-	-	09/52								

TOTAL 3

Kitson   Cardiff Railway   0-4-0ST

Kitson design for Cardiff Railway, introduced 1898
Loco Weight: 28t 5c *Driving Wheels:* 3' 2½" *Cylinders:* (O) 14" x 21" *Valve Gear:* Hawthorn - Kitson

Number	1948	1952	1955	1959	1963	1965	w/dwn
1338	TN	83B	83B	83B	87D	-	09/63

TOTAL 1

Sharp Stewart Port Talbot Railway 0-8-2T

Sharp Stewart design for Port Talbot Railway, introduced 1902.

Loco Weight: 75t 17c *Driving Wheels:* 4' 3" *Cylinders:* (O) 20" x 26" *Valve Gear:* Stephenson (Slide Valves)

Number	1948	1952	1955	1959	1963	1965	w/dwn
1358	DG	-	-	-	-	-	02/48

TOTAL 1

1361 Churchward 0-6-0ST

Introduced in 1910 by Churchward for dock shunting.

Loco Weight: 35t 4c *Driving Wheels:* 3' 8" *Cylinders:* (O) 16" x 20" *Valve Gear:* Stephenson (Slide Valves)

Number	1948	1952	1955	1959	1963	1965	w/dwn	Number	1948	1952	1955	1959	1963	1965	w/dwn
1361	LA	83D	83D	83D	-	-	05/61	1364	LA	83D	83D	83D	-	-	01/61
1362	NA	83A	83B	83B	-	-	05/61	1365	LA	83D	83D	82C	-	-	12/62
1363	LA	83D	83D	83D	-	-	12/62								

TOTAL 5

1366 Collett 0-6-0PT

Collett development of 1361 Class, introduced 1934.

Loco Weight: 35t 15c *Driving Wheels:* 3' 8" *Cylinders:* (O) 16" x 20" *Valve Gear:* Stephenson (Slide Valves)

Number	1948	1952	1955	1959	1963	1965	w/dwn	Number	1948	1952	1955	1959	1963	1965	w/dwn
1366	SDN	82C	83B	83B	-	-	01/61	1369	SDN	82C	82C	82C	72F	-	11/64
1367	WEY	82F	82F	71G	72F	-	10/64	1370	WEY	82F	82F	71G	-	-	01/60
1368	WEY	82F	82F	71G	72F	-	10/64	1371	SDN	82C	82C	82C	-	-	11/60

TOTAL 6

1400 Collett 0-4-2T

Introduced in 1932 by Collett. Push pull fitted.

Loco Weight: 41t 6c *Driving Wheels:* 5' 2" *Cylinders:* (I) 16" x 24" *Valve Gear:* Stephenson (Slide Valves)

Number	1948	1952	1955	1959	1963	1965	w/dwn	Number	1948	1952	1955	1959	1963	1965	w/dwn
1400	SDN	82C	82C	-	-	-	06/57	1427	NA	83A	83A	83A	-	-	06/60
1401	CNYD	82D	85B	-	-	-	11/58	1428	CNYD	89A	87E	85B	-	-	06/59
1402	CHEL	85B	85B	-	-	-	10/56	1429	EXE	83C	83C	83C	-	-	03/59
1403	WEY	82C	82F	-	-	-	11/57	1430	BRD	82A	86A	-	-	-	09/58
1404	HFD	85B	85B	-	-	-	02/56	1431	FGD	87J	87J	81C	-	-	04/61
1405	EXE	83C	83C	-	-	-	09/58	1432	OSW	89A	89A	89A	89D	-	07/63
1406	GLO	85B	85B	-	-	-	03/58	1433	SDN	82C	82C	82C	-	-	01/61
1407	RDG	81D	81D	81D	-	-	06/60	1434	CHR	84J	84J	83D	-	-	07/62
1408	WOS	85A	85A	-	-	-	03/58	1435	EXE	83C	83C	81F	-	-	01/62
1409	LYD	85B	85B	82A	85B	-	10/63	1436	SDN	82C	82C	-	-	-	10/58
1410	STB	84J	81C	82C	-	-	06/61	1437	SLO	81B	81F	81F	-	-	02/59
1411	CNYD	34E	81B	-	-	-	10/56	1438	STB	84F	84F	82C	-	-	11/62
1412	OSW	89A	89A	82A	-	-	06/60	1439	NA	83A	83A	-	-	-	08/57
1413	GLO	85B	85B	-	-	-	03/56	1440	EXE	83C	83C	83C	84C	-	12/63
1414	STB	84F	84F	-	-	-	04/57	1441	LYD	85B	85B	85B	-	-	06/60
1415	BRD	82A	82A	-	-	-	02/57	1442	SLO	81F	81F	81F	83C	-	05/65
1416	CNYD	84J	84J	-	-	-	10/56	1443	SHL	81C	81C	-	-	-	06/57
1417	OSW	6C	6C	6C	-	-	02/59	1444	RDG	81D	81D	81D	81F	-	10/64
1418	WOS	85A	84A	-	-	-	10/58	1445	HFD	85C	85C	85C	81B	-	09/64
1419	FGD	83E	83E	83E	-	-	04/61	1446	SDN	82C	82C	-	-	-	09/58
1420	CHYS	88A	81F	81C	86C	-	11/64	1447	RDG	81D	81D	81D	86C	-	03/64
1421	NPT	86D	86A	83D	83C	-	12/63	1448	OXF	81B	81B	81B	-	-	06/60
1422	PPRD	86G	86G	-	-	-	06/57	1449	EXE	83C	83C	89C	-	-	06/60
1423	FGD	87J	87J	89A	-	-	01/59	1450	OXF	81B	81B	81B	83C	-	06/65
1424	GLO	85B	85B	85B	85B	-	11/63	1451	EXE	83C	83C	83C	83C	-	07/64
1425	CHYS	88A	81F	-	-	-	02/56	1452	FGD	87J	87J	83A	-	-	06/60
1426	SLO	81C	81C	85B	-	-	04/62	1453	SDN	82F	82F	71G	85B	-	11/64

Page 22

No.	1948	1952	1955	1959	1963	1965	w/dwn	No.	1948	1952	1955	1959	1963	1965	w/dwn
1454	WEY	82F	82A	82A	-	-	12/60	1465	MCH	89C	89C	-	-	-	09/58
1455	HFD	85C	85C	85C	85C	-	05/64	1466	NA	83A	83A	83A	83C	-	12/63
1456	LYD	85B	81C	85C	-	-	02/59	1467	WEY	82F	82F	71G	-	-	04/59
1457	CNYD	84J	6C	6C	-	-	02/59	1468	EXE	83C	83C	83C	-	-	03/62
1458	BAN	84F	84F	84J	89D	-	11/64	1469	EXE	83C	83C	-	-	-	09/58
1459	OSW	89A	89A	-	-	-	09/58	1470	NA	83A	83A	83A	-	-	10/62
1460	HFD	85C	85C	-	-	-	02/56	1471	LTS	86D	86D	83C	83C	-	10/63
1461	AYN	88A	85A	-	-	-	05/58	1472	CARM	87G	87G	71G	85B	-	11/64
1462	SHL	81C	81C	82C	-	-	09/62	1473	BAN	84J	34E	14D	-	-	08/62
1463	BRD	82A	82A	82A	-	-	04/61	1474	MCH	81C	81C	71G	81C	-	09/64
1464	GLO	85B	85B	82C	-	-	06/60								-

TOTAL 75

1500   Hawksworth   0-6-0PT

Heavy shunter introduced by Hawksworth in 1949. One of a couple of new Great Western designs which were built after that company ceased to exist.

Loco Weight: 58t 4c *Driving Wheels:* 4' 7½" *Cylinders:* (O) 17½" x 24" *Valve Gear:* Walschaerts (Piston Valves)

No.	1948	1952	1955	1959	1963	1965	w/dwn	No.	1948	1952	1955	1959	1963	1965	w/dwn
1500	06/49	81A	81A	81A	81A	-	12/63	1505	08/49	81A	81A	81A	-	-	05/62
1501	07/49	81C	81C	81C	-	-	01/61	1506	09/49	86B	86B	86B	81A	-	12/63
1502	07/49	81E	81E	81E	-	-	01/61	1507	09/49	86B	86B	86B	81A	-	12/63
1503	08/49	81A	81A	81A	81A	-	12/63	1508	09/49	86E	86E	86C	-	-	09/62
1504	08/49	81A	81A	81A	81A	-	05/63	1509	09/49	86A	86A	86A	-	-	08/59

TOTAL 10

Possibly the most famous class of locomotive on the Great Western was the 'CASTLE' Class, of which one of the first batch, No. 4079 'Pendennis Castle' is seen here. She was built at Swindon Works in February 1924, withdrawn during May 1964, and is now preserved.

Transport Publishing Ltd. Collection

1501   Dean / Armstrong   0-6-0PT

Dean / Armstrong design dating from 1872. After 1910, they were rebuilt with pannier tanks.

Loco Weight : 42t 17c   Driving Wheels : 4' 7½"   Cylinders : (I) 17" x 24"   Valve Gear : Stephenson (Slide Valves)

Number	1948	1952	1955	1959	1963	1965	w/dwn	Number	1948	1952	1955	1959	1963	1965	w/dwn
1531	OXF	-	-	-	-	-	12/49	1538	SPM	-	-	-	-	-	11/48
1532	CNYD	-	-	-	-	-	07/48	1542	SDN	-	-	-	-	-	02/51

Continued with Number 1742

1600   Hawksworth   0-6-0PT

Hawksworth design introduced in 1949. A classic G.W. style pannier tank built new by B.R..

Loco Weight : 41t 12c   Driving Wheels : 4' 1½"   Cylinders : (I) 16½" x 24"   Valve Gear : Stephenson (Slide Valves)

No.	1948	1952	1955	1959	1963	1965	w/dwn	No.	1948	1952	1955	1959	1963	1965	w/dwn
1600	10/49	88C	88C	88C	-	-	03/59	1635	02/51	89A	84J	84J	-	-	10/59
1601	10/49	87H	87H	87H	-	-	08/60	1636	02/51	89A	89C	89C	81B	-	06/64
1602	10/49	87H	87H	89A	-	-	09/60	1637	02/51	87H	87H	87H	-	-	06/60
1603	10/49	89C	89A	89A	-	-	06/59	1638	03/51	87F	87F	87F	89D	6C	08/66
1604	10/49	89A	89A	89A	-	-	07/60	1639	03/51	85B	85B	85B	85A	-	11/64
1605	11/49	81C	85A	85B	-	-	02/62	1640	03/51	87C	87C	87C	-	-	07/61
1606	11/49	87H	87H	87F	-	-	09/61	1641	03/51	87D	87D	87D	88E	-	11/64
1607	11/49	87F	87F	87F	87F	-	08/65	1642	04/51	85B	85B	85B	-	-	01/62
1608	11/49	83A	83A	83A	85B	-	09/63	1643	04/51	87C	87F	87F	87F	-	10/65
1609	11/49	87F	87F	87F	-	-	07/62	1644	04/51	87F	87F	87F	-	-	10/59
1610	11/49	88E	88E	88E	-	-	12/59	1645	04/51	87A	87A	87A	-	-	10/62
1611	11/49	87H	87H	87H	87F	-	10/65	1646	05/51	87D	84J	60C	-	-	12/62
1612	11/49	85B	85B	87F	88E	-	07/65	1647	05/51	82C	87C	87C	-	-	04/61
1613	12/49	87G	87F	87F	87H	-	03/65	1648	05/51	82C	87C	87C	87H	-	05/63
1614	12/49	87F	87F	87F	86A	-	02/64	1649	05/51	82B	82B	60C	-	-	12/62
1615	12/49	88C	88C	87F	-	-	06/61	1650	11/54	-	83D	83D	85B	-	02/64
1616	12/49	85B	85B	85B	-	-	10/59	1651	12/54	-	87K	87F	87F	-	10/65
1617	12/49	81F	85C	85C	86C	--	11/63	1652	12/54	-	87D	87D	-	-	01/60
1618	12/49	87F	87F	84K	-	-	05/62	1653	12/54	-	86A	86A	-	-	12/62
1619	12/49	84H	84F	87F	89B	-	05/63	1654	12/54	-	87F	87F	81B	-	06/64
1620	06/50	88E	88E	88E	-	-	06/60	1655	01/55	-	87F	87F	-	-	07/65
1621	06/50	84F	84F	84F	-	-	01/63	1656	01/55	-	86A	86A	-	-	06/64
1622	06/50	87F	87F	87F	81B	-	06/64	1657	01/55	-	85C	86C	-	-	11/64
1623	06/50	85B	85B	85B	85B	-	06/65	1658	02/55	-	82C	82C	-	-	11/64
1624	06/50	89C	83E	83E	-	-	02/62	1659	02/55	-	84J	-	-	-	10/60
1625	08/50	85B	85B	85C	-	-	06/60	1660	02/55	-	84J	89B	6C	-	02/66
1626	08/50	83E	83E	83E	-	-	08/62	1661	03/55	-	85A	85A	-	-	07/64
1627	08/50	85B	85B	85B	81F	-	06/64	1662	03/55	-	85C	86C	-	-	12/63
1628	08/50	87H	87F	87F	89B	6C	09/66	1663	03/55	-	84K	89D	-	-	01/65
1629	09/50	88A	85A	85A	-	-	06/60	1664	03/55	-	83E	82C	-	-	11/64
1630	01/51	85B	85B	85B	81F	-	06/64	1665	04/55	-	87F	87F	-	-	07/64
1631	01/51	85B	85B	85B	85B	-	11/64	1666	04/55	-	87F	89D	-	-	02/64
1632	01/51	85B	85B	85B	89B	-	04/65	1667	05/55	-	85C	86C	-	-	11/64
1633	01/51	87F	87F	87F	-	-	10/62	1668	05/55	-	83B	89D	-	-	01/65
1634	02/51	87C	87C	87C	-	-	06/61	1669	05/55	-	84K	87A	-	-	10/65

TOTAL 70

Companion volumes :

Part 2 : Southern Region, Nos. 30001 - 36005, & W1 - W36
Part 3 : London Midland & Scottish Regions, Nos. 40000 - 58937
Part 4 : Eastern, North Eastern & Scottish Regions, Nos. 60001 - 69999
Part 5 : B.R. Standard and 'Austerity' Locomotives, Nos. 70000 - 92250
Part 6 : B.R. Diesel & Electric Locomotives (1948 - 1968)

Available direct from the Publisher or from Transport Bookshops everywhere.

1854 0-6-0PT

Continued from Number 907.

Number	1948	1952	1955	1959	1963	1965	w/dwn	Number	1948	1952	1955	1959	1963	1965	w/dwn
1705	CED	-	-	-	-	-	11/50	1720	NPT	-	-	-	-	-	12/49
1706	CNYD	-	-	-	-	-	06/48	1726	PILL	-	-	-	-	-	04/48
1709	PILL	-	-	-	-	-	11/50	1730	TDU	-	-	-	-	-	08/48
1713	NPT	-	-	-	-	-	06/48	1731	SDN	-	-	-	-	-	06/49
1715	NEA	-	-	-	-	-	10/49								

Continued with Number 1752

1501 0-6-0PT

Continued from Number 1542.

Number	1948	1952	1955	1959	1963	1965	w/dwn	Number	1948	1952	1955	1959	1963	1965	w/dwn
1742	OXF	-	-	-	-	-	02/50	1747	CNYD	-	-	-	-	-	05/50
1745	STB	-	-	-	-	-	08/48	1749	STB	-	-	-	-	-	10/48

Continued with Number 1773

1854 0-6-0PT

Continued from Number 1731.

Number	1948	1952	1955	1959	1963	1965	w/dwn	Number	1948	1952	1955	1959	1963	1965	w/dwn
1752	STJ	-	-	-	-	-	03/50	1760	TNO	-	-	-	-	-	07/50
1753	TR	-	-	-	-	-	04/48	1762	XY	-	-	-	-	-	04/48
1754	DYD	-	-	-	-	-	12/49	1764	PILL	-	-	-	-	-	10/49
1758	SDN	-	-	-	-	-	03/49	1769	ABDR	-	-	-	-	-	04/48

Continued with Number 1799

1501 0-6-0PT

Continued from Number 1749.

Number	1948	1952	1955	1959	1963	1965	w/dwn	Number	1948	1952	1955	1959	1963	1965	w/dwn
1773	CNYD	-	-	-	-	-	03/50	1782	TR	-	-	-	-	-	11/50
1780	CNYD	-	-	-	-	-	08/48	1789	WEY	-	-	-	-	-	10/50

TOTAL 12

1854 0-6-0PT

Continued from Number 1769.

Number	1948	1952	1955	1959	1963	1965	w/dwn
1799	LA	-	-	-	-	-	12/49

Continued with Number 1855

1813 Dean 0-6-0ST

Introduced by Dean for G.W.R. in 1883. This was originally a side tank design which was later rebuilt as saddle tank.

Loco Weight : 44t 8c *Driving Wheels :* 4' 7½" *Cylinders :* (I) 17" x 24" *Valve Gear :* Stephenson (Slide Valves)

Number	1948	1952	1955	1959	1963	1965	w/dwn
1835	STB	-	-	-	-	-	01/49

TOTAL 1

Continued from Number 1799

Number	1948	1952	1955	1959	1963	1965	w/dwn	Number	1948	1952	1955	1959	1963	1965	w/dwn
1855	NEA	-	-	-	-	-	12/50	1884	CED	-	-	-	-	-	08/49
1858	NEA	-	-	-	-	-	10/50	1888	CED	-	-	-	-	-	12/49
1861	DID	-	-	-	-	-	11/51	1889	CDF	-	-	-	-	-	12/48
1862	NPT	-	-	-	-	-	12/50	1891	CDF	-	-	-	-	-	12/49
1863	SRD	-	-	-	-	-	09/49	1894	NPT	-	-	-	-	-	02/49
1867	DYD	-	-	-	-	-	11/48	1896	PILL	-	-	-	-	-	12/49
1870	STJ	-	-	-	-	-	10/50	1897	CED	-	-	-	-	-	01/49
1878	MTHR	-	-	-	-	-	11/49	1900	SBZ	-	-	-	-	-	04/48

TOTAL 40

1901

0-6-0PT, 0-6-0ST *

Continued from Number 992

Number	1948	1952	1955	1959	1963	1965	w/dwn	Number	1948	1952	1955	1959	1963	1965	w/dwn
1903	CARM	87G	-	-	-	-	06/52	1990	LA	-	-	-	-	-	11/49
1907	LLY	-	-	-	-	-	01/50	1991	LLY	87F	-	-	-	-	01/53
1909	TN	-	-	-	-	-	11/49	1993	BRY	-	-	-	-	-	04/51
1912	PDN	-	-	-	-	-	12/49	1996	WTD	85B	-	-	-	-	01/53
1917	BHD	-	-	-	-	-	03/51	2000	AYN	-	-	-	-	-	12/49
1919	WOS	-	-	-	-	-	11/49	2001	WOS	85A	-	-	-	-	08/52
1925 *	SHL	-	-	-	-	-	04/51	2002	LLY	-	-	-	-	-	02/52
1930	SBZ	-	-	-	-	-	08/49	2004	BHD	-	-	-	-	-	01/52
1935	OXF	81F	-	-	-	-	10/53	2006	BHD	-	-	-	-	-	12/49
1941	CARM	-	-	-	-	-	02/51	2007 *	WOS	-	-	-	-	-	12/49
1943	GLO	-	-	-	-	-	03/51	2008	CED	88C	6C	-	-	-	03/58
1945	DG	-	-	-	-	-	11/49	2009	GLO	-	-	-	-	-	01/51
1949	BHD	-	-	-	-	-	04/50	2010	WTD	87H	-	-	-	-	03/53
1957	LLY	-	-	-	-	-	04/51	2011	WTD	6C	6C	-	-	-	08/56
1964	WTD	-	-	-	-	-	02/52	2012	LLY	87F	87F	-	-	-	06/58
1965	MCH	-	-	-	-	-	01/50	2013	WTD	-	-	-	-	-	05/50
1967	LLY	-	-	-	-	-	06/51	2014	SDN	-	-	-	-	-	11/51
1968	BHD	-	-	-	-	-	09/51	2016	WOS	-	-	-	-	-	01/52
1969	SHL	-	-	-	-	-	08/49	2017	SDN	-	-	-	-	-	03/51
1973	LA	-	-	-	-	-	12/49	2018	WTD	-	-	-	-	-	12/49
1979	WTD	-	-	-	-	-	08/50	2019	LLY	-	-	-	-	-	12/49
1989	GLO	-	-	-	-	-	09/50								

TOTAL 44

2021

Dean

0-6-0PT

Introduced 1897. Dean design for Great Western Railway, originally built as saddle tanks, all later rebuilt with pannier tanks.

Loco Weight: 39t 15c *Driving Wheels:* 4' 1½" *Cylinders:* (I) 16½" x 24" *Valve Gear:* Stephenson (Slide Valves)

Number	1948	1952	1955	1959	1963	1965	w/dwn	Number	1948	1952	1955	1959	1963	1965	w/dwn
2021	PPRD	-	-	-	-	-	06/51	2033	PILL	-	-	-	-	-	03/51
2022	CED	-	-	-	-	-	12/49	2034	LYD	85A	85C	-	-	-	08/55
2023	WES	-	-	-	-	-	01/52	2035	PPRD	86G	86A	-	-	-	03/55
2025	LYD	-	-	-	-	-	05/52	2037	WOS	-	-	-	-	-	07/50
2026	HFD	-	-	-	-	-	04/51	2038	TN	83D	-	-	-	-	04/53
2027	LLY	87F	87F	-	-	-	02/57	2039	LYD	-	-	-	-	-	04/50
2029	HFD	-	-	-	-	-	11/49	2040	HFD	85B	6C	-	-	-	10/56
2030	WLN	-	-	-	-	-	02/52	2042	LLY	6C	-	-	-	-	04/53
2031	SPM	82B	-	-	-	-	01/53	2043	LYD	85C	6C	-	-	-	01/55
2032	OSW	-	-	-	-	-	06/51	2044	LYD	-	-	-	-	-	07/51

Number	1948	1952	1955	1959	1963	1965	w/dwn		Number	1948	1952	1955	1959	1963	1965	w/dwn
2045	LYD	-	-	-	-	-	12/49		2100	WOS	85A	-	-	-	-	06/52
2047	CARM	-	-	-	-	-	12/49		2101	WOS	85D	6C	-	-	-	03/56
2048	CED	-	-	-	-	-	05/52		2102	LYD	-	-	-	-	-	11/49
2050	SBZ	-	-	-	-	-	10/51		2104	BHD	-	-	-	-	-	05/51
2051	WOS	-	-	-	-	-	07/51		2106	BHD	6C	-	-	-	-	08/52
2052	BHD	-	-	-	-	-	05/50		2107	STB	84F	6C	-	-	-	06/56
2053	WES	82D	-	-	-	-	04/54		2108	BHD	6C	-	-	-	-	12/54
2054	OSW	-	-	-	-	-	03/51		2109	SRD	-	-	-	-	-	02/52
2055	SLO	-	-	-	-	-	01/51		2110	SRD	-	-	-	-	-	07/50
2056	CARM	-	-	-	-	-	03/51		2111	CARM	87G	-	-	-	-	03/53
2059	LLY	-	-	-	-	-	11/49		2112	SLO	81B	-	-	-	-	09/54
2060	SDN	82C	-	-	-	-	12/54		2113	PILL	-	-	-	-	-	03/50
2061	SRD	84A	84H	-	-	-	04/55		2114	LYD	-	-	-	-	-	12/49
2063	NPT	-	-	-	-	-	05/51		2115	WOS	85A	-	-	-	-	06/52
2064	SPM	-	-	-	-	-	11/49		2117	ABDR	-	-	-	-	-	06/51
2065	BAN	-	-	-	-	-	11/49		2121	LYD	85B	-	-	-	-	06/52
2066	CHYS	-	-	-	-	-	09/51		2122	NPT	86A	-	-	-	-	11/52
2067	SRD	6C	-	-	-	-	11/52		2123	CED	88B	-	-	-	-	10/52
2068	OSW	89A	-	-	-	-	01/53		2124	CED	-	-	-	-	-	07/50
2069	CARM	87G	87G	6C	-	-	04/59		2126	LLY	-	-	-	-	-	09/50
2070	SPM	82B	82B	-	-	-	08/55		2127	TN	83B	-	-	-	-	09/52
2071	TYS	-	-	-	-	-	06/50		2129	BHD	6C	-	-	-	-	03/53
2072	BRD	82A	6C	-	-	-	07/56		2130	CED	-	-	-	-	-	05/50
2073	NPT	-	-	-	-	-	06/51		2131	LYD	-	-	-	-	-	11/51
2075	OSW	-	-	-	-	-	03/51		2132	LYD	-	-	-	-	-	08/50
2076	RDG	-	-	-	-	-	10/51		2134	DG	6C	6C	-	-	-	05/57
2079	DYD	87B	-	-	-	-	11/52		2135	SPM	82B	-	-	-	-	01/53
2080	LYD	-	-	-	-	-	03/52		2136	PILL	86A	6C	-	-	-	04/55
2081	LLY	87F	-	-	-	-	09/54		2137	LLY	-	-	-	-	-	12/49
2082	DG	6C	6C	-	-	-	06/55		2138	HFD	85C	85C	-	-	-	05/56
2083	LLY	-	-	-	-	-	11/51		2140	CED	-	-	-	-	-	05/52
2085	LLY	6C	-	-	-	-	08/53		2141	CED	-	-	-	-	-	10/50
2086	CED	-	-	-	-	-	05/52		2144	LYD	85C	85A	-	-	-	05/55
2088	EXE	83C	83B	-	-	-	08/55		2146	GLO	87C	-	-	-	-	03/53
2089	BHD	-	-	-	-	-	09/51		2147	CED	88B	-	-	-	-	03/53
2090	STB	86A	86A	-	-	-	03/55		2148	PZ	-	-	-	-	-	02/52
2091	LYD	-	-	-	-	-	04/50		2150	LLY	-	-	-	-	-	01/52
2092	STB	6C	6C	-	-	-	08/55		2151	MCH	-	-	-	-	-	05/52
2093	KDR	-	-	-	-	-	01/52		2152	TYS	-	-	-	-	-	11/51
2094	PPRD	-	-	-	-	-	05/52		2153	LYD	-	-	-	-	-	12/50
2095	SRD	-	-	-	-	-	04/51		2154	PILL	-	-	-	-	-	01/52
2096	HFD	-	-	-	-	-	05/50		2155	LYD	-	-	-	-	-	11/50
2097	NA	83E	83D	-	-	-	03/55		2156	SRD	6C	-	-	-	-	02/53
2098	LLY	-	-	-	-	-	05/51		2159	PPRD	-	-	-	-	-	08/51
2099	HFD	6C	-	-	-	-	06/54		2160	LYD	85C	85A	-	-	-	02/57

TOTAL 110

Burry Port & Gwendraeth Valley Railway 0-6-0T

1912 Design for Burry Port & Gwendraeth Valley Railway.
2162/5/7/8 were rebuilt by the Great Western Railway.

Loco Weight : 37t 15c Driving Wheels : 3' 9" Cylinders : (O) 16" x 24" Valve Gear : Stephenson (Slide Valves)

Number	1948	1952	1955	1959	1963	1965	w/dwn		Number	1948	1952	1955	1959	1963	1965	w/dwn
2162	LLY	87F	87F	-	-	-	03/55		2167	LLY	87F	-	-	-	-	02/53
2165	LLY	87F	87F	-	-	-	03/55		2168	LLY	87F	87F	-	-	-	05/56
2166	SED	87D	87D	-	-	-	05/55									

TOTAL 5

Burry Port & Gwendraeth Valley Railway   0-6-0ST

1907 Avonside design for Burry Port & Gwendraeth Railway, later rebuilt by G.W.R.
Loco Weight: 38t 5c *Driving Wheels:* 3' 6" *Cylinders:* (O) 15" x 22" *Valve Gear:* Stephenson (slide valves)

Number	1948	1952	1955	1959	w/dwn
2176	LLY	87F	87F	-	03/55

TOTAL 1

2181   0-6-0PT

Introduced 1939, '2021' Class locos with increased brake power for heavy gradients.
Loco Weight: 39t 15c *Driving Wheels:* 4' 1½" *Cylinders:* (I) 16½" x 24" *Valve Gear:* Stephenson (slide valves)

Number	1948	1952	1955	1959	1963	1965	w/dwn	Number	1948	1952	1955	1959	1963	1965	w/dwn
2181	SBZ	-	-	-	-	-	02/52	2186	STB	84J	84J	-	-	-	04/55
2182	SBZ	83E	83E	-	-	-	08/55	2187	STB	-	-	-	-	-	02/52
2183	CNYD	83A	84J	-	-	-	05/55	2188	CNYD	-	-	-	-	-	02/52
2184	CNYD	-	-	-	-	-	11/50	2189	STB	-	-	-	-	-	10/50
2185	STB	84J	-	-	-	-	12/52	2190	CNYD	-	-	-	-	-	04/51

TOTAL 10

Burry Port & Gwendraeth Valley Railway   0-6-0ST

R.A. Carr design for Burry Port & Gwendraeth Railway, introduced in 1900
Loco Weight: 38t 0c *Driving Wheels:* 3' 6" *Cylinders:* (O) 15" x 22" *Valve Gear:* Stephenson (slide valves)

Number & Name	1948	1952	1955	1959	W/dwn
2192 Ashburnham	NEA	-	-	-	04/51

TOTAL 1

Burry Port & Gwendraeth Valley Railway   0-6-0ST

Introduced 1901, R.A. Carr design for Burry Port & Gwendraeth Railway.
Loco Weight: 35t 12c *Driving Wheels:* 3' 6" *Cylinders:* (O) 15" x 22" *Valve Gear:* Stephenson (slide valves)

Number & Name	1948	1952	1955	1959	W/dwn
2193 Burry Port	LLY	-	-	-	02/52

TOTAL 1

Burry Port & Gwendraeth Valley Railway   0-6-0ST

Introduced 1903, Eager design for Burry Port & Gwendraeth Railway.
Loco Weight: 31t 7c *Driving Wheels:* 3' 6" *Cylinders:* (O) 15" x 20" *Valve Gear:* Stephenson (slide valves)

Number & Name	1948	1952	1955	1959	W/dwn
2194 Kidwelly	TN	83B	-	-	02/53
2195 Cym Mawr	SDN	82C	-	-	01/53

TOTAL 2

Burry Port & Gwendraeth Valley Railway   0-6-0ST

Introduced 1906, Avonside Engine Company design for Burry Port & Gwendraeth Railway.
Loco Weight: 38t 0c *Driving Wheels:* 3' 6" *Cylinders:* (O) 15" x 22" *Valve Gear:* Stephenson (slide valves)

Number & Name	1948	1952	1955	1959	W/dwn
2196 Gwendraeth	LLY	87F	87F	-	01/56

TOTAL 1

Burry Port & Gwendraeth Valley Railway 0-6-0ST

Hudswell Clark design for Burry Port & Gwendraeth Valley Railway, introduced 1909.

Loco Weight: 36t 8c *Driving Wheels:* 3' 9" *Cylinders:* (O) 15" x 22" *Valve Gear:* Stephenson (Slide Valves)

Number & Name	1948	1952	1955	1959	W/dwn
2197 Pioneer	LLY	87F	-	-	10/52

TOTAL 1

Burry Port & Gwendraeth Valley Railway 0-6-0ST

Hudswell Clark design for Burry Port & Gwendraeth Valley Railway, introduced 1910. Later rebuilt by G.W.R.

Loco Weight: 37t 15c *Driving Wheels:* 3' 9" *Cylinders:* (O) 15" x 22" *Valve Gear:* Stephenson (Slide Valves)

Number	1948	1952	1955	1959	1963	W/dwn
2198	LLY	87F	87F	87F	-	03/59

TOTAL 1

2251   Collett   0-6-0

Mixed Traffic design by Collett, introduced 1930. Built over a period of nearly twenty years, the last two were delivered to British Railways.

Loco Weight: 43t 8c *Driving Wheels:* 5' 2" *Cylinders:* (I) 17½" x 24" *Valve Gear:* Stephenson (Slide Valves)

No.	1948	1952	1955	1959	1963	1965	w/dwn	No.	1948	1952	1955	1959	1963	1965	w/dwn
2200	ABH	89C	89C	89C	-	-	09/62	2236	CARM	87G	81F	84K	89C	-	05/65
2201	OSW	89C	82B	89C	81E	-	06/64	2237	WOS	85A	85A	89C	-	-	06/59
2202	DID	81F	84C	89C	-	-	10/60	2238	TYS	84E	84E	84E	-	-	06/59
2203	TYS	84E	82B	82C	-	-	09/60	2239	NPT	86A	86A	89A	-	-	05/62
2204	MCH	89C	89C	89C	82G	-	12/63	2240	DID	81E	81E	81E	-	-	06/62
2205	WOS	85A	85A	82B	-	-	06/59	2241	WOS	85A	85A	85C	86C	-	02/64
2206	TYS	89C	84G	85A	-	-	12/61	2242	WOS	85A	85A	85C	86C	-	05/65
2207	WOS	85A	85D	85B	-	-	04/61	2243	HFD	81A	81A	81A	-	-	01/63
2208	RDG	81D	83B	87H	-	-	06/59	2244	OSW	89A	84G	89C	82C	-	06/65
2209	TYS	84J	84C	85A	-	-	08/62	2245	RDG	81D	81D	81D	85B	-	05/63
2210	OSW	89A	89A	84G	84D	-	06/65	2246	STB	84F	84C	81E	85A	-	12/63
2211	TN	83B	83C	84C	84D	-	11/64	2247	WOS	85A	85A	85A	82G	-	02/64
2212	TN	83B	83B	81D	-	-	12/62	2248	GLO	85B	85B	85B	87G	-	09/64
2213	TN	83B	83B	82B	-	-	11/60	2249	OXF	85C	85C	85C	86C	-	09/64
2214	TN	83B	81E	81E	89A	-	05/65	2250	SDN	82C	82B	82B	-	-	08/62
2215	TN	82B	82B	82C	-	-	10/61	2251	SPM	82B	82B	89C	82E	-	12/63
2216	CARM	87G	87G	87G	-	-	01/62	2252	DID	81E	81E	81E	-	-	12/59
2217	CARM	87G	89C	89C	82E	-	11/64	2253	SPM	82B	85A	85B	85B	-	03/65
2218	NPT	86A	86A	86A	86A	-	11/64	2254	CARM	85B	85B	85B	-	-	01/59
2219	MCH	89C	89A	89A	82G	-	03/64	2255	OSW	89A	89A	89C	-	-	05/62
2220	SPM	82B	87H	87H	-	-	12/61	2256	BAN	84C	84C	84C	-	-	09/62
2221	DID	81E	81E	81E	81E	-	11/64	2257	TYS	84E	84E	84E	81D	-	09/64
2222	DID	81E	81A	81A	85A	-	05/65	2258	SPM	82B	85A	82C	-	-	12/58
2223	ABH	87J	87J	87J	-	-	05/62	2259	CNYD	84J	84C	84C	-	-	04/59
2224	SDN	82C	87G	87G	-	-	09/63	2260	ABH	89C	89C	89C	-	-	11/61
2225	SPM	82B	85C	89B	-	-	06/59	2261	TN	83B	82B	82B	81D	-	09/64
2226	DID	81E	87H	87E	-	-	08/59	2262	CHR	85A	82C	81D	-	-	12/59
2227	CNYD	86A	86A	86A	-	-	04/61	2263	WOS	85A	85A	87H	-	-	01/59
2228	SALOP	84G	87H	87H	-	-	06/59	2264	RDG	81D	81D	89C	-	-	09/60
2229	SALOP	84G	87H	87H	-	-	09/62	2265	SPM	82B	82B	82B	-	-	09/60
2230	EXE	83C	83C	84C	-	-	01/62	2266	TN	83B	85C	85C	-	-	10/59
2231	SALOP	84G	86E	86E	86E	-	02/65	2267	TN	83B	83B	85A	-	-	11/61
2232	SRD	84F	84G	89C	85B	-	09/64	2268	TN	83B	83B	82D	82D	-	05/65
2233	SALOP	89C	89A	89C	-	-	11/61	2269	SPM	82B	82B	82B	-	-	01/59
2234	SALOP	84G	84G	84C	-	-	05/62	2270	STB	84F	84C	84C	-	-	09/62
2235	SALOP	84G	89B	83B	-	-	08/59	2271	CARM	87G	89C	89C	-	-	09/62

Continued with Number 3200.

No.	1948	1952	1955	1959	1963	1965	w/dwn	No.	1948	1952	1955	1959	1963	1965	w/dwn
2272	CARM	87G	87G	87G	-	-	08/59	2286	HFD	85C	89A	89C	86C	-	09/64
2273	LDR	87E	87G	87G	82D	-	12/63	2287	CNYD	89B	89B	89B	87G	-	05/65
2274	WOS	85A	85C	84G	-	-	09/60	2288	WTD	87H	87H	87H	-	-	12/61
2275	TN	83B	83B	89A	-	-	02/60	2289	DID	81E	81F	84G	84C	-	05/64
2276	PDN	81A	81A	81A	-	-	09/62	2290	WOS	85A	85A	87G	-	-	06/59
2277	WOS	85A	85A	85A	82E	-	12/63	2291	CARM	.85B	85B	85B	82C	-	09/64
2278	WOS	85A	85A	87J	-	-	09/59	2292	TYS	89C	86E	86E	-	-	06/62
2279	STB	84F	84E	84E	-	-	01/59	2293	SPM	82B	82B	82C	-	-	07/59
2280	NPT	86A	86A	89C	-	-	09/59	2294	WOS	85A	85A	84K	-	-	09/62
2281	STB	85C	85C	89C	-	-	11/59	2295	BAN	85B	85A	85C	-	-	07/62
2282	PDN	81A	81A	81A	-	-	05/60	2296	TYS	84E	84E	85A	-	-	10/59
2283	ABH	87H	87H	87H	87H	-	12/63	2297	TYS	84J	84C	84C	-	-	09/60
2284	CRM	87G	87E	87E	-	-	06/59	2298	ABH	89C	89C	89C	86A	-	12/63
2285	SHL	81C	81C	89C	-	-	11/59	2299	RDG	81D	81D	81D	-	-	09/59

Continued with Number 3200.

2301   Dean Goods   0-6-0

Dean design introduced in 1883, later superheated. Many saw service in France during W.W.I.

Loco Weight: 36t 16c   *Driving Wheels:* 5' 2"   *Cylinders:* (I) 17½" x 24"   *Valve Gear:* Stephenson (Slide Valves)

No.	1948	1952	1955	1959	1963	1965	w/dwn	No.	1948	1952	1955	1959	1963	1965	w/dwn
2322	SPM	-	-	-	-	-	06/51	2460	STJ	86E	-	-	-	-	04/54
2323	MCH	89C	-	-	-	-	06/53	2462	BRD	82B	-	-	-	-	01/53
2327	OSW	89A	-	-	-	-	04/53	2464	MCH	-	-	-	-	-	12/49
2339	WOS	-	-	-	-	-	03/52	2468	BCN	89B	-	-	-	-	01/53
2340	SPM	82B	-	-	-	-	06/54	2474	CARM	87G	81D	-	-	-	04/55
2343	BCN	89B	-	-	-	-	02/53	2482	OSW	89A	-	-	-	-	12/52
2349	HFD	-	-	-	-	-	03/52	2483	OSW	89A	-	-	-	-	09/52
2350	LYD	85C	-	-	-	-	01/53	2484	CDF	89A	-	-	-	-	05/54
2351	BCN	89B	-	-	-	-	02/53	2513	CHR	84K	89B	-	-	-	07/55
2354	OSW	89A	-	-	-	-	04/53	2515	LYD	85C	-	-	-	-	02/53
2356	MCH	-	-	-	-	-	07/48	2516	OSW	89A	89A	-	-	-	05/56
2382	OSW	-	-	-	-	-	04/50	2523	BCN	-	-	-	-	-	09/49
2385	PPRD	-	-	-	-	-	10/51	2532	DID	81E	-	-	-	-	05/54
2386	OSW	-	-	-	-	-	12/50	2534	SPM	82D	-	-	-	-	01/53
2401	BCN	89B	-	-	-	-	01/53	2537	CDF	86C	-	-	-	-	01/53
2407	NPT	-	-	-	-	-	01/52	2538	CDF	89A	89A	-	-	-	05/57
2408	BAN	89A	-	-	-	-	01/53	2541	HFD	85C	-	-	-	-	06/54
2409	CARM	89A	-	-	-	-	04/53	2543	OSW	89A	-	-	-	-	02/53
2411	CARM	87A	-	-	-	-	04/54	2551	WOS	85A	-	-	-	-	09/53
2414	STJ	86E	-	-	-	-	03/53	2556	OSW	89A	-	-	-	-	06/53
2426	SPM	82B	-	-	-	-	12/53	2568	SDN	82C	-	-	-	-	05/53
2431	CARM	-	-	-	-	-	11/51	2569	BCN	-	-	-	-	-	10/48
2444	BRD	82D	-	-	-	-	11/52	2570	CDF	-	-	-	-	-	01/49
2445	WES	82B	-	-	-	-	03/53	2572	MCH	89A	-	-	-	-	12/52
2449	OSW	89A	-	-	-	-	01/53	2573	RDG	81D	-	-	-	-	02/53
2452	BCN	89B	-	-	-	-	10/52	2578	SPM	82B	-	-	-	-	09/53
2458	WOS	85A	-	-	-	-	05/54	2579	OXF	81F	-	-	-	-	01/53

TOTAL 54

2600   Aberdare   2-6-0

Dean design of 1900, which was unusual for a 2-6-0 in having double framing.

Loco Weight: 56t 15c   *Driving Wheels:* 4' 7½"   *Cylinders:* (I) 18" x 26"   *Valve Gear:* Stephenson (Slide Valves)

No.	1948	1952	1955	1959	1963	1965	w/dwn	No.	1948	1952	1955	1959	1963	1965	w/dwn
2612	BAN	-	-	-	-	-	01/48	2643	BAN	-	-	-	-	-	07/48
2620	STB	-	-	-	-	-	08/49	2651	WOS	-	-	-	-	-	06/49
2623	OXY	-	-	-	-	-	02/48	2655	STB	-	-	-	-	-	06/49

Number	1948	1952	1955	1959	1963	1965	w/dwn	Number	1948	1952	1955	1959	1963	1965	w/dwn
2656	GLO	-	-	-	-	-	03/48	2667	CDF	-	-	-	-	-	10/49
2662	CHR	-	-	-	-	-	07/48	2669	PPRD	-	-	-	-	-	05/48
2665	OXY	-	-	-	-	-	01/48	2680	HFD	-	-	-	-	-	06/48

TOTAL 12

2700   Dean   0-6-0PT

Dean saddletank, introduced in 1896. Later rebuilt with pannier tanks.

Loco Weight : 45t 13c   *Driving Wheels :* 4' 7½"   *Cylinders :* (I) 17½" x 24"   *Valve Gear :* Stephenson (Slide Valves)

No.	1948	1952	1955	1959	1963	1965	w/dwn	No.	1948	1952	1955	1959	1963	1965	w/dwn
2702	SPM	-	-	-	-	-	01/50	2754	CED	-	-	-	-	-	10/50
2704	CNYD	-	-	-	-	-	03/50	2755	TN	-	-	-	-	-	08/48
2706	STB	-	-	-	-	-	10/48	2756	GLO	-	-	-	-	-	05/49
2707	LLY	-	-	-	-	-	07/50	2757	SLO	-	-	-	-	-	02/50
2708	TN	-	-	-	-	-	07/49	2760	MTHR	-	-	-	-	-	10/50
2709	SPM	-	-	-	-	-	09/48	2761	TDU	-	-	-	-	-	03/50
2712	STB	-	-	-	-	-	03/50	2764	PILL	-	-	-	-	-	07/48
2713	CNYD	-	-	-	-	-	09/49	2767	PPRD	-	-	-	-	-	01/49
2714	HFD	-	-	-	-	-	05/48	2769	TDU	-	-	-	-	-	03/49
2715	DYD	-	-	-	-	-	07/50	2771	STB	-	-	-	-	-	06/50
2716	CNYD	-	-	-	-	-	09/50	2772	LMTN	-	-	-	-	-	11/49
2717	CNYD	-	-	-	-	-	10/48	2774	WOS	-	-	-	-	-	04/48
2719	TYS	-	-	-	-	-	11/50	2776	LA	-	-	-	-	-	04/48
2721	DYD	-	-	-	-	-	08/50	2780	SBZ	-	-	-	-	-	07/50
2722	NEA	-	-	-	-	-	11/50	2781	CED	-	-	-	-	-	06/48
2724	CED	-	-	-	-	-	02/49	2785	NA	-	-	-	-	-	04/48
2728	PPRD	-	-	-	-	-	04/48	2786	SPM	-	-	-	-	-	12/49
2730	LLY	-	-	-	-	-	04/48	2787	PANT	-	-	-	-	-	12/49
2734	PILL	-	-	-	-	-	08/48	2789	SED	-	-	-	-	-	05/49
2738	PILL	-	-	-	-	-	12/49	2790	SLO	-	-	-	-	-	06/50
2739	PPRD	-	-	-	-	-	05/48	2791	SRD	-	-	-	-	-	04/50
2743	WOS	-	-	-	-	-	10/50	2792	DYD	-	-	-	-	-	06/50
2744	SALOP	-	-	-	-	-	11/50	2793	PILL	-	-	-	-	-	01/48
2745	SALOP	-	-	-	-	-	01/50	2794	NPT	-	-	-	-	-	11/49
2746	LLY	-	-	-	-	-	07/48	2795	NPT	-	-	-	-	-	01/49
2748	TN	-	-	-	-	-	04/48	2797	NEA	-	-	-	-	-	06/48
2749	PPRD	-	-	-	-	-	04/48	2798	DG	-	-	-	-	-	11/49
2751	LLY	-	-	-	-	-	04/48	2799	WOS	-	-	-	-	-	03/50
2752	PZ	-	-	-	-	-	03/48								

TOTAL 57

28xx   Churchward   2-8-0

Introduced 1903, Churchward design for G.W.R..

Number 2884 onwards were introduced by Collett in 1938, the most noticeable difference being the fitting of side window cabs. (Weight was increased to 76t 5c)

In 1947 twenty were converted for oil burning and were renumbered into the 48xx series. They were renumbered back to original series between 1948 and 1949.

Loco Weight : 75t 10c   *Driving Wheels :* 4' 7½"   *Cylinders :* (O) 18½" x 30"   *Valve Gear :* Stephenson (Slide Valves)

Number	1948	1952	1955	1959	1963	1965	w/dwn	Notes
2800	PPRD	87B	87B	-	-	-	04/58	
2801	ABDR	86G	86G	86G	-	-	12/58	
2802	PPRD	86G	86G	81E	-	-	12/58	
2803	WES	81F	86E	86E	-	-	04/59	
2804	STJ	86E	84F	84F	-	-	07/59	
2805	BAN	86B	86C	83A	-	-	05/60	

Number	1948	1952	1955	1959	1963	1965	w/dwn	Notes
2806	ABDR	86C	86E	86E	-	-	03/60	
2807	HFD	85A	85A	86A	86E	-	03/63	
2808	ABDR	86J	86E	87F	-	-	09/59	
2809	STJ	83A	83A	83D	-	-	01/60	
2810	ABDR	84K	86J	86J	-	-	09/59	
2811	ABDR	86E	86E	82D	-	-	10/59	
2812	CHR	84K	84C	84E	-	-	01/59	
2813	PPRD	87B	86E	86C	-	-	11/60	
2814	TN	83B	83B	-	-	-	08/58	
2815	STJ	81D	86E	86E	-	-	12/59	
2816	BAN	84C	84C	84C	-	-	10/59	
2817	WEY	86A	84C	86G	-	-	03/59	
2818	WES	82B	82C	82C	86A	-	10/63	
2819	STJ	86A	84B	84B	-	-	01/61	
2820	CDF	86C	81D	-	-	-	11/58	
2821	CDF	81D	86G	86C	-	-	09/60	
2822	ABDR	84K	84C	83B	83B	-	11/64	
2823	ABDR	84G	84C	86A	-	-	04/59	
2824	STJ	87F	81D	81D	-	-	08/59	
2825	OXY	81D	8A	86G	-	-	03/59	
2826	PDN	84E	84G	86E	-	-	09/59	
2827	OXF	81F	84C	-	-	-	08/58	
2828	ABDR	86J	86J	86J	-	-	01/59	
2829	STJ	86E	86E	85B	-	-	02/59	
2830	OXY	84B	84B	84B	-	-	01/59	
2831	ABDR	86J	86J	86J	-	-	01/60	
2832	LLY	84B	84G	86E	-	-	11/59	Renumbered from 4806, 04/49
2833	BHD	84B	84B	86G	-	-	03/59	
2834	LA	86A	84C	86G	-	-	11/62	Renumbered from 4808, 01/50
2835	PDN	84C	84C	82C	-	-	05/60	
2836	ABDR	86J	86J	86J	81E	-	06/64	
2837	CDF	86C	86C	86C	-	-	05/60	
2838	STJ	86E	86E	86E	-	-	08/59	
2839	SPM	86E	86E	86A	86G	-	06/64	Renumbered from 4804, 10/48
2840	PDN	84J	84J	84J	-	-	06/59	
2841	ABDR	84G	84B	84B	81D	-	12/63	
2842	NPT	86A	86A	86A	81E	-	09/63	
2843	SHL	83D	83D	83D	-	-	06/59	
2844	SPM	86E	86E	86E	-	-	02/60	
2845	PDN	81C	82B	86A	84C	-	07/63	Renumbered from 4809, 12/49
2846	SPM	82B	83A	83A	-	-	11/60	
2847	LA	84C	84C	86C	-	-	03/60	Renumbered from 4811, 06/49
2848	LA	84E	84E	86G	-	-	06/59	Renumbered from 4807, 07/49
2849	STJ	84E	84E	84E	-	-	08/62	Renumbered from 4803, 04/49
2850	PDN	87F	84C	84B	-	-	02/60	
2851	NPT	86A	86A	84E	84C	-	06/63	
2852	STB	84F	82C	82C	81E	-	10/63	
2853	SPM	84J	84J	84C	-	-	05/62	Renumbered from 4810, 06/49
2854	STJ	84B	84B	85B	86E	-	10/63	Renumbered from 4801, 02/49
2855	PDN	87F	85A	86G	-	-	12/62	
2856	PDN	84F	84E	84E	84B	-	04/64	
2857	LA	84C	84C	86G	87A	-	04/63	
2858	SHL	84B	86A	86A	-	-	01/63	
2859	SPM	86E	86E	86C	86G	-	12/64	
2860	CDF	81F	86E	86E	-	-	04/62	
2861	OXF	86A	86A	86A	86E	-	03/63	
2862	LLY	86G	86E	86E	86E	-	04/64	Renumbered from 4802, 09/48
2863	LLY	86B	86J	86J	-	-	06/59	Renumbered from 4805, 05/49
2864	CDF	86G	86E	86C	-	-	06/59	

A gleaming Collett 0-6-0 No. 2222 stands in the sunshine after a repaint into lined green livery.

Transport Publishing Ltd. Collection

28xx 2-6-0 No. 2829.

Transport Publishing Ltd. Collection

Number	1948	1952	1955	1959	1963	1965	w/dwn	Notes
2865	NPT	84B	82C	82C	-	-	01/63	
2866	NPT	86A	86E	86E	84C	-	03/63	
2867	LA	84E	84C	86C	86A	-	07/63	
2868	PDN	84B	82B	86A	-	-	06/59	
2869	BAN	83A	83A	86E	-	-	06/59	
2870	ABDR	86J	86J	86J	-	-	06/59	
2871	BAN	84J	84J	84J	83B	-	05/63	
2872	LLY	87F	86E	86E	86E	-	08/63	Renumbered from *4800, 09/48*
2873	EXE	84F	86C	86E	81C	-	12/64	
2874	BAN	84F	84F	86C	87A	-	05/63	
2875	PDN	83A	83A	83A	84C	-	04/64	
2876	NPT	86A	86J	86J	88J	-	01/65	
2877	CDF	86C	86C	86C	-	-	01/60	
2878	BAN	84J	84J	84J	-	-	06/59	
2879	NPT	86A	82B	82C	82C	-	08/64	
2880	ABDR	81C	81C	81F	-	-	06/59	
2881	OXF	83A	83A	83A	-	-	01/60	
2882	BAN	84B	84B	84E	83B	-	12/63	
2883	CHR	86B	86E	86E	-	-	11/62	
2884	STJ	86G	86G	86G	86E	-	04/64	
2885	BAN	84F	84F	84E	86A	-	01/64	
2886	CHR	84C	84C	84E	82D	-	06/64	
2887	STJ	86E	86E	86E	88L	-	06/64	
2888	LLY	86G	86E	87F	84C	-	02/63	Renumbered from *4850, 09/48*
2889	CDF	86A	82B	86C	81D	-	04/63	
2890	CDF	84K	84K	84C	82C	-	04/65	
2891	CDF	86C	86C	86C	86A	-	10/64	
2892	STJ	86C	86C	86C	86E	-	05/63	
2893	PPRD	86G	86E	86C	81E	-	11/64	
2894	NPT	86A	87B	86A	86A	-	08/63	
2895	BRD	86E	86E	86C	86E	-	04/65	
2896	NPT	86A	86C	86E	86G	-	06/64	
2897	SALOP	84C	84C	84E	86G	-	03/63	
2898	BAN	84C	82B	86A	81E	-	10/64	
2899	BAN	81C	81C	81C	81C	-	03/65	

Continued with Number 3800

2900   'Saint'   4-6-0

Introduced 1903 by Churchward, design based on pioneer loco No. 100 (later 2900 Saint Martin). Nos. 2979 - 2989 were originally built as 4-4-2, later rebuilt to 4-6-0.

Loco Weight : 72t 0c   *Driving Wheels :* 6' 8½"   *Cylinders :* (O) 18½" x 30"   *Valve Gear :* Stephenson (piston valves)

Number & Name		1948	1952	1955	1959	1963	1965	w/dwn	Notes
2902	Lady of the Lake	LMTN	-	-	-	-	-	08/49	
2903	Lady of Lyons	TYS	-	-	-	-	-	11/49	
2905	Lady Macbeth	CDF	-	-	-	-	-	04/48	
2906	Lady of Lynn	CDF	86C	-	-	-	-	08/52	
2908	Lady of Quality	SDN	-	-	-	-	-	12/50	
2912	Saint Ambrose	WEY	-	-	-	-	-	02/51	
2913	Saint Andrew	SDN	-	-	-	-	-	05/48	
2915	Saint Bartholomew	CHR	-	-	-	-	-	10/50	
2916	Saint Benedict	TYS	-	-	-	-	-	07/48	
2920	Saint David	HFD	85C	-	-	-	-	10/53	
2924	Saint Helena	HFD	-	-	-	-	-	03/50	
2926	Saint Nicholas	CHR	-	-	-	-	-	09/51	
2927	Saint Patrick	SDN	-	-	-	-	-	12/51	
2928	Saint Sebastian	WES	-	-	-	-	-	08/48	
2929	Saint Stephen	BRD	-	-	-	-	-	12/49	
2930	Saint Vincent	CHR	-	-	-	-	-	11/49	

Number & Name		1948	1952	1955	1959	1963	1965	w/dwn	Notes
2931	Arlington Court	BRD	-	-	-	-	-	02/51	
2932	Ashton Court	HFD	-	-	-	-	-	06/51	
2933	Bilbury Court	LMTN	84D	-	-	-	-	01/53	
2934	Butleigh Court	SDN	82C	-	-	-	-	06/52	
2935	Caynham Court	SDN	-	-	-	-	-	12/48	
2936	Cefntilla Court	NPT	-	-	-	-	-	04/51	
2937	Clevedon Court	HFD	85C	-	-	-	-	06/53	
2938	Corsham Court	GLO	85C	-	-	-	-	08/52	
2939	Croome Court	BRD	-	-	-	-	-	12/50	
2940	Dorney Court	CDF	-	-	-	-	-	01/52	
2941	Easton Court	WES	-	-	-	-	-	12/49	
2942	Fawley Court	BRD	-	-	-	-	-	12/49	
2943	Hampton Court	CDF	-	-	-	-	-	01/51	
2944	Highnam Court	HFD	-	-	-	-	-	11/51	
2945	Hillingdon Court	SDN	82C	-	-	-	-	06/53	
2946	Langford Court	WES	-	-	-	-	-	11/49	
2947	Madresfield Court	SDN	-	-	-	-	-	04/51	
2948	Stackpole Court	HFD	-	-	-	-	-	11/51	
2949	Stanford Court	SDN	-	-	-	-	-	01/52	
2950	Taplow Court	BRD	82A	-	-	-	-	09/52	
2951	Tawstock Court	HFD	85B	-	-	-	-	06/52	
2952	Twineham Court	STJ	-	-	-	-	-	09/51	
2953	Titley Court	CHR	-	-	-	-	-	02/52	
2954	Tockenham Court	SDN	82C	-	-	-	-	06/52	
2955	Tortworth Court	WEY	-	-	-	-	-	03/50	
2979	Quentin Durward	NPT	-	-	-	-	-	01/51	
2980	Cœur de Lion	GLO	-	-	-	-	-	05/48	
2981	Ivanhoe	BAN	-	-	-	-	-	03/51	
2987	Bride of Lammermoor	HFD	-	-	-	-	-	10/49	
2988	Rob Roy	TYS	-	-	-	-	-	05/48	
2989	Talisman	CHR	-	-	-	-	-	09/48	

TOTAL 47

ROD   Robinson G.C.R.   2-8-0

Robinson G.C.R. design built from 1917 for Railway Operating Division (Royal Engineers) for use in France and the Western Front. After war service, one hundred were purchased by G.W.R. All subsequently received Great Western boiler fittings. **3005** swapped identity with **3033** in 1949.

Loco Weight : 73t 11c   *Driving Wheels :* 4' 8"   *Cylinders :* (O) 21" x 26"   *Valve Gear :* Stephenson (Piston Valves)

No.	1948	1952	1955	1959	1963	1965	w/dwn	No.	1948	1952	1955	1959	1963	1965	w/dwn
3002	PPRD	-	-	-	-	-	04/48	3025	RDG	86G	-	-	-	-	07/54
3004	CARM	-	-	-	-	-	02/48	3026	CNYD	84C	-	-	-	-	12/54
3005	TYS	-	-	-	-	-	08/48	3027	WOS	-	-	-	-	-	05/48
3006	CARM	-	-	-	-	-	06/48	3028	CNYD	84F	84B	-	-	-	08/56
3008	SRD	-	-	-	-	-	09/48	3029	WOS	85A	84B	-	-	-	05/56
3009	CARM	-	-	-	-	-	06/48	3030	WOS	-	-	-	-	-	07/48
3010	CARM	87G	87G	-	-	-	03/56	3031	OXY	84B	84B	-	-	-	05/56
3011	CARM	87G	87G	-	-	-	10/58	3032	WES	82B	82B	-	-	-	10/55
3012	PPRD	86G	84E	-	-	-	05/56	3033	OXY	84J	-	-	-	-	05/53
3013	SPM	-	-	-	-	-	09/48	3034	SPM	82B	-	-	-	-	02/53
3014	WES	82B	87G	-	-	-	10/55	3035	WES	-	-	-	-	-	08/48
3015	CARM	87A	87G	-	-	-	10/58	3036	ABDR	86G	86G	-	-	-	03/58
3016	OXY	84E	84B	-	-	-	10/56	3037	PPRD	-	-	-	-	-	08/48
3017	SPM	84C	82B	-	-	-	10/56	3038	CDF	86G	86G	-	-	-	07/56
3018	PPRD	86G	87G	-	-	-	01/57	3039	OXY	-	-	-	-	-	08/48
3019	WES	-	-	-	-	-	04/48	3040	PPRD	86G	86G	-	-	-	06/56
3020	SRD	84C	-	-	-	-	06/54	3041	SPM	82B	84G	-	-	-	03/58
3021	WOS	-	-	-	-	-	07/48	3042	CDF	86G	86G	-	-	-	10/56
3022	SPM	85A	85B	-	-	-	06/56	3043	SRD	84C	86G	-	-	-	09/56
3023	PPRD	86G	84E	-	-	-	10/55	3044	CDF	86G	86G	-	-	-	10/56
3024	OXY	81E	86G	-	-	-	10/58	3046	SPM	-	-	-	-	-	08/48

No.	1948	1952	1955	1959	1963	1965	w/dwn	No.	1948	1952	1955	1959	1963	1965	w/dwn
3047	RDG	81D	-	-	-	-	06/53	3049	TYS	-	-	-	-	-	11/48
3048	WOS	85A	85B	-	-	-	05/56								

TOTAL 45

31xx Collett Rebuild 2-6-2T

Introduced in 1938 by Collett, these locos were rebuilds (with smaller driving wheels & higher boiler pressure), of Churchward's 3150 class (see below)

Loco Weight: 81t 9c *Driving Wheels:* 5' 3" *Cylinders:* (O) 18½" x 30" *Valve Gear:* Stephenson (Piston Valves)

Number	1948	1952	1955	1959	1963	1965	w/dwn	Number	1948	1952	1955	1959	1963	1965	w/dwn
3100	TDU	86F	86F	-	-	-	05/57	3103	NPT	86A	86A	86A	-	-	01/60
3101	TYS	84E	84E	-	-	-	08/57	3104	OXY	84A	84A	-	-	-	06/57
3102	OXY	84A	84A	-	-	-	10/58								

TOTAL 5

3150 Churchward 2-6-2T

Introduced in 1905 by Churchward for suburban passenger service. Developed from the original 31xx Class, but had larger boiler. All were eventually superheated.

Loco Weight: 81t 12c *Driving Wheels:* 5' 8" *Cylinders:* (O) 18½" x 30" *Valve Gear:* Stephenson (Piston Valves)

Number	1948	1952	1955	1959	1963	1965	w/dwn	Number	1948	1952	1955	1959	1963	1965	w/dwn
3150	STJ	86E	86E	-	-	-	09/57	3172	STJ	86E	86E	-	-	-	10/57
3151	TYS	-	-	-	-	-	03/52	3174	STJ	86E	86E	-	-	-	03/58
3153	GLO	85B	-	-	-	-	02/53	3175	GLO	-	-	-	-	-	03/49
3154	STJ	-	-	-	-	-	10/50	3176	STJ	86E	86E	-	-	-	11/57
3157	STJ	86E	-	-	-	-	10/52	3177	STJ	86E	86E	-	-	-	10/57
3158	TYS	-	-	-	-	-	04/48	3178	STJ	-	-	-	-	-	01/51
3159	STJ	-	-	-	-	-	11/49	3180	TYS	84E	85B	-	-	-	10/57
3160	SRD	84A	-	-	-	-	06/53	3182	STJ	-	-	-	-	-	08/49
3161	STJ	86E	-	-	-	-	12/52	3183	STJ	86E	86E	-	-	-	10/57
3163	STJ	85B	85B	-	-	-	06/57	3184	STJ	-	-	-	-	-	07/48
3164	GLO	85B	85B	-	-	-	03/56	3185	STJ	86E	86E	-	-	-	02/56
3165	STJ	-	-	-	-	-	07/48	3186	LA	83D	83D	-	-	-	06/57
3167	STJ	86E	-	-	-	-	08/52	3187	LA	83D	83D	-	-	-	11/57
3168	STJ	-	-	-	-	-	09/50	3188	STJ	86E	-	-	-	-	11/52
3169	BHD	-	-	-	-	-	07/50	3189	STJ	-	-	-	-	-	09/49
3170	STJ	86E	86A	-	-	-	08/58	3190	STJ	86E	86E	-	-	-	03/58
3171	GLO	85B	85B	-	-	-	07/57								

TOTAL 33

2251 0-6-0

Continued from Number 2299.

No.	1948	1952	1955	1959	1963	1965	w/dwn	No.	1948	1952	1955	1959	1963	1965	w/dwn
3200	MCH	89C	89A	89A	89D	-	01/65	3210	DID	81E	81E	81E	82G	-	11/64
3201	MCH	89C	89C	89A	86A	-	05/65	3211	DID	81E	81E	81E	-	-	09/62
3202	OSW	89C	89C	89A	-	-	06/60	3212	DID	81E	81E	81E	86E	-	10/63
3203	CNYD	84G	85B	85B	85B	-	12/63	3213	GLO	85B	85A	85A	85A	-	12/63
3204	GLO	85B	85A	84K	86C	-	02/63	3214	WOS	85A	85A	85A	87H	-	10/63
3205	GLO	85B	85B	85A	86C	-	05/65	3215	SDN	82B	82B	82B	-	-	01/63
3206	CNYD	84J	81E	81E	82G	-	12/63	3216	BAN	84C	87G	85A	82G	-	12/63
3207	MCH	89C	89C	89A	-	-	12/62	3217	SALOP	84G	81F	85A	84D	-	11/64
3208	OSW	89A	89A	89A	89D	-	05/65	3218	01/48	84C	85A	85A	82E	-	05/65
3209	HFD	85C	85C	89A	89C	-	06/64	3219	01/48	85A	81D	81D	81D	-	12/63

TOTAL 120

33xx   'Bulldog'   4-4-0

Introduced by William Dean in 1898.

Loco Weight: 51t 16c   *Driving Wheels:* 5' 8"   *Cylinders:* (I) 18" x 26"   *Valve Gear:* Stephenson (slide valves)

Number & Name	1948	w/dwn	Number & Name	1948	w/dwn
3335	EXE	10/48	3421	SDN	04/48
3341 Blasius	NA	11/49	3426	RDG	12/49
3363 Alfred Baldwin	WES	10/49	3430 Inchcape	NA	12/48
3364 Frank Bibby	WES	06/49	3431	LA	12/48
3366	CHR	04/48	3432	HFD	12/49
3376 River Pym	DID	09/48	3438	WES	10/49
3377	SALOP	03/51	3440	WOS	06/48
3379 River Fal	GLO	06/48	3441 Blackbird	LA	02/49
3382	WOS	11/49	3442 Bullfinch	SALOP	07/48
3383	NA	12/49	3443 Chaffinch	TN	05/49
3386	RDG	11/49	3444 Cormorant	TN	06/51
3391 Dominion of Canada	LA	05/48	3445 Flamingo	LA	10/48
3393 Australia	WOS	11/49	3446 Goldfinch	LA	12/48
3395 Tasmania	EXE	08/48	3447 Jackdaw	NEY	04/51
3396 Natal Colony	DID	03/48	3448 Kingfisher	DID	01/49
3400	NA	05/49	3449 Nightingale	CHEL	06/51
3401 Vancouver	LA	11/49	3450 Peacock	STB	12/49
3406 Calcutta	PPRD	01/51	3451 Pelican	EXE	04/51
3407 Madras	NA	12/49	3452 Penguin	SDN	04/48
3408 Bombay	DID	04/48	3453 Seagull	PPRD	11/51
3417 Lord Mildmay of Fleet	WLN	04/48	3454 Skylark	HFD	11/51
3418 Sir Arthur Yorke	RDG	08/49	3455 Starling	NEA	06/50
3419	DID	08/49			

TOTAL 45

94xx   Hawksworth   0-6-0PT

Taper boilered shunting pannier tank introduced in 1947 by Hawksworth.

Loco Weight: 55t 7c   *Driving Wheels:* 4' 7½"   *Cylinders:* (I) 17½" x 24"   *Valve Gear:* Stephenson (slide valves)

No.	1948	1952	1955	1959	1963	1965	w/dwn	No.	1948	1952	1955	1959	1963	1965	w/dwn
3400	12/55	-	-	84G	88B	-	11/64	3405	04/56	-	-	88A	88B	-	11/64
3401	01/56	-	-	88A	88B	-	11/64	3406	05/56	-	-	88A	88B	-	11/64
3402	02/56	-	-	88A	88B	-	11/64	3407	08/56	-	-	88A	-	-	10/62
3403	02/56	-	-	88A	88B	-	09/64	3408	08/56	-	-	88A	-	-	09/62
3404	03/56	-	-	88A	-	-	07/62	3409	10/56	-	-	88A	88B	-	10/64

Continued with Number 8400

3440   'City'   4-4-0

G. J. Churchward design of 1903, this locomotive is reputed to be the first to travel at more than 100 m.p.h., but there has always been controversy over this. When withdrawn in 1931 it was preserved at York Railway Museum, but was returned to stock in 1957 to work special trains.

Unlike the other six working preserved locos, (G.N.S.R. 49, H.R. 103, Midland 1000, C.R. 123, L.S.W.R. T9 120, and N.B.R. 256), City of Truro was put to work on normal service & parcel trains when not working special trains.

It was also far travelled, ending up in Glasgow for over a week during 1959, and sharing Dawsholm shed with the four Scottish preserved locos when not in use hauling special trains between Glasgow Central and Kelvin Hall Station for the Scottish Industries Exhibition.

When finally retired, it reverted to the number it carried in York Museum, 3717.

Loco Weight: 55t 6c   *Driving Wheels:* 6' 8½"   *Cylinders:* (I) 18" x 26"   *Valve Gear:* Stephenson (Slide Valves)

Number & Name	In service	1959	Preserved	
3440 City of Truro	02/57	82C	05/61	TOTAL 1

517 Armstrong 0-4-2T

G. Armstrong design for the G.W.R., dating from 1876

Loco Weight: 35t 4c *Driving Wheels:* 5' 2" *Cylinders:* (I) 16" x 24" *Valve Gear:* Stephenson (Slide Valves)

Number	1948	1952	1955	1959	1963	1965	w/dwn	Number	1948	1952	1955	1959	1963	1965	w/dwn
3574	WOS	-	-	-	-	-	12/49	3577	SED	-	-	-	-	-	05/49
3575	STJ	-	-	-	-	-	10/49								

TOTAL 3

35xx Dean 2-4-0T

Introduced by William Dean in 1899

Loco Weight: 41t 7c *Driving Wheels:* 5' 2" *Cylinders:* (I) 16" x 24" *Valve Gear:* Stephenson (Slide Valves)

Number	1948	1952	1955	1959	1963	1965	w/dwn	Number	1948	1952	1955	1959	1963	1965	w/dwn
3561	SDN	-	-	-	-	-	10/49	3588	OXF	-	-	-	-	-	12/49
3562	SHL	-	-	-	-	-	02/49	3589	OXF	-	-	-	-	-	08/48
3582	TN	-	-	-	-	-	11/49	3592	CARM	-	-	-	-	-	04/49
3585	OXF	-	-	-	-	-	11/49	3597	CHYS	-	-	-	-	-	08/48
3586	LTS	-	-	-	-	-	12/49	3599	RYR	-	-	-	-	-	10/49

TOTAL 10

57xx Collett Standard Pannier Tank 0-6-0PT

Introduced 1929 by Collett , this was numerically the largest class built for the Great Western, and was used on every type of service from shunting to local passenger. They were to be seen everywhere on the former Great Western system, and also on Southern Region metals as well.

Thirteen were sold to **LONDON TRANSPORT** (*see appendix one*), and many were sold to the National Coal Board and other companies for further service.

Numbers **3600 - 3799, 4600 - 4699, 8750 - 8799, and 9600 - 9799** all had modified cabs and were vacuum brake fitted.   Numbers **9700 - 9710** were condensing locos for use on Metropolitan lines.

Numbers **6750 - 6779** were built with modified cab, but had no steam brake, and were for shunting use only.   Likewise, numbers **6700 - 6749** had no steam brakes and were built with original cabs.

Loco Weight: Between 40t 00c - 50t 15c   *Driving Wheels:* 4' 7½"   *Cylinders:* (I) 17½" x 24"
Valve Gear: Stephenson (Slide Valves)

No.	1948	1952	1955	1959	1963	1965	w/dwn	No.	1948	1952	1955	1959	1963	1965	w/dwn
3600	PDN	83A	83A	84K	87A	-	12/63	3622	DID	81E	81E	81E	81C	-	09/64
3601	HFD	85D	85D	85D	84G	-	10/64	3623	SPM	82B	82B	82B	-	-	09/62
3602	SALOP	84G	84G	84G	-	-	02/62	3624	TYS	84D	84D	84D	-	-	05/62
3603	EXE	83C	83C	86J	88J	-	07/64	3625	TYS	84E	84E	84E	84E	2A	07/66
3604	SPM	82B	82B	82B	87D	-	12/63	3626	BHD	6C	6C	6C	87B	-	08/63
3605	ABDR	86J	86J	85A	84B	2B	10/66	3627	TDU	86F	86F	86F	-	-	02/63
3606	EXE	83C	83C	83C	-	-	12/62	3628	PPRD	86G	86G	86G	-	-	01/63
3607	WOS	85A	85A	85A	84G	2C	10/66	3629	LA	83D	83D	82D	-	-	01/63
3608	OXF	81F	81F	81B	81B	-	06/65	3630	BAN	84K	84K	6E	-	-	09/62
3609	GLO	85B	85B	85B	-	-	08/60	3631	LMTN	84D	84D	84D	84B	-	07/65
3610	ABDR	86J	86J	86J	87B	-	02/65	3632	SPM	82B	82B	82B	-	-	12/62
3611	NEA	87A	87A	87A	-	-	08/62	3633	SED	87D	87D	87C	71G	-	10/63
3612	ABEEG	86D	86D	86D	88G	-	10/64	3634	NPT	86A	86A	86A	86A	-	07/64
3613	TYS	84H	84H	87B	87B	-	05/64	3635	PDN	83E	83E	83E	87D	-	04/65
3614	SPM	82B	82B	82D	-	-	03/62	3636	NPT	86A	86A	86A	-	-	02/62
3615	SRD	84A	84A	84A	88C	-	10/65	3637	FGD	87J	87J	87J	-	-	10/62
3616	ABEEG	86F	86F	86F	88H	-	09/65	3638	BCN	89B	89B	89B	-	-	01/61
3617	LTS	86D	86D	86D	88G	-	09/64	3639	LA	83D	83D	87H	-	-	01/63
3618	PDN	81C	81C	81C	81C	-	05/64	3640	ABEEG	86G	86G	86G	-	-	05/62
3619	PDN	84D	84D	84D	84G	2C	09/66	3641	SED	87D	87D	87D	-	-	08/62
3620	SHL	81C	81C	81C	81C	-	06/65	3642	LLY	87F	87F	87F	87B	-	04/65
3621	NEA	87A	87A	87A	87A	-	11/64	3643	SPM	82B	82B	82B	82E	-	11/65

No.	1948	1952	1955	1959	1963	1965	w/dwn	No.	1948	1952	1955	1959	1963	1965	w/dwn
3644	PDN	86D	86D	86D	88G	-	06/65	3704	SHL	81C	81C	81C	-	-	01/61
3645	SDN	82C	82C	82C	-	-	05/62	3705	LA	83E	83E	83E	86B	-	03/65
3646	PDN	84K	84E	84C	81A	-	05/64	3706	BCN	89B	89B	89B	86A	-	11/63
3647	NPT	86A	86J	86H	86F	-	06/65	3707	CED	88B	88B	88E	88E	-	09/64
3648	PDN	81A	81A	81A	88H	-	12/63	3708	CDF	86G	86G	86G	86G	-	07/65
3649	STB	84F	84F	84F	-	-	01/61	3709	DID	81E	81E	81E	89A	6C	08/66
3650	TYS	84E	88B	82B	87A	-	09/63	3710	PDN	84F	84F	84F	88C	-	05/63
3651	PPRD	86G	86G	86G	86G	-	04/63	3711	PPRD	86H	86H	86H	81A	-	05/63
3652	SLO	86F	86C	86B	87A	-	10/63	3712	NPT	86A	86A	86A	87H	-	12/63
3653	TYS	84E	81E	81E	81F	-	10/63	3713	LDR	87E	87E	87E	-	-	02/62
3654	NEY	87H	87H	87H	87H	-	08/65	3714	NPT	86A	86A	86A	86A	-	12/63
3655	ABDR	86J	86J	86J	-	-	12/62	3715	RDG	81A	87A	87A	81D	-	03/65
3656	LTS	86D	86D	86D	-	-	02/62	3716	CDF	86H	86H	86J	88J	-	12/63
3657	TYS	84E	87H	84E	-	-	05/61	3717	PPRD	86G	86G	86G	86G	-	06/65
3658	PDN	84F	84F	84F	84F	-	09/65	3718	DYD	87B	87B	87B	-	-	05/62
3659	PDN	83A	83A	83A	83C	-	10/65	3719	LLY	87F	87F	87F	-	-	01/63
3660	TYS	84E	84E	84E	84E	-	04/63	3720	SPM	82B	82B	82A	82G	-	12/63
3661	DG	87F	87F	87F	83L	-	04/65	3721	DID	81E	81E	81E	85B	-	04/64
3662	NPT	86A	86A	86A	86A	-	08/65	3722	OXF	81F	81F	81F	-	-	05/62
3663	RGD	86B	86B	86B	-	-	12/62	3723	PDN	81D	81D	81D	-	-	04/62
3664	TYS	84A	84A	84A	86F	-	05/64	3724	SDN	82C	82C	82C	-	-	05/61
3665	CHR	84K	84K	6E	81C	-	01/64	3725	HFD	85A	85A	85A	85A	-	01/65
3666	SDN	82C	82C	82C	-	-	12/62	3726	NPT	86A	86A	82B	-	-	01/62
3667	STB	84F	84F	84F	-	-	05/61	3727	SHL	81C	81C	88A	88C	-	04/64
3668	TDU	86F	86F	86F	88C	-	07/63	3728	HFD	85C	85C	85C	86A	-	04/65
3669	PDN	83B	83B	83B	83B	-	09/65	3729	ABEEG	86C	84F	84F	86A	-	03/63
3670	ABEEG	86C	86C	86C	-	-	05/61	3730	PPRD	86G	86G	88E	88E	-	11/64
3671	YEO	82E	82E	71H	72C	-	07/65	3731	WES	82B	82B	82B	87A	-	05/64
3672	PDN	88A	88A	88A	88B	-	04/64	3732	WLN	84H	84H	84H	-	-	05/62
3673	TYS	84E	84E	84E	84E	-	05/64	3733	YEO	82E	82E	71H	72C	-	12/63
3674	TDU	86F	86F	86B	-	-	12/62	3734	PDN	88A	88B	88E	88E	-	04/64
3675	LA	83D	83D	83D	82E	85B	12/65	3735	WES	82D	82D	82D	82D	-	09/65
3676	SPM	82B	82B	82A	-	-	05/61	3736	RDG	83B	83B	83B	83B	-	03/63
3677	SLO	83C	83C	82A	82E	81F	12/65	3737	SDN	82C	82C	71G	71G	-	09/64
3678	LDR	87E	87E	87E	87F	-	12/63	3738	PDN	81D	81D	81D	88H	-	08/65
3679	SED	87D	87D	87C	72A	-	03/63	3739	SDN	82C	82C	82C	82D	-	10/64
3680	ABEEG	86H	86D	86D	88G	-	05/64	3740	STB	81B	81B	85B	-	-	01/59
3681	SLO	88B	88B	88D	88B	82F	03/66	3741	OXF	87A	87A	87A	-	-	09/62
3682	SDN	82C	82C	82C	87B	85A	12/65	3742	BHD	6C	6C	6C	82F	-	11/64
3683	ABEEG	86G	86G	86H	86G	-	10/64	3743	TYS	84F	84F	84F	-	-	05/62
3684	SDN	82C	82C	82C	-	-	05/62	3744	OXY	84B	84H	84H	84H	2B	08/66
3685	PDN	81A	86G	86G	86G	-	04/64	3745	OXY	84B	84F	84F	85B	-	12/64
3686	LA	83D	83D	83D	86F	-	07/65	3746	SPM	82C	82C	82C	82D	-	07/64
3687	OXF	87A	87A	87A	87A	-	06/65	3747	ABDR	86J	86H	86H	86A	-	02/65
3688	PDN	81A	81A	81A	-	-	09/62	3748	SDN	82B	82B	82A	88L	-	05/64
3689	TYS	84E	84E	84E	88L	-	05/64	3749	WLN	84H	84H	84K	89B	-	11/65
3690	PPRD	86F	86F	86F	88C	-	06/65	3750	SHL	81C	81C	81C	-	-	09/62
3691	LTS	86H	86A	86A	86A	-	04/65	3751	BAN	84F	84F	81E	81E	-	09/65
3692	PPRD	86G	82F	82B	87B	-	05/64	3752	LLY	87F	87F	87F	82E	-	07/64
3693	TYS	84E	84E	84E	87A	-	07/64	3753	ABDR	86J	86J	86J	88J	-	01/65
3694	BAN	84C	84C	87K	-	-	09/62	3754	PDN	81A	81A	81A	81A	-	11/65
3695	TDU	86F	86J	86J	88E	-	07/64	3755	CDF	86C	86C	86C	-	-	10/62
3696	WES	82D	82D	82D	82E	-	11/65	3756	SRD	84A	84A	84A	88H	-	03/63
3697	RDG	81B	81B	81B	-	-	05/62	3757	NEA	84H	84H	84H	-	-	03/64
3698	LLY	87F	87F	87F	87F	-	04/64	3758	WES	82D	82B	82B	82C	82F	03/66
3699	TDU	86F	86J	86J	88J	-	02/65	3759	SPM	82B	82A	82A	71G	85B	12/65
3700	NPT	86A	86B	86K	86A	-	02/65	3760	SRD	84H	84H	84H	-	-	09/62
3701	LDR	87E	87E	87E	87F	-	05/64	3761	LLY	87F	87F	87F	87F	-	05/64
3702	SALOP	84G	84G	83F	82E	-	04/62	3762	CHR	84K	84K	87B	87B	-	12/63
3703	LTS	86G	86G	86G	-	-	05/62	3763	SPM	82B	82F	82C	81E	-	06/65

No.	1948	1952	1955	1959	1963	1965	w/dwn	No.	1948	1952	1955	1959	1963	1965	w/dwn
3764	SPM	82B	82B	82B	-	-	01/63	3782	SALOP	84G	84G	84G	89A	2B	10/66
3765	SPM	82B	82B	82B	82E	-	07/63	3783	RDG	88B	88B	88E	-	-	09/62
3766	PDN	87A	87A	87A	87A	-	08/63	3784	SPM	82B	82A	82B	88L	-	06/65
3767	BCN	89B	89B	89B	86A	-	10/65	3785	LDR	87E	87E	87E	-	-	07/62
3768	LDR	87E	87E	87F	87A	-	05/64	3786	CHR	84K	84K	6E	86E	-	03/63
3769	SLO	84E	84E	84K	-	-	10/62	3787	LA	83D	83D	83D	-	-	01/63
3770	RDG	89B	89B	89B	89D	-	04/65	3788	SALOP	84G	84G	84G	89A	-	11/65
3771	LLY	87F	87F	87F	-	-	01/63	3789	HFD	85C	85C	89A	89B	-	10/65
3772	TDU	86F	86F	86A	86A	-	06/65	3790	LA	83D	83D	83D	87A	-	06/65
3773	SPM	82B	82B	82B	-	-	10/62	3791	DYD	87B	87B	87B	87B	-	12/63
3774	NEA	87A	87A	87A	-	-	05/62	3792	OXY	84B	84A	84A	84A	-	11/65
3775	WLN	85A	85A	85A	85B	85B	12/65	3793	OXY	84B	84A	-	-	-	09/58
3776	ABEEG	86D	86D	82B	84H	2B	04/66	3794	EXE	83C	83C	83C	83C	-	12/64
3777	LLY	87F	87F	87F	87F	-	12/63	3795	SPM	82B	82A	82B	82E	-	05/63
3778	SRD	84A	84A	84A	84B	-	03/64	3796	NPT	86A	83A	83A	87F	-	03/65
3779	PPRD	86G	86G	86G	86G	-	12/63	3797	LDR	87E	87E	87E	87D	-	11/64
3780	SDN	82C	82C	82C	-	-	12/62	3798	SLO	86A	86A	86A	87A	-	10/64
3781	DG	87C	87C	87C	87F	-	08/63	3799	SHL	81C	81C	81C	-	-	01/61

Continued with Number 4600.

28xx

2-8-0

Continued from Number 2899.

Number	1948	1952	1955	1959	1963	1965	w/dwn	Notes
3800	NPT	86A	86A	86A	86A	-	08/64	
3801	NPT	86A	86C	86C	86E	-	08/64	
3802	BAN	84B	84B	84B	84E	-	08/65	
3803	BAN	86C	86C	87F	86E	-	07/63	
3804	NPT	86A	86A	86A	88L	-	07/64	
3805	NPT	86A	86A	86A	86A	-	09/64	
3806	STJ	86E	86E	86A	84C	-	12/63	
3807	NPT	86A	86A	86A	86A	-	02/65	
3808	STJ	86E	86E	86A	86A	-	07/65	
3809	CDF	86C	86C	86C	84C	-	10/64	
3810	NPT	86A	86C	86C	88L	-	11/64	
3811	LA	87F	87F	87F	86E	-	09/63	
3812	CDF	86C	86C	86E	86E	-	06/65	
3813	LA	84B	84B	84B	84B	-	07/65	Renumbered from 4855, 06/49
3814	CDF	86C	86C	81F	86E	-	12/64	
3815	STJ	86E	86E	86E	89B	-	05/64	
3816	NPT	86A	86C	86C	88J	-	07/65	
3817	CDF	86C	86C	86C	89B	-	08/65	
3818	STJ	86E	86E	86E	86A	-	05/65	Renumbered from 4852, 09/48
3819	BAN	84C	84C	82D	81E	-	12/64	
3820	PDN	84C	84K	84C	81E	-	07/65	Renumbered from 4856, 06/49
3821	BAN	84F	84F	84F	84C	-	10/64	
3822	PPRD	86G	86G	86G	87A	-	01/64	
3823	CDF	86C	82B	81F	86E	-	07/65	
3824	CDF	86C	86A	86G	86A	-	06/64	
3825	BAN	84B	84B	84F	84C	-	09/64	
3826	PPRD	86G	86G	86G	86G	-	01/65	
3827	BAN	84F	84F	86A	-	-	11/62	
3828	PPRD	86G	86G	86G	84C	-	10/64	
3829	BAN	84E	84C	84B	84E	-	03/64	
3830	NPT	86A	86A	86A	86A	-	06/65	
3831	NPT	84C	84C	84E	84B	-	09/63	Renumbered from 4857, 05/49
3832	PDN	86E	86E	86A	86A	-	04/64	
3833	NPT	86A	86A	86A	86A	-	07/63	

Number	1948	1952	1955	1959	1963	1965	w/dwn	Notes
3834	EXE	83A	83A	83A	81C	-	04/64	
3835	OXF	81F	84C	86C	86E	-	01/65	
3836	OXF	86A	86C	81C	86E	-	11/65	
3837	PDN	84E	81E	84B	86A	-	07/65	Renumbered from *4854*, *08/49*
3838	OXF	86E	86E	86E	86E	-	11/64	
3839	PDN	85A	84E	84E	88J	-	12/63	Renumbered from *4853*, *11/49*
3840	RDG	83A	83A	83A	81E	-	07/65	
3841	RDG	83A	83A	83A	86G	-	03/64	
3842	WES	86C	86C	86C	82C	-	07/65	
3843	RDG	86E	86E	86C	88J	-	10/63	
3844	RDG	86E	86E	86E	86G	-	10/65	
3845	RDG	81D	81E	86C	84C	-	06/64	
3846	RDG	81D	86C	84B	89B	-	10/63	
3847	OXF	81F	86E	86E	88J	-	03/64	
3848	OXF	85A	85A	85B	86E	-	07/65	
3849	WES	86E	86E	86E	84C	-	05/65	
3850	WES	86E	86E	86E	88J	-	08/65	
3851	PDN	87F	87F	87F	86E	-	07/65	
3852	PDN	86E	86E	86E	84C	-	04/64	
3853	PDN	86E	86E	86E	88J	-	12/63	
3854	SHL	82C	82B	86G	81C	-	06/65	
3855	SHL	81C	86G	86C	84C	-	08/65	
3856	SHL	81C	81C	84C	86E	-	10/64	
3857	SHL	81C	81C	81F	84C	-	03/64	
3858	SHL	84K	84K	84C	81D	-	09/63	
3859	SHL	84K	84C	86G	86E	-	05/65	
3860	SHL	84B	84B	86C	88J	-	08/64	
3861	BAN	84C	84B	84B	86G	-	07/65	
3862	PPRD	86G	83D	83D	88L	-	02/65	
3863	WES	84B	84B	84B	86E	-	10/65	
3864	LA	83A	83A	83A	86E	-	07/65	
3865	STJ	82C	84B	84B	84E	-	03/65	Renumbered from *4851*, *04/49*
3866	OXF	86E	86E	86E	88J	-	07/65	

TOTAL 167

4000   'Star'   4-6-0

Introduced 1907 by Churchward. This class was the predecessor of the famous 'Castle' class which was introduced in 1923. Fifteen 'Stars' were subsequently rebuilt as 'Castles'.

Loco Weight : 79t 17c   Driving Wheels : 6' 8½"   Cylinders : (4) 16" x 26"   Valve Gear : Walschaerts (piston valves)

Number & Name	1948	1952	1955	1959	1963	1965	w/dwn	Notes
4003 **Lode Star**	LDR	-	-	-	-	-	07/51	
4004 **Morning Star**	OXF	-	-	-	-	-	04/48	
4007 **Swallowfield Park**	WOS	-	-	-	-	-	09/51	
4012 **Knight of the Thistle**	NA	-	-	-	-	-	10/49	
4013 **Knight of St. Patrick**	CHR	-	-	-	-	-	05/50	
4015 **Knight of St. John**	SDN	-	-	-	-	-	02/51	
4017 **Knight of Liege**	SDN	-	-	-	-	-	11/49	
4018 **Knight of the Grand Cross**	SRD	-	-	-	-	-	04/51	
4019 **Knight Templar**	BRD	-	-	-	-	-	10/49	
4020 **Knight Commander**	BRD	-	-	-	-	-	03/51	
4021 **British Monarch**	OXF	81F	-	-	-	-	10/52	
4022 *Belgian Monarch*	SDN	-	-	-	-	-	02/52	Name removed *05/40*
4023 *Danish Monarch*	LDR	87E	-	-	-	-	06/52	Name removed *11/40*
4025 *Italian Monarch*	SRD	-	-	-	-	-	08/50	Name removed *06/40*
4026 *Japanese Monarch*	TN	-	-	-	-	-	02/50	Name removed *01/41*
4028 *Roumanian Monarch*	WES	-	-	-	-	-	11/51	Name removed *11/40*
4030 *Swedish Monarch*	BRD	-	-	-	-	-	05/50	Name removed *11/40*
4031 **Queen Mary**	SRD	-	-	-	-	-	06/51	
4033 **Queen Victoria**	BRD	-	-	-	-	-	06/51	
4034 **Queen Adelaide**	BRD	82C	-	-	-	-	09/52	

Number & Name	1948	1952	1955	1959	1963	1965	w/dwn	Notes
4035 Queen Charlotte	BRD	-	-	-	-	-	10/51	
4036 Queen Elizabeth	SDN	-	-	-	-	-	03/52	
4038 Queen Berengaria	WES	-	-	-	-	-	04/52	
4039 Queen Matilda	LDR	-	-	-	-	-	11/50	
4040 Queen Boadicea	SALOP	-	-	-	-	-	06/51	
4041 Prince of Wales	BRD	-	-	-	-	-	04/51	
4042 Prince Albert	BRD	-	-	-	-	-	11/51	
4043 Prince Henry	BRD	-	-	-	-	-	01/52	
4044 Prince George	SALOP	84G	-	-	-	-	02/53	
4045 Prince John	WES	-	-	-	-	-	11/50	
4046 Princess Mary	SALOP	-	-	-	-	-	11/51	
4047 Princess Louise	BRD	-	-	-	-	-	07/51	
4048 Princess Victoria	LDR	87E	-	-	-	-	01/53	
4049 Princess Maud	OXF	84A	-	-	-	-	06/53	
4050 Princess Alice	LDR	-	-	-	-	-	02/52	
4051 Princess Helena	WOS	-	-	-	-	-	10/50	
4052 Princess Beatrice	OXF	84G	-	-	-	-	06/53	
4053 Princess Alexandra	SRD	84A	-	-	-	-	07/54	
4054 Princess Charlotte	EXE	-	-	-	-	-	01/52	
4055 Princess Sophia	SDN	-	-	-	-	-	02/51	
4056 Princess Margaret	TN	82A	82A	-	-	-	10/57	
4057 Princess Elizabeth	SDN	-	-	-	-	-	02/52	
4058 Princess Augusta	TYS	-	-	-	-	-	04/51	
4059 Princess Patricia	GLO	85B	-	-	-	-	09/52	
4060 Princess Eugenie	SRD	82A	-	-	-	-	10/52	
4061 Glastonbury Abbey	SALOP	84A	84A	-	-	-	03/57	
4062 Malmesbury Abbey	SDN	82C	82C	-	-	-	11/56	

TOTAL 47

4073

4-6-0

Continued from Number 111.

Number & Name	1948	1952	1955	1959	1963	1965	w/dwn	Notes
4000 North Star	SRD	84A	84A	-	-	-	05/57	
4016 The Somerset Light Infantry (Prince Alberts)	NA	-	-	-	-	-	09/51	
4032 Queen Alexandra	LA	-	-	-	-	-	09/51	
4037 The South Wales Borderers	PDN	81A	81A	83A	-	-	09/62	
4073 Caerphilly Castle	PDN	82A	82A	86C	-	-	05/60	
4074 Caldicote Castle	LDR	87E	87E	87E	81A	-	05/63	DC 04/59
4075 Cardiff Castle	PDN	82A	82A	82A	-	-	11/61	
4076 Carmarthen Castle	PDN	84K	83A	87E	-	-	02/63	
4077 Chepstow Castle	NA	83A	83D	83D	-	-	08/62	
4078 Pembroke Castle	LDR	87E	87E	81D	-	-	07/62	
4079 Pendennis Castle	HFD	85B	84A	82A	82C	-	05/64	
4080 Powderham Castle	BRD	82D	82A	82A	88L	-	08/64	DC 08/58
4081 Warwick Castle	LDR	87E	87E	83C	-	-	01/63	
4082 Windsor Castle	GLO	85A	81A	81A	81A	-	09/64	Became 7013 02/52
4083 Abbotsbury Castle	CDF	84A	84A	83A	-	-	12/61	
4084 Aberystwyth Castle	BRD	82A	82A	83A	-	-	10/60	
4085 Berkeley Castle	RDG	81D	81D	85B	-	-	05/62	
4086 Builth Castle	WOS	85A	83D	82C	-	-	04/62	
4087 Cardigan Castle	LA	83D	83D	83D	83D	-	10/63	DC 02/58
4088 Dartmouth Castle	LA	83D	83D	85A	82C	-	05/64	DC 05/58
4089 Donnington Castle	BRD	83A	81A	81A	81A	-	10/64	
4090 Dorchester Castle	LA	83G	84A	81A	88L	-	06/63	DC 03/57
4091 Dudley Castle	PDN	82A	82A	81A	-	-	01/59	
4092 Dunraven Castle	WOS	84A	84A	81D	-	-	12/61	
4093 Dunster Castle	BRD	85A	87E	87E	82B	-	09/64	DC 12/57
4094 Dynevor Castle	CDF	86C	84A	87E	-	-	03/62	
4095 Harlech Castle	LDR	87E	87E	83G	-	-	12/62	
4096 Highclere Castle	BRD	82A	82A	81A	-	-	01/63	
4097 Kenilworth Castle	PZ	81A	81A	87E	-	-	05/60	DC 06/58
4098 Kidwelly Castle	NA	83A	83A	83A	81A	-	12/63	
4099 Kilgerran Castle	NA	83A	83A	87E	-	-	09/62	

Continued with Number 5000

57xx 0-6-0PT No. 3602 marks time in Birmingham Snow Hill Station, awaiting its next turn of duty.

photo courtesy Steve Davies

45xx 2-6-2T No. 4562 keeps company with another unidentified member of the class.

Transport Publishing Ltd. Collection

51xx — Collett — 2-6-2T

Developed from Churchward 31xx class of 1903, 5101-5148 were rebuilds, rest were built new.

Loco Weight: 75t 10c *Driving Wheels:* 5' 8" *Cylinders:* (O) 18" x 30" *Valve Gear:* Stephenson (Piston Valves)

No.	1948	1952	1955	1959	1963	1965	w/dwn	No.	1948	1952	1955	1959	1963	1965	w/dwn
4100	WOS	85D	85D	85B	85B	-	11/65	4140	GLO	85B	84A	84F	84F	-	11/63
4101	TYS	84E	88D	85B	85B	-	07/64	4141	CHEL	85B	85B	85B	85B	-	03/63
4102	LMTN	84C	84C	82C	-	-	09/62	4142	BRD	86E	86A	85A	85A	-	12/63
4103	SRD	84A	84A	84D	82E	-	09/64	4143	BRD	88D	88D	88A	83B	-	06/64
4104	STB	84F	84F	84F	85A	-	05/64	4144	STJ	86E	86E	86F	86E	-	06/65
4105	SRD	84A	84G	83A	84C	-	01/64	4145	TDU	86A	83A	83A	-	-	12/62
4106	TYS	84E	87E	87E	-	-	09/62	4146	STB	84F	84F	84F	-	-	08/62
4107	TYS	84E	87E	87E	87H	-	06/65	4147	TYS	84E	81F	81F	84G	-	09/65
4108	SRD	84A	84A	83A	88H	-	10/64	4148	STJ	86A	85B	81F	84A	-	09/65
4109	NA	83A	83A	83A	85B	-	04/64	4149	STB	84C	84C	84C	84C	-	03/63
4110	SRD	84E	84E	84H	83B	-	06/65	4150	STB	84F	82F	83A	86E	-	06/65
4111	TYS	84E	84E	84E	84E	-	09/65	4151	BRD	86E	86E	86E	86E	-	04/65
4112	LMTN	84D	84D	84D	-	-	08/62	4152	BRD	88D	88D	85A	-	-	09/62
4113	TN	83B	85A	85A	85A	-	11/65	4153	KDR	85D	85D	85D	84G	-	11/64
4114	WOS	85A	85D	85D	84G	-	11/63	4154	WLN	84H	85A	85A	84C	-	10/65
4115	SRD	84A	84K	83A	86E	-	06/65	4155	BRD	85A	84H	84E	84E	-	09/65
4116	TYS	84E	84E	85B	-	-	09/62	4156	STJ	86A	86E	86E	86E	-	06/65
4117	TN	83B	83B	83A	-	-	09/61	4157	TYS	84E	82A	83B	82D	-	06/65
4118	SALOP	84G	84D	84D	-	-	09/62	4158	STJ	86G	84H	84H	84E	-	06/65
4119	STJ	86E	86E	86E	86E	-	09/63	4159	CHR	84E	82A	83B	86E	-	06/64
4120	BHD	6C	6C	84H	84D	-	11/64	4160	09/48	88C	88D	88A	88B	-	06/65
4121	BHD	86G	86E	86F	88H	-	06/65	4161	09/48	88C	88D	84A	85B	-	11/65
4122	BHD	6C	6C	87H	87H	-	06/64	4162	09/48	88F	88D	84D	-	-	07/60
4123	BHD	6C	6C	85B	-	-	11/61	4163	09/48	88C	88D	88A	-	-	10/62
4124	BHD	6C	6C	85A	85A	-	08/64	4164	09/48	87B	88D	86E	-	-	01/60
4125	BHD	6C	6C	81F	84D	-	06/65	4165	10/48	84E	84K	85B	84A	-	10/65
4126	BHD	6C	6C	88A	-	-	01/62	4166	10/48	83A	82D	71G	88B	-	06/64
4127	BHD	6C	6C	86E	-	-	01/63	4167	10/48	83F	83E	83E	84E	-	05/64
4128	BHD	6C	6C	83B	86E	-	06/64	4168	11/48	86A	86A	84F	84F	-	09/65
4129	BHD	6C	6C	88A	-	-	09/62	4169	11/48	87A	87A	87A	87A	-	05/65
4130	STJ	86B	86A	86E	86E	-	07/64	4170	10/49	84E	84E	84E	-	-	09/60
4131	PPRD	86G	87H	82B	82E	-	09/64	4171	10/49	84D	84D	84D	84D	-	10/64
4132	NEA	87H	87H	87H	87H	-	06/64	4172	10/49	84E	84E	84E	84E	-	01/65
4133	NA	83A	82D	71G	84D	-	10/64	4173	10/49	84F	84F	84F	84G	-	12/64
4134	LDR	87G	87G	87G	87A	-	05/63	4174	11/49	85B	85B	83A	82D	-	06/65
4135	PPRD	86G	86G	86G	86C	-	05/64	4175	11/49	85D	85D	85D	84G	-	10/65
4136	TN	83B	83B	83G	86E	-	06/64	4176	11/49	83C	83B	83A	84D	-	10/65
4137	STJ	86A	86E	86E	86E	-	10/64	4177	11/49	88C	88C	83A	88B	-	05/65
4138	PPRD	86G	86G	-	-	-	07/58	4178	11/49	87G	84E	83A	84D	-	10/65
4139	WOS	85A	82A	-	-	-	07/58	4179	12/49	83A	83A	83A	84A	-	02/65

Continued with Number 5101

42xx — Churchward — 2-8-0T

Introduced in 1910. **5205** onward introduced in 1923 with 19" x 30" Cylinders, and weighed 82t 2c.

Loco Weight: 81t 12c *Driving Wheels:* 4' 7½" *Cylinders:* (O) 17" x 24" *Valve Gear:* Stephenson (Piston Valves)

No.	1948	1952	1955	1959	1963	1965	w/dwn	No.	1948	1952	1955	1959	1963	1965	w/dwn
4200	STJ	86E	86E	86A	-	-	03/59	4218	TDU	86F	86F	86F	-	-	09/62
4201	PILL	86B	86B	86B	-	-	10/59	4221	NEA	87A	87A	87A	-	-	08/59
4203	NPT	86A	86A	86A	-	-	01/61	4222	ABEEG	86F	86F	86F	88H	-	10/64
4206	NPT	86A	83E	83E	-	-	12/59	4223	CARM	86C	87F	87F	-	-	08/59
4207	LDR	87E	86C	86C	-	-	10/61	4224	NPT	86C	88C	86F	-	-	02/59
4208	LTS	86D	86D	86D	-	-	11/59	4225	NPT	86A	86C	86C	-	-	01/63
4211	PILL	86B	86A	86A	-	-	08/59	4226	PILL	86B	86C	86C	-	-	03/59
4212	LDR	87B	87B	87B	-	-	06/59	4227	CDF	86H	86H	86A	86A	-	02/65
4213	LLY	87F	87F	87F	88H	-	01/64	4228	ABDR	86J	86J	86J	88H	-	12/63
4214	TDU	86H	86B	86B	86F	-	05/64	4229	PILL	86B	86G	86A	-	-	03/61
4215	SBZ	86F	86H	86E	-	-	10/59	4230	NPT	86A	86G	86G	-	-	09/62
4217	ABEEG	86H	86F	86E	-	-	07/59	4231	ABEEG	86C	86C	86C	-	-	12/59

No.	1948	1952	1955	1959	1963	1965	w/dwn	No.	1948	1952	1955	1959	1963	1965	w/dwn
4232	NEA	87A	87A	87D	87D	-	10/63	4269	PILL	86B	86H	86F	-	-	12/62
4233	PILL	86B	86B	86B	86B	-	10/64	4270	NPT	86C	86C	86C	-	-	09/62
4235	PILL	86B	86B	86B	-	-	08/62	4271	NPT	86H	86A	86A	86B	-	12/63
4236	CDF	86F	86F	86F	-	-	09/62	4272	NEA	86J	86J	86J	88L	-	10/63
4237	PILL	86B	86B	86H	86F	-	04/64	4273	TDU	86F	86F	86D	88H	-	10/64
4238	PPRD	86H	86H	86B	86B	-	12/63	4274	NEA	87A	87A	87A	-	-	06/62
4241	TDU	86F	86F	86F	86E	-	04/64	4275	PPRD	86E	86E	87A	87A	-	01/64
4242	NPT	86A	86A	87A	88L	-	03/64	4276	NPT	86F	86F	86B	-	-	12/62
4243	ABEEG	86E	87A	87A	88H	-	05/64	4277	DYD	86E	86A	86H	86F	-	06/64
4246	PILL	86B	86A	86A	-	-	12/62	4278	LLY	87F	87F	87F	87B	-	07/64
4247	NPT	86A	83E	86A	88H	-	04/64	4279	NEA	87A	87A	87A	88J	-	01/64
4248	NPT	86A	86A	86A	86E	-	05/63	4280	PILL	86B	86B	86B	-	-	01/63
4250	LDR	87E	86H	86H	-	-	09/62	4281	LLY	87F	87A	87A	-	-	12/60
4251	TDU	86F	86F	86F	88H	-	06/63	4282	SED	86E	87A	87A	87A	-	09/63
4252	NEA	87A	87A	87A	87A	-	09/63	4283	SED	87F	86A	86A	86A	-	10/64
4253	PILL	86B	86B	86B	86B	-	04/63	4284	NEA	87A	87A	87A	87A	-	09/64
4254	LLY	87F	86C	86C	86B	-	04/65	4285	ABDR	86C	86B	86H	86F	-	04/65
4255	DYD	86C	86A	86J	87A	-	04/64	4286	DYD	86E	86A	86A	87F	-	09/64
4256	LDR	87B	87B	87B	87B	-	01/64	4287	ABEEG	86H	86H	86H	-	-	01/61
4257	ABDR	86J	86J	86J	88J	-	10/63	4288	NEA	87A	87A	87A	-	-	11/60
4258	PILL	86B	86B	86B	86A	-	04/65	4289	NPT	86A	86E	86E	-	-	10/62
4259	NEA	87A	86A	86B	86B	-	03/64	4290	CDF	86J	86A	86A	-	-	02/63
4260	NPT	86F	87F	87F	-	-	06/59	4291	PILL	86B	86B	86H	-	-	09/62
4261	LTS	86D	86D	86D	-	-	03/59	4292	DYD	87B	87B	87B	87B	-	10/64
4262	STJ	82B	82B	86J	88H	-	04/64	4293	NEA	87A	87A	87B	-	-	08/62
4263	NPT	86B	86B	86F	88H	-	02/64	4294	NPT	86A	86A	83E	86B	-	09/64
4264	ABDR	86J	86J	87A	86B	-	07/63	4295	LDR	87A	87A	87A	87F	-	12/64
4265	LDR	87B	87B	87B	86A	-	06/63	4296	SED	87B	87B	87B	87B	-	12/63
4266	CARM	86J	86C	86C	-	-	08/62	4297	ABDR	86J	86J	86C	86A	-	02/65
4267	ABEEG	88C	88C	86A	-	-	10/62	4298	SBZ	83E	86E	86F	87F	-	06/63
4268	NPT	86C	86D	86D	88G	-	08/65	4299	DG	87C	87C	87C	86A	-	12/63

Continued with Number 5200

43xx   Churchward   2-6-0

Introduced in 1911 by Churchward, various batches had different weight distribution.
9300 - 9319 had side window cabs and were renumbered 7332 - 7341(in order) during 1956 - 59

Loco Weight : 62t 0c - 65t 6c   *Driving Wheels :* 5' 8"   *Cylinders :* (O) 18½" x 30"   *Valve Gear :* Stephenson (piston valves)

No.	1948	1952	1955	1959	1963	1965	w/dwn	No.	1948	1952	1955	1959	1963	1965	w/dwn
4303	PPRD	86C	-	-	-	-	11/52	4358	NEY	87C	87H	85B	-	-	08/59
4318	DID	86C	-	-	-	-	06/52	4365	WES	-	-	-	-	-	04/48
4320	CHEL	-	-	-	-	-	01/49	4375	CNYD	84F	84F	-	-	-	01/58
4326	DID	81E	84F	-	-	-	03/57	4377	WES	82D	82D	89C	-	-	01/59
4337	BHD	-	-	-	-	-	11/51	4381	SDN	82C	-	-	-	-	05/53
4353	BHD	-	-	-	-	-	11/48	4386	BHD	-	-	-	-	-	04/48

Continued with Number 5300

44xx   Churchward   2-6-2T

introduced in 1904 by Churchward, designed for secondary branches.

Loco Weight : 56t 13c   *Driving Wheels :* 4' 1½"   *Cylinders :* (O) 17" x 24"   *Valve Gear :* Stephenson (piston valves)

No.	1948	1952	1955	1959	1963	1965	w/dwn	No.	1948	1952	1955	1959	1963	1965	w/dwn
4400	WLN	-	-	-	-	-	04/51	4406	WLN	86F	83D	-	-	-	08/55
4401	WLN	83C	-	-	-	-	09/54	4407	LA	83D	-	-	-	-	03/53
4402	LA	-	-	-	-	-	12/49	4408	TDU	86F	-	-	-	-	01/53
4403	WLN	83D	-	-	-	-	01/53	4409	WLN	-	-	-	-	-	02/51
4404	TDU	-	-	-	-	-	03/52	4410	EXE	83C	83D	-	-	-	08/55
4405	NA	83A	83A	-	-	-	08/55								

     TOTAL 11

4500   Churchward   2-6-2T

1906 Churchward design for G.W.R.. Developed from 4400 class. All eventually superheated.

Loco Weight : 57t 0c   *Driving Wheels :* 4' 7½"   *Cylinders :* (O) 17" x 24"   *Valve Gear :* Stephenson (Piston Valves)

No.	1948	1952	1955	1959	1963	1965	w/dwn
4500	PZ	83G	-	-	-	-	08/53
4501	MCH	89C	-	-	-	-	03/53
4502	SDN	-	-	-	-	-	10/51
4503	SBZ	-	-	-	-	-	01/51
4504	WOS	83F	-	-	-	-	06/52
4505	SBZ	83E	83E	-	-	-	10/57
4506	WTD	87H	87H	-	-	-	03/55
4507	SDN	82F	82E	71G	-	-	10/63
4508	WES	83E	83E	83F	-	-	10/59
4509	PZ	-	-	-	-	-	06/51
4510	SDN	82D	-	-	-	-	03/53
4511	MCH	81F	-	-	-	-	11/53
4512	MCH	89C	-	-	-	-	02/53
4513	MCH	-	-	-	-	-	10/50
4514	ABEEG	86H	-	-	-	-	02/53
4515	WTD	87H	-	-	-	-	04/53
4516	SBZ	83E	-	-	-	-	12/52
4517	LA	83E	-	-	-	-	02/53
4518	NPT	83D	-	-	-	-	10/52
4519	WTD	87H	87H	87H	-	-	02/59
4520	WES	82F	-	-	-	-	01/53
4521	SDN	82A	85B	-	-	-	12/55
4522	ABEEG	86G	86H	-	-	-	02/55
4523	TR	83F	83E	-	-	-	10/55
4524	LA	83D	83D	-	-	-	06/58
4525	PZ	83G	-	-	-	-	06/53
4526	NA	83E	83E	-	-	-	01/58
4527	WEY	82E	-	-	-	-	03/53
4528	LA	-	-	-	-	-	12/50
4529	SBZ	-	-	-	-	-	03/52
4530	EXE	83D	83D	-	-	-	03/55
4531	LA	-	-	-	-	-	02/50
4532	TR	83A	82A	-	-	-	02/55
4533	PPRD	86G	86G	-	-	-	03/55
4534	GLO	85B	83D	-	-	-	02/55
4535	BRD	82A	82A	-	-	-	02/55
4536	BRD	82D	82D	82D	-	-	04/59
4537	PZ	83G	83G	-	-	-	02/55
4538	SDN	82C	82C	-	-	-	05/57
4539	BRD	81D	82A	-	-	-	10/55
4540	PZ	83C	83G	83C	-	-	03/59
4541	PPRD	86G	87H	-	-	-	10/55
4542	LA	83D	83D	-	-	-	08/55
4543	SDN	-	-	-	-	-	08/50
4544	SDN	82A	-	-	-	-	09/52
4545	PZ	83G	83G	-	-	-	09/58
4546	WOS	85A	89A	-	-	-	01/58
4547	NA	83A	83A	83E	-	-	02/60
4548	PZ	83G	83G	-	-	-	11/57
4549	MCH	89C	89C	89C	-	-	12/61
4550	SDN	82C	82C	87H	-	-	10/60
4551	SDN	82D	82D	-	-	-	02/58
4552	SBZ	83E	83E	83E	-	-	09/61
4553	WTD	87H	87H	83D	-	-	12/58
4554	TR	83F	83F	-	-	-	09/58
4555	MCH	89C	89C	82D	83D	-	11/63
4556	WTD	87H	87H	87H	-	-	06/60
4557	TDU	86F	87H	87H	-	-	09/62
4558	WOS	81F	82A	87H	-	-	07/62
4559	SBZ	83E	83E	83E	-	-	10/60
4560	MCH	89C	89C	89C	-	-	08/59
4561	TR	83F	83F	83F	-	-	05/62
4562	WEY	82F	82A	71G	-	-	03/60
4563	BRD	82A	83G	83G	-	-	10/61
4564	CHEL	85B	85B	89C	83E	-	09/64
4565	SBZ	83E	83E	83E	-	-	10/61
4566	PZ	83G	83G	83G	-	-	04/62
4567	CHEL	85A	85A	82D	-	-	09/62
4568	SBZ	83E	83E	83G	-	-	02/59
4569	TR	83E	83E	83E	87H	-	07/64
4570	SBZ	83E	83G	83G	-	-	01/63
4571	MCH	89C	85A	85A	-	-	03/61
4572	WES	82D	82D	82D	-	-	12/58
4573	WES	82D	82C	85B	-	-	08/61
4574	PZ	83G	83G	83F	-	-	02/63

TOTAL 75

4575   Collett   2-6-2T

1927 Collett development of 4500 class for G.W.R..

Loco Weight : 61t 0c   *Driving Wheels :* 4' 7½"   *Cylinders :* (O) 17" x 24"   *Valve Gear :* Stephenson (Piston Valves)

No.	1948	1952	1955	1959	1963	1965	w/dwn
4575	MCH	89C	89C	89C	-	-	08/60
4576	WTD	87H	87H	-	-	-	09/58
4577	BRD	82A	82A	83G	-	-	11/59
4578	CHEL	85D	88C	-	-	-	08/58
4579	WTD	87H	87H	-	-	-	09/58
4580	BRD	82A	88A	-	-	-	06/58
4581	TR	83B	88A	-	-	-	04/58
4582	NA	83A	82A	-	-	-	04/58
4583	LA	83D	83D	-	-	-	01/58
4584	KDR	83E	83E	83E	-	-	02/59
4585	SDN	83E	83E	83E	-	-	10/59
4586	KDR	85B	85B	-	-	-	04/56
4587	NA	83A	83F	83F	-	-	08/60
4588	TR	83F	83F	83F	-	-	07/62
4589	TR	83F	88A	83C	-	-	09/60
4590	SDN	83D	83D	-	-	-	10/58
4591	LA	83D	83D	83D	83D	-	07/64
4592	SDN	82A	82A	83D	-	-	01/60
4593	NPT	86H	86H	86G	83B	-	09/64
4594	KDR	85A	85A	87H	-	-	11/60

No.	1948	1952	1955	1959	1963	1965	w/dwn	No.	1948	1952	1955	1959	1963	1965	w/dwn
4595	BRD	82A	82A	-	-	-	12/58	4598	SBZ	83E	83F	-	-	-	12/56
4596	WOS	85D	85D	-	-	-	09/57	4599	NPT	85A	89C	89C	-	-	03/59
4597	ABEEG	86G	82A	-	-	-	01/58								

Continued with Number 5500

57xx

0-6-0PT

Continued from Number 3799.

No.	1948	1952	1955	1959	1963	1965	w/dwn	No.	1948	1952	1955	1959	1963	1965	w/dwn
4600	HFD	85C	85C	86G	86G	-	07/64	4650	SLO	81B	81B	81B	86F	-	07/65
4601	DID	88C	88C	88E	-	-	11/62	4651	SDN	82C	82C	82C	87B	-	09/63
4602	SALOP	84G	84K	6E	84F	-	11/64	4652	CDF	86H	86H	86H	88H	-	04/64
4603	SPM	82A	82B	82B	86G	-	04/64	4653	LA	83D	83D	87A	87A	-	11/64
4604	SHL	83B	83B	83B	86F	-	07/65	4654	NEY	87H	87H	87H	87H	-	12/63
4605	TYS	84H	84H	84H	-	-	10/62	4655	WEY	82B	82B	82B	72A	-	06/65
4606	PDN	81D	81D	81D	81E	-	02/65	4656	LA	83D	83D	83D	-	-	12/62
4607	SPM	82B	82D	82D	82D	-	09/65	4657	HFD	85C	85C	85C	86A	-	07/64
4608	SHL	81C	81C	81C	81C	-	09/64	4658	LA	83D	83D	83D	87H	-	05/64
4609	PDN	81D	81D	81D	81D	-	05/65	4659	GLO	85B	85B	85C	86C	-	05/64
4610	SHL	81C	81C	88C	70B	-	10/64	4660	WEY	82A	82B	82B	87A	-	07/64
4611	PPRD	86A	86A	86A	86A	-	06/65	4661	RDG	81D	81D	81D	81D	-	12/63
4612	SPM	82C	82C	82C	87A	-	08/65	4662	PILL	86F	86C	86D	88G	-	09/65
4613	WOS	85A	85A	85A	85A	-	12/64	4663	SHL	83B	83B	83B	88H	-	06/65
4614	WOS	85A	85D	85A	85B	-	07/64	4664	WOS	85B	85A	85A	85A	-	07/65
4615	PDN	81A	81A	81A	81A	-	10/64	4665	PDN	81D	81D	81D	84F	-	06/65
4616	CHYS	88D	88D	88A	71G	-	10/64	4666	PDN	87C	87C	87C	72A	-	06/65
4617	SLO	84J	84J	84J	89A	-	10/63	4667	PDN	88A	88A	88A	88C	-	04/64
4618	CED	88A	88A	88A	88L	-	10/63	4668	PPRD	86G	86G	86G	86G	87F	07/65
4619	SPM	82B	82B	82A	82E	-	09/64	4669	TDU	86F	86F	86F	88H	-	06/65
4620	TYS	86D	86D	86D	88G	-	07/65	4670	RDG	81D	81D	81D	81D	-	10/64
4621	NEA	87A	87A	87A	87A	-	07/65	4671	NPT	86A	86A	86A	86A	86E	11/65
4622	CDF	86C	86C	86C	83B	-	05/64	4672	SALOP	84G	84G	88A	70A	-	07/63
4623	SALOP	84G	84G	84G	86C	-	06/65	4673	SHL	81C	81C	81C	83C	-	06/65
4624	SPM	82B	82F	71G	71G	-	09/64	4674	LTS	86D	86D	86D	88G	-	11/64
4625	KDR	85A	85A	85A	-	-	05/62	4675	TDU	86F	86F	86F	88H	-	06/65
4626	SPM	82B	88B	88E	70E	-	03/64	4676	OXF	81F	81F	87K	87F	-	10/65
4627	GLO	85B	85B	85B	86A	-	10/64	4677	CDF	86C	87J	87J	87A	-	03/63
4628	GLO	85B	85B	85B	85A	-	05/64	4678	HFD	85C	85C	85C	86C	-	07/64
4629	WOS	85A	85A	85A	85B	-	09/63	4679	LA	83D	83D	83D	86A	-	05/65
4630	CED	88D	88D	88D	70E	-	11/65	4680	PDN	81F	81B	85B	85A	85A	12/65
4631	BAN	84C	84C	88E	72C	-	06/65	4681	DYD	87B	87B	87B	70A	-	12/63
4632	MTHR	88D	88D	88D	-	-	01/62	4682	ABEEG	86H	86H	86B	87A	-	09/63
4633	CDF	86C	86C	86C	88L	-	04/63	4683	TYS	84J	84J	84J	89B	-	10/65
4634	TDU	86F	86F	88A	82G	-	09/64	4684	DYD	87B	87B	87B	87B	-	07/65
4635	MTHR	88D	88D	88D	88D	2A	07/66	4685	ABEEG	86H	86H	86H	-	-	05/62
4636	WES	82D	82D	82D	82D	-	09/65	4686	ABEEG	86H	88B	88E	-	-	08/59
4637	CDF	86D	86D	86D	88B	-	05/64	4687	STB	84F	84F	84F	84F	-	11/64
4638	STB	81B	81B	81B	81B	-	06/65	4688	RDG	82B	82B	82B	88J	-	12/63
4639	PPRD	86G	86G	86G	86G	-	06/65	4689	YEO	82E	82E	71H	71G	-	12/65
4640	DYD	87B	87B	87B	87B	-	12/63	4690	RDG	88D	88D	88D	88D	-	10/63
4641	KDR	85C	85D	81D	-	-	05/62	4691	PDN	81B	81B	81B	82G	-	09/64
4642	PDN	86G	86G	86G	86G	-	01/64	4692	RDG	88C	88C	88C	70A	-	09/64
4643	TDU	86F	86H	86B	86B	-	04/65	4693	LA	83D	83D	84K	87A	-	04/64
4644	PDN	81A	81A	81A	87J	-	10/63	4694	DG	87C	87C	87C	72A	-	06/65
4645	OXF	84J	84J	84J	89B	-	11/65	4695	SHL	81C	81C	87B	87B	-	06/64
4646	BAN	84F	84F	84F	84F	2C	11/66	4696	STB	84F	84F	84F	84F	2C	11/66
4647	SPM	82D	82D	82D	-	-	10/62	4697	SDN	82C	82C	82C	82C	-	07/65
4648	TYS	84E	84E	84E	84E	-	09/64	4698	PDN	81A	81B	88A	70A	-	11/65
4649	RDG	81E	81E	81E	81F	-	09/64	4699	PDN	81A	87H	87H	87A	-	06/64

Continued with Number 5700

47xx Churchward 2-8-0

Introduced by Churchward in 1919 as a mixed traffic class. Although a successful design, only nine were ever built. 4700 originally had a smaller boiler than the rest of the class.

Loco Weight: 82t 0c *Driving Wheels:* 5' 8" *Cylinders:* (O) 19" x 30" *Valve Gear:* Stephenson (piston valves)

Number	1948	1952	1955	1959	1963	1965	w/dwn	Number	1948	1952	1955	1959	1963	1965	w/dwn
4700	PDN	81A	81A	81A	-	-	10/62	4705	PDN	81A	81A	83D	81C	-	12/63
4701	PDN	81A	81A	81A	81A	-	09/63	4706	EXE	82B	82B	82B	81C	-	02/64
4702	PDN	81A	81A	81A	-	-	06/62	4707	PDN	81A	81A	81C	81C	-	05/64
4703	LA	83D	82B	82B	81A	-	05/64	4708	OXY	84B	81A	81A	-	-	10/62
4704	BHD	81A	81A	81A	81A	-	05/64								

TOTAL 9

49xx 'Hall' 4-6-0

4900 was a 1924 rebuild by Collett of 2925 Saint Martin, with 6' 0" wheels and a side window cab. This loco weighed 72t 10c. 4901 onwards (introduced 1928}, were based on this prototype rebuild, but had modified footplating and higher pitched boilers.

Loco Weight: 75t 0c *Driving Wheels:* 6' 0" *Cylinders:* (o) 18½" x 30" *Valve Gear:* Stephenson (piston valves)

Number & Name	1948	1952	1955	1959	1963	1965	w/dwn	Notes
4900 Saint Martin	PDN	84C	85A	81A	-	-	04/59	
4901 Adderley Hall	CDF	86C	86G	84A	-	-	09/60	
4902 Aldenham Hall	OXF	81F	81F	81F	81E	-	09/63	
4903 Astley Hall	OXF	81F	81F	81F	81A	-	10/64	
4904 Binnegar Hall	OXF	84G	84E	84G	83B	-	12/63	
4905 Barton Hall	SDN	84K	85C	83A	82B	-	11/63	
4906 Bradfield Hall	TR	83F	83F	83E	-	-	09/62	
4907 Broughton Hall	PDN	82F	85C	81C	86C	-	08/63	Renumbered from3903, 04/50
4908 Broome Hall	LLY	81A	83G	83G	81E	-	10/63	
4909 Blakesley Hall	BAN	82C	82A	82B	-	-	09/62	
4910 Blaisdon Hall	CARM	87G	87G	87E	81E	-	12/63	
4912 Berrington Hall	PPRD	82C	84A	84A	-	-	08/62	
4913 Baglan Hall	CDF	86C	86C	84G	-	-	09/62	
4914 Cranmore Hall	RDG	82A	82A	82B	82B	-	12/63	
4915 Condover Hall	CARM	87G	84G	81A	-	-	02/63	
4916 Crumlin Hall	OXY	82C	86A	86A	86C	-	08/64	
4917 Crosswood Hall	TYS	82B	82D	82D	-	-	09/62	
4918 Dartington Hall	CHR	84C	84B	82A	88L	-	06/63	
4919 Donnington Hall	SALOP	84B	84B	81A	82C	-	10/64	
4920 Dumbleton Hall	RDG	81D	83B	83B	83D	82E	12/65	
4921 Eaton Hall	OXF	81F	81F	81F	-	-	09/62	
4922 Enville Hall	CARM	87G	87G	82A	82B	-	07/63	
4923 Evenley Hall	OXY	81A	81A	87E	84B	-	05/64	
4924 Eydon Hall	TYS	84E	84B	84C	82C	-	10/63	
4925 Eynsham Hall	SDN	82C	82C	81C	-	-	08/62	
4926 Fairleigh Hall	WES	82D	84A	86G	-	-	09/61	
4927 Farnborough Hall	WES	82D	82D	82A	87F	-	09/63	
4928 Gatacre Hall	OXF	81F	82C	83D	87B	-	12/63	
4929 Goytrey Hall	TR	85B	85B	85B	85B	-	03/65	
4930 Hagley Hall	TYS	82B	82D	83B	82C	-	12/63	
4931 Hanbury Hall	RDG	81C	83G	83G	-	-	07/62	
4932 Hatherton Hall	PPRD	83C	83B	83B	-	-	11/64	
4933 Himley Hall	PPRD	82D	81F	82D	82B	-	08/64	
4934 Hindlip Hall	TYS	82F	86C	81C	-	-	09/62	
4935 Ketley Hall	PDN	81E	81E	87G	81E	-	03/63	
4936 Kinlet Hall	TR	83F	83D	83D	88L	-	01/64	
4937 Lanelay Hall	NEY	87G	84G	87E	-	-	09/62	
4938 Liddington Hall	OXF	81F	81F	81F	-	-	12/62	
4939 Littleton Hall	TYS	81C	81D	81E	-	-	02/63	

Number & Name	1948	1952	1955	1959	1963	1965	w/dwn	Notes
4940 Ludford Hall	SBZ	83E	83B	83B	-	-	11/59	
4941 Llangedwyn Hall	NPT	81A	87F	87F	-	-	10/62	
4942 Maindy Hall	BRD	82A	82A	84C	81E	-	12/63	
4943 Marrington Hall	PDN	84B	81A	86G	86G	-	12/63	
4944 Middleton Hall	OXY	81C	81C	83C	-	-	09/62	
4945 Milligan Hall	SDN	82C	81E	82D	-	-	11/61	
4946 Moseley Hall	PZ	83G	86C	86C	89A	-	06/63	
4947 Nanhoran Hall	PZ	82B	82B	82A	-	-	09/62	
4948 Northwick Hall	LA	81D	83C	83C	-	-	09/62	Renumbered from 3902, 09/48
4949 Packwood Hall	PZ	83B	83B	82A	82B	-	09/64	
4950 Patshull Hall	SRD	84B	83D	83G	81E	-	05/64	
4951 Pendeford Hall	PDN	82A	86A	84B	82C	-	06/64	
4952 Peplow Hall	CDF	86E	87F	85A	-	-	09/62	
4953 Pitchford Hall	CDF	86C	86C	82C	88L	-	04/63	
4954 Plaish Hall	CDF	83C	81E	81F	84E	-	11/64	
4955 Plaspower Hall	TN	84B	84B	83A	86G	-	10/63	
4956 Plowdon Hall	OXY	81C	81C	82A	82D	-	07/63	
4957 Postlip Hall	SDN	87H	86A	84B	-	-	03/62	
4958 Priory Hall	PDNT	82C	82B	87G	86G	-	09/64	
4959 Purley Hall	YS	84E	84B	81E	81E	-	12/64	
4960 Pyle Hall	SRD	84C	81D	81D	-	-	09/62	
4961 Pyrland Hall	PDN	82A	82A	81D	-	-	12/62	
4962 Ragley Hall	PDN	81D	81D	81D	87J	-	10/65	
4963 Rignall Hall	WES	86C	84B	84B	-	-	06/62	
4964 Rodwell Hall	OXY	84E	84E	84C	86G	-	10/63	
4965 Rood Ashton Hall	SPM	83G	83D	81E	-	-	03/62	
4966 Shakenhurst Hall	LA	83D	84B	84B	87A	-	11/63	
4967 Shirenewton Hall	TYS	82B	81A	83A	-	-	09/62	
4968 Shotton Hall	SPM	86C	86C	84G	-	-	07/62	Renumbered from 3900, 03/49
4969 Shrugborough Hall	SPM	82C	81F	81D	-	-	09/62	
4970 Sketty Hall	PZ	83B	83B	83B	87B	-	07/63	
4971 Stanway Hall	LA	83B	83B	83B	-	-	08/62	Renumbered from 3901, 04/49
4972 Saint Brides Hall	LA	83D	82C	82C	82D	-	02/64	Renumbered from 3904, 10/48
4973 Sweeney Hall	OXF	82C	82C	86C	-	-	07/62	
4974 Talgarth Hall	CDF	86C	86C	86G	-	-	04/62	
4975 Umberslade Hall	CDF	86C	85C	83D	81D	-	06/63	
4976 Warfield Hall	CHR	84K	85C	83G	81C	-	05/64	
4977 Watcombe Hall	GLO	84C	84C	81A	-	-	05/62	
4978 Westwood Hall	PDN	87E	83D	83B	83D	-	09/64	
4979 Wooton Hall	CDF	86C	81C	81F	81F	-	12/63	
4980 Wrottesley Hall	WOS	84C	84C	82B	82B	-	07/63	
4981 Abberley Hall	CARM	87G	87E	87J	87J	-	10/63	
4982 Acton Hall	FGD	87H	86A	86C	-	-	05/62	
4983 Albert Hall	NA	82B	82B	87G	87H	-	12/63	
4984 Albrighton Hall	CARM	87G	87G	84B	-	-	09/62	
4985 Allesley Hall	PDN	82D	83B	83B	86G	-	09/64	
4986 Aston Hall	SPM	82B	81A	84A	-	-	05/62	
4987 Brockley Hall	OXY	84D	84C	81D	-	-	04/62	
4988 Bulwell Hall	WEY	82F	82F	82B	87F	-	02/64	
4989 Cherwell Hall	RDG	81D	81D	81D	81C	-	11/64	
4990 Clifton Hall	SPM	86E	86G	84A	-	-	04/62	
4991 Cobham Hall	OXY	84B	86G	83B	82B	-	12/63	
4992 Crosby Hall	TYS	83D	83D	83C	82B	-	04/65	
4993 Dalton Hall	TYS	81D	81D	81D	82B	-	02/65	
4994 Downton Hall	RDG	81D	81E	81E	81E	-	03/63	
4995 Easton Hall	RDG	81D	81D	81F	-	-	06/62	
4996 Eden Hall	OXY	85B	85B	81G	83B	-	09/63	
4997 Elton Hall	NEY	87H	84A	84B	-	-	10/61	
4998 Eyton Hall	PDN	81E	81D	81D	84C	-	10/63	
4999 Gopsall Hall	TYS	82B	82B	86C	-	-	09/62	

Continued with Number 5900　　　　　　　*Page 49*

Continued from Number 4099.

Number & Name	1948	1952	1955	1959	1963	1965	w/dwn	Notes
5000 Launceston Castle	PDN	82A	82A	82C	85B	-	10/64	
5001 Llandovery Castle	CDP	86C	86C	84G	-	-	02/63	DC 06/61
5002 Ludlow Castle	LDR	87E	87E	82C	82C	-	09/64	
5003 Lulworth Castle	TN	83C	83C	86C	-	-	08/62	
5004 Llanstephan Castle	PDN	81A	81A	87E	-	-	04/62	
5005 Manorbier Castle	CDF	86C	86C	82C	-	-	02/60	
5006 Tregenna Castle	LDR	86C	81A	87G	-	-	04/62	
5007 Rougemont Castle	CDF	86C	86C	81A	-	-	09/62	
5008 Raglan Castle	PDN	84A	84A	81A	-	-	09/62	DC 03/61
5009 Shrewsbury Castle	LA	82C	82C	82C	-	-	10/60	
5010 Restormel Castle	CDP	84A	84A	81A	-	-	10/59	
5011 Tintagel Castle	NA	83A	83A	83A	-	-	09/62	
5012 Berry Pomeroy Castle	EXE	83D	81F	81F	-	-	04/62	
5013 Abergavenny Castle	LDR	87E	87E	87E	-	-	07/62	
5014 Goodrich Castle	PDN	81A	81A	81A	81A	-	02/65	
5015 Kingswear Castle	SRD	84A	84A	82A	88L	-	04/63	
5016 Montgomery Castle	LDR	87E	87E	87E	-	-	09/62	DC 02/60
5017 St Donats Castle / The Gloucester Regiment 28th 61st	WOS	85B	85B	85B	-		09/62	Renamed 03/54
5018 St. Mawes Castle	SRD	85B	85B	81D	81D	-	03/64	
5019 Treago Castle	BRD	82A	82A	84A	-	-	09/62	DC 02/61
5020 Trematon Castle	CDF	86C	86C	83D	-	-	11/62	
5021 Whittington Castle	SALOP	83D	83C	83D	-	-	09/62	
5022 Wigmore Castle	PDN	84A	84A	84A	84A	-	06/63	DC 02/59
5023 Brecon Castle	PDN	83D	83D	82C	-	-	02/63	
5024 Carew Castle	BRD	83A	83A	83A	-	-	05/62	
5025 Chirk Castle	BRD	82A	82A	81F	81F	-	11/63	
5026 Criccieth Castle	LA	81F	81F	84A	84A	-	11/64	DC 10/59
5027 Farleigh Castle	PDN	84A	82A	81A	-	-	11/62	DC 04/61
5028 Llantilio Castle	NA	83A	83A	83D	-	-	05/60	
5029 Nunney Castle	PDN	81A	81A	85A	88L	-	12/63	
5030 Shirburn Castle	CDF	86C	86C	87G	-	-	09/62	
5031 Totnes Castle	SRD	84A	84K	84A	84A	-	10/63	DC 06/59
5032 Usk Castle	SALOP	84A	84A	83A	-	-	09/62	DC 05/59
5033 Broughton Castle	CHR	84K	84K	81F	-	-	09/62	DC 10/60
5034 Corfe Castle	NA	81D	81A	81A	-	-	09/62	DC 02/60
5035 Coity Castle	PDN	81A	81A	81A	-	-	05/62	
5036 Lyonshall Castle	PDN	81D	81D	81D	-	-	09/62	DC 12/60
5037 Monmouth Castle	PDN	82A	85A	85A	87F	-	03/64	
5038 Morlais Castle	PDN	81A	81A	84G	81D	-	09/63	
5039 Rhuddlan Castle	PDN	87G	87G	87E	87F	-	06/64	
5040 Stokesay Castle	PDN	81A	81A	81A	82B	-	10/63	
5041 Tiverton Castle	LA	83A	83A	87E	81A	-	12/63	
5042 Winchester Castle	GLO	85B	85B	85B	87F	-	06/65	
5043 Earl of Mount Edgcumbe	PDN	87G	87G	81A	88L	-	12/63	DC 10/56
5044 Earl of Dunraven	PDN	81A	81A	81A	-	-	04/62	
5045 Earl of Dudley	PDN	84A	84A	84A	-	-	09/62	
5046 Earl Cawdor	CDF	86C	86C	84A	-	-	09/62	
5047 Earl of Dartmouth	NA	83A	84A	84A	-	-	09/62	
5048 Earl of Devon	BRD	82A	82A	82A	-	-	08/62	
5049 Earl of Plymouth	CDF	86C	86C	83A	82B	-	03/63	DC 09/59
5050 Earl of St. Germans	LA	84G	84G	84G	82B	-	08/63	
5051 Earl Bathurst	LDR	87E	87E	87E	87F	-	05/63	
5052 Earl of Radnor	CDF	86C	86C	81A	-	-	09/62	
5053 Earl Cairns	SRD	84A	83D	83A	-	-	07/62	
5054 Earl of Ducie	CDF	86C	86C	82A	87F	-	10/64	
5055 Earl of Eldon	PDN	81A	81A	83A	81A	-	09/64	

Number & Name	1948	1952	1955	1959	1963	1965	w/dwn	Notes
5056 Earl of Powis	PDN	81A	81A	81A	81A	-	11/64	DC 10/60
5057 Earl Waldegrave	LA	83D	82A	82A	81A	-	03/64	DC 07/58
5058 Earl of Clancarty	NA	83D	83D	83D	85B	-	03/63	
5059 Earl of St. Aldwyn	EXE	83C	83A	84A	-	-	06/62	
5060 Earl of Berkeley	LA	81A	81A	81A	81A	-	04/63	DC 07/61
5061 Earl of Birkenhead	SALOP	84K	84K	81D	-	-	09/62	DC 09/58
5062 Earl of Shaftesbury	NA	83B	82C	82A	-	-	08/62	
5063 Earl Baldwin	WOS	85A	82A	84A	84A	-	02/65	
5064 Bishop's Castle	SALOP	82A	82A	82C	-	-	09/62	DC 09/58
5065 Newport Castle	PDN	81A	81A	81A	-	-	01/63	
5066 Wardour Castle / Sir Felix Pole	PDN	81A	81A	81A	-	-	09/62	Renamed 04/56 DC 04/59
5067 St. Fagans Castle	SDN	82A	82A	82A	-	-	07/62	
5068 Beverston Castle	SDN	82C	82C	82C	-	-	09/62	DC 07/59
5069 Isambard Kingdom Brunel	PDN	81A	83D	83D	-	-	02/62	DC 11/58
5070 Sir Daniel Gooch	SRD	84A	84A	84A	81A	-	03/64	
5071 Spitfire	NA	83A	83A	85B	82B	-	10/63	DC 06/59
5072 Hurricane	LDR	87E	87E	84A	-	-	10/62	
5073 Blenheim	SALOP	84G	84G	82A	88L	-	02/64	DC 07/59
5074 Hampden	BRD	82A	86C	81A	88L	-	05/64	DC 09/61
5075 Wellington	SRD	84K	84K	83D	-	-	09/62	
5076 Gladiator	BRD	82A	82A	82A	81D	-	09/64	
5077 Fairey Battle	TN	86C	82A	87E	-	-	07/62	
5078 Beaufort	NA	83A	83A	86C	-	-	11/62	DC 12/61
5079 Lysander	LA	83A	83A	83A	-	-	05/60	
5080 Defiant	CDF	86C	86C	87G	87F	-	04/63	
5081 Lockheed Hudson	PDN	81A	85A	85A	88L	-	10/63	
5082 Swordfish	BRD	82A	81A	81A	-	-	07/62	
5083 Bath Abbey	BRD	82C	82C	81D	-	-	01/59	
5084 Reading Abbey	BRD	82C	82C	81A	-	-	07/62	DC 10/58
5085 Evesham Abbey	PDN	81A	82A	82A	82B	-	02/64	
5086 Viscount Horne	SALOP	85A	85A	-	-	-	11/58	
5087 Tintern Abbey	PDN	81A	81A	81A	87F	-	08/63	
5088 Llanthony Abbey	SRD	84A	84A	84A	-	-	09/62	DC 06/58
5089 Westminster Abbey	LDR	86C	87E	84A	84A	-	11/64	
5090 Neath Abbey	LA	83D	85A	82A	-	-	05/62	
5091 Cleeve Abbey	BRD	82C	84G	87E	88L	-	10/64	
5092 Tresco Abbey	WOS	85A	85A	82A	88L	-	07/63	DC 10/61
5093 Upton Castle	LDR	81A	81A	81A	81A	-	09/63	
5094 Tretower Castle	NA	82A	82A	85B	-	-	09/62	DC 06/60
5095 Barbury Castle	LA	81A	81A	86C	-	-	08/62	DC 11/58
5096 Bridgwater Castle	BRD	82A	82A	82A	88L	-	06/64	DC 01/59
5097 Sarum Castle	SALOP	84G	84G	84G	88L	-	03/63	DC 06/61
5098 Clifford Castle	EXE	83D	83D	83D	87F	-	06/64	DC 01/59
5099 Compton Castle	PDN	86C	86C	86C	-	-	02/63	

Continued with Number 7000

51xx

2-6-2T

Continued from Number 4179.

No.	1948	1952	1955	1959	1963	1965	w/dwn	No.	1948	1952	1955	1959	1963	1965	w/dwn
5101	STB	84F	84F	84D	84D	-	06/63	5111	SRD	-	-	-	-	-	10/48
5102	TYS	84E	87A	87A	-	-	03/60	5112	WOS	85B	84A	-	-	-	10/55
5103	SRD	84K	84K	86G	-	-	12/60	5113	NA	83A	83A	-	-	-	10/55
5104	LMTN	84D	84D	82B	-	-	11/60	5114	WOS	-	-	-	-	-	09/50
5105	STB	84F	84F	-	-	-	10/58	5117	CHR	-	-	-	-	-	05/49
5106	TYS	84E	84A	83D	-	-	03/60	5119	SHL	-	-	-	-	-	06/48
5107	STB	84F	84F	-	-	-	06/57	5121	TYS	-	-	-	-	-	10/48
5108	NA	83A	83A	-	-	-	07/58	5122	STB	-	-	-	-	-	09/50
5109	LMTN	84H	84H	-	-	-	06/57	5125	TYS	-	-	-	-	-	07/52
5110	KDR	85D	85D	85D	-	-	12/60	5127	WLN	-	-	-	-	-	05/48

No.	1948	1952	1955	1959	1963	1965	w/dwn
5128	RHY	-	-	-	-	-	11/48
5129	TYS	-	-	-	-	-	07/51
5130	LMTN	-	-	-	-	-	08/48
5131	STB	-	-	-	-	-	10/48
5132	NA	-	-	-	-	-	08/51
5134	STB	-	-	-	-	-	04/51
5135	WLN	-	-	-	-	-	08/49
5136	STB	-	-	-	-	-	10/51
5137	WLN	-	-	-	-	-	10/51
5138	STB	84H	-	-	-	-	11/52
5139	WLN	84H	-	-	-	-	11/52
5140	SBZ	83A	-	-	-	-	06/53
5141	STB	84C	-	-	-	-	10/52
5142	NA	-	-	-	-	-	05/52
5143	SRD	-	-	-	-	-	12/51
5144	LMTN	-	-	-	-	-	01/52
5146	STB	-	-	-	-	-	05/48
5147	STB	84F	-	-	-	-	01/53
5148	LA	83D	83D	83D	-	-	12/59
5150	NA	83A	83A	83A	-	-	08/60
5151	SRD	84A	84A	84A	-	-	08/62
5152	TYS	84E	84E	84C	85A	-	11/63
5153	NA	83A	83A	83A	84G	-	11/64
5154	SALOP	84G	84G	83A	85B	-	08/63
5155	STB	84F	86E	86E	-	-	01/60
5156	TYS	84E	84E	-	-	-	09/58
5157	NA	83A	83B	-	-	-	07/58
5158	SBZ	83A	83A	83A	-	-	04/61
5159	THT	88F	88F	-	-	-	04/56
5160	STB	86A	84F	-	-	-	11/58
5161	LMTN	84D	84D	-	-	-	04/57
5162	TYS	87E	88F	-	-	-	07/58
5163	LMTN	84D	84E	84E	-	-	11/59
5164	TYS	84E	84E	83A	86G	-	04/63
5165	STB	84F	84F	-	-	-	02/58
5166	TYS	84E	84E	86E	-	-	05/61
5167	STB	84F	84F	84H	-	-	01/62
5168	SALOP	84G	84G	-	-	-	08/58
5169	BRD	86E	86E	86E	-	-	09/60
5170	STB	84F	84C	84C	-	-	12/59
5171	TYS	84E	87G	-	-	-	07/58
5172	TN	83B	83B	-	-	-	10/58
5173	WOS	85A	86A	86A	-	-	08/62
5174	CHR	84K	84K	6E	-	-	11/61
5175	TYS	84E	83D	83D	-	-	04/61
5176	CHR	6C	6C	84F	-	-	01/61
5177	TYS	84E	84K	85B	-	-	05/61
5178	WLN	84H	84H	83A	-	-	03/60
5179	CHR	84K	84K	85A	-	-	07/60
5180	STB	84F	84F	87H	-	-	07/62
5181	CHR	84K	84E	86E	-	-	08/62
5182	TYS	84E	82A	85B	-	-	05/62
5183	STJ	88F	88C	83A	-	-	05/62
5184	CHR	84K	84D	84D	85B	-	10/64
5185	LMTN	84D	84D	83B	-	-	03/60
5186	CHR	84K	84K	82A	-	-	08/59
5187	LMTN	84A	84A	84A	-	-	05/62
5188	TYS	84E	84A	86A	-	-	07/62
5189	STB	84F	84F	84F	-	-	08/59
5190	TYS	84E	82F	81F	-	-	09/62
5191	STB	84F	84F	86E	86E	-	07/64
5192	LMTN	84D	84E	84E	84F	-	06/63
5193	STB	84F	83D	83E	-	-	06/62
5194	LMTN	84D	84D	85B	-	-	04/61
5195	BRY	88C	88F	83A	-	-	06/61
5196	STB	84F	83A	83A	-	-	12/59
5197	STB	84F	82A	82A	-	-	07/60
5198	TYS	84E	84E	85B	-	-	06/61
5199	TYS	84F	84F	84F	85B	-	03/63

TOTAL 169

42xx

2-8-0T

Continued from Number 4299.

No.	1948	1952	1955	1959	1963	1965	w/dwn
5200	CDF	86B	86B	86B	86B	-	04/65
5201	NPT	86E	86A	86A	87F	-	06/63
5202	TDU	86H	86C	86B	86F	-	06/65
5203	LLY	87F	87F	87F	86A	-	12/63
5204	LLY	87F	87F	87F	-	-	12/62
5205	STJ	86E	86E	86A	85A	-	12/63
5206	NPT	86A	86A	86H	86F	-	05/65
5207	CARM	86H	86C	86C	-	-	01/61
5208	NPT	86A	86F	86F	88H	-	06/65
5209	LLY	87F	87F	87F	87F	-	07/65
5210	SED	87D	87D	87D	87D	-	09/64
5211	LDR	87D	87D	87D	87D	-	05/64
5212	LLY	86A	86E	86E	-	-	05/62
5213	LLY	87F	87F	87F	86A	-	10/64
5214	SED	86E	86E	86E	86E	-	09/64
5215	LLY	87F	87F	87F	87F	-	07/64
5216	DYD	87B	87B	87B	87B	-	10/63
5217	NPT	86A	86A	86A	86A	-	05/63
5218	NPT	86A	86C	86C	86F	-	09/64
5219	LDR	87E	87F	87F	-	-	12/62
5220	LLY	87B	87B	87B	88L	-	12/63
5221	SED	87D	87D	87B	87A	-	10/63
5222	NPT	86A	86A	87F	87A	-	05/64
5223	LLY	87F	87B	87F	87A	-	03/65
5224	NPT	86A	86E	86E	88L	-	04/63
5225	NEA	87A	87A	87A	88L	-	08/63
5226	LLY	82C	82C	85C	85A	-	03/65
5227	SED	87D	86A	86A	-	-	02/63
5228	LLY	86E	86A	86A	86A	-	04/64
5229	NPT	86A	86A	86A	86A	-	05/63
5230	LLY	87F	87F	87F	87D	-	07/64
5231	CARM	86B	86B	86B	86F	-	04/64
5232	SED	87D	87D	87D	86A	-	01/63
5233	NPT	86A	86A	86A	86A	-	08/63
5234	NPT	86A	86A	86A	86A	-	06/63
5235	PILL	86B	86B	86B	86A	-	09/65
5236	CDF	86F	86A	86E	86A	-	10/63
5237	ABDR	86J	86J	86J	88J	-	09/64

No.	1948	1952	1955	1959	1963	1965	w/dwn
5238	NPT	86A	86A	86A	86A	-	01/64
5239	NEA	87A	87A	87A	87A	-	04/63
5240	LLY	87F	82C	87D	88J	-	02/64
5241	SPM	86D	86H	86H	86F	-	06/65
5242	NEA	87A	87A	87A	87F	-	12/64
5243	NPT	86A	86A	85C	88H	-	11/64
5244	PILL	86B	86B	86B	86B	-	05/64
5245	ABDR	86J	86J	85C	85A	-	10/64
5246	SED	87D	87D	87A	87B	-	12/63
5247	LLY	87F	87F	87F	-	-	02/63
5248	LLY	87F	87F	87F	88G	-	10/63
5249	CDF	86C	87F	87F	88J	-	10/63
5250	DYD	86B	86B	86B	86B	-	12/63
5251	NPT	86A	86A	86A	86B	-	01/64

No.	1948	1952	1955	1959	1963	1965	w/dwn
5252	PILL	86B	86B	86B	86F	-	05/65
5253	SED	86E	86E	86E	86E	-	04/63
5254	NEA	87B	87B	87B	87B	-	07/64
5255	NPT	86A	86A	86A	86A	-	05/63
5256	NPT	86A	86A	86A	86B	-	03/65
5257	DYD	87B	87B	86B	87B	-	10/64
5258	ABDR	86J	86J	86J	-	-	12/62
5259	ABEEG	86A	86A	86A	86F	-	03/64
5260	DYD	86A	86A	86C	88L	-	03/63
5261	LLY	87F	87F	86A	86E	-	03/65
5262	STJ	86E	86E	87D	88J	-	08/63
5263	ABDR	86J	86J	86J	86F	-	12/63
5264	NPT	86A	86A	87B	86E	-	09/64

TOTAL 151

43xx

2-6-0

Continued from Number 4386.

No.	1948	1952	1955	1959	1963	1965	w/dwn
5300	OXY	84G	-	-	-	-	01/53
5302	BAN	-	-	-	-	-	05/48
5303	KDR	-	-	-	-	-	05/51
5305	WEY	82F	-	-	-	-	06/52
5306	WES	82D	82A	82C	86E	-	06/64
5307	CDF	84C	82B	-	-	-	11/56
5309	WLN	84B	-	-	-	-	01/53
5310	NEY	87H	87G	-	-	-	07/58
5311	WES	82A	84K	82A	-	-	10/60
5312	GLO	85B	84B	-	-	-	10/58
5313	OXY	84F	84F	-	-	-	05/58
5314	WEY	82F	82F	-	-	-	07/57
5315	CNYD	84J	84K	82B	-	-	02/59
5316	BHD	6C	6C	-	-	-	06/56
5317	BAN	84C	84C	-	-	-	11/56
5318	LA	86E	86A	86G	-	-	09/61
5319	CNYD	84J	84J	84G	-	-	11/59
5320	RDG	-	-	-	-	-	09/48
5321	EXE	83C	83B	87F	-	-	08/59
5322	SDN	82C	81F	81E	86G	-	04/64
5323	OXF	81F	82B	-	-	-	06/58
5324	BAN	84C	87H	81D	-	-	09/60
5325	BRD	82B	83B	-	-	-	08/57
5326	WES	82D	81D	81E	-	-	03/62
5327	BRD	82C	82D	-	-	-	07/56
5328	WEY	82F	84G	-	-	-	07/58
5330	DID	81E	81D	86G	89B	-	06/64
5331	OXY	84K	84G	84G	-	-	11/60
5332	WLN	84C	84C	87F	-	-	10/61
5333	OXY	84E	84E	84E	-	-	05/60
5334	CNYD	84J	86C	-	-	-	11/57
5335	CDF	87F	87F	-	-	-	10/58
5336	GLO	85B	84B	82B	86E	-	09/64
5337	WEY	82F	82F	86C	-	-	10/60
5338	WEY	82F	82D	-	-	-	08/58
5339	CARM	87G	83A	83C	-	-	11/60
5340	WEY	-	-	-	-	-	09/48
5341	LDR	84B	84B	84E	-	-	07/59
5343	BRD	-	-	-	-	-	07/48
5344	CHR	84K	84K	-	-	-	09/58
5345	CHEL	85B	85B	82B	-	-	06/59

No.	1948	1952	1955	1959	1963	1965	w/dwn
5346	TYS	-	-	-	-	-	05/51
5347	GLO	85B	85B	-	-	-	04/58
5348	HFD	-	-	-	-	-	01/52
5349	BAN	-	-	-	-	-	05/48
5350	NA	82B	82B	85C	-	-	12/59
5351	SPM	82B	82C	82C	-	-	06/61
5353	NEY	87H	87G	87G	-	-	05/60
5355	PPRD	86G	85B	85D	-	-	04/59
5356	RDG	87E	83D	82B	-	-	10/59
5357	NEY	87H	87F	87H	-	-	09/62
5358	SPM	82B	82D	82D	-	-	07/62
5359	WEY	-	-	-	-	-	10/51
5360	SHL	87G	83A	-	-	-	09/58
5361	BAN	84C	84C	83F	-	-	01/60
5362	STJ	86E	83A	-	-	-	07/58
5364	NPT	-	-	-	-	-	07/51
5365	CNYD	-	-	-	-	-	03/51
5367	SDN	82C	82B	-	-	-	09/58
5368	NEY	87H	81D	-	-	-	09/58
5369	TYS	84E	84E	84E	86G	-	11/63
5370	TYS	84E	84E	84E	-	-	09/60
5371	SDN	84F	84F	-	-	-	07/58
5372	NEY	87H	87H	-	-	-	07/58
5373	BAN	-	-	-	-	-	06/50
5374	SPM	-	-	-	-	-	06/48
5375	RDG	81D	84B	85A	-	-	10/59
5376	LA	83F	83D	83F	-	-	06/62
5377	HFD	85C	85C	-	-	-	09/58
5378	CDF	87F	84B	84E	-	-	09/59
5379	OXY	84F	84F	-	-	-	05/58
5380	DID	81E	81E	81E	81E	-	09/63
5381	DID	81E	84B	86G	-	-	09/59
5382	CDF	86C	86A	86E	-	-	04/59
5384	WEY	82F	82F	71G	-	-	10/60
5385	RDG	82D	82D	82B	-	-	07/62
5386	OXY	84B	84E	-	-	-	10/58
5388	CDF	86C	86C	86G	-	-	03/59
5390	OXY	81D	84B	-	-	-	08/58
5391	NA	86E	84A	-	-	-	03/57
5392	NEY	87H	87F	-	-	-	08/58

No.	1948	1952	1955	1959	1963	1965	w/dwn	Notes
5393	BHD	6C	6C	6C	-	-	10/59	Renumbered from *8393*, *09/48*

No.	1948	1952	1955	1959	1963	1965	w/dwn	No.	1948	1952	1955	1959	1963	1965	w/dwn
5394	GLO	85B	85B	85D	-	-	*01/59*	5397	DID	81E	81E	-	-	-	*07/58*
5395	FGD	89C	89C	-	-	-	*10/55*	5398	GLO	85B	85B	85B	-	-	*02/59*
5396	SDN	82C	82C	85A	-	-	*05/60*	5399	CHR	84K	84C	6E	-	-	*09/62*

Continued with Number 6300

54xx   Collett   0-6-0PT

Introduced 1931 by Collett , this class was fitted with push - pull equipment for branch passenger work.

Loco Weight : 46t 12c   *Driving Wheels :* 5' 2"   *Cylinders :* (I) 16½" x 24"   *Valve Gear :* Stephenson (Slide Valves)

No.	1948	1952	1955	1959	1963	1965	w/dwn	No.	1948	1952	1955	1959	1963	1965	w/dwn
5400	LDR	87G	87G	89A	-	-	*04/59*	5413	SHL	81F	81F	-	-	-	*10/57*
5401	SHL	81C	89A	-	-	-	*02/57*	5414	SHL	81C	86A	82D	-	-	*10/59*
5402	WES	82D	82D	-	-	-	*09/58*	5415	SHL	81C	81C	-	-	-	*07/57*
5403	WES	82D	82D	-	-	-	*08/57*	5416	SHL	81C	84J	82D	72C	-	*08/63*
5404	BAN	84C	84C	-	-	-	*12/57*	5417	SHL	85B	84B	85B	-	-	*01/61*
5405	SHL	81C	89A	-	-	-	*10/57*	5418	SHL	81C	81C	85B	-	-	*06/61*
5406	WES	82D	82D	-	-	-	*09/57*	5419	WES	82D	82D	-	-	-	*02/58*
5407	BAN	84C	84C	84C	-	-	*06/60*	5420	SHL	81C	81C	84C	85B	-	*10/63*
5408	LDR	85B	85B	-	-	-	*12/56*	5421	SHL	88E	83B	85B	-	-	*09/62*
5409	SHL	81B	34E	14D	-	-	*06/59*	5422	WES	82D	82D	89A	-	-	*06/60*
5410	SHL	81C	81C	81C	72C	-	*10/63*	5423	WES	82D	82D	82D	-	-	*06/59*
5411	SHL	83B	83B	-	-	-	*06/58*	5424	BAN	84C	84C	84C	-	-	*04/59*
5412	LA	83B	83C	83C	-	-	*04/62*								

TOTAL 25

4575   2-6-2T

Continued from Number 4599.

No.	1948	1952	1955	1959	1963	1965	w/dwn	No.	1948	1952	1955	1959	1963	1965	w/dwn
5500	TR	83F	83F	83F	-	-	*10/59*	5525	EXE	83C	82A	83B	-	-	*09/62*
5501	TN	83B	83B	-	-	-	*07/58*	5526	TR	83F	83F	83F	-	-	*06/62*
5502	SBZ	83E	83E	-	-	-	*07/58*	5527	BRD	82A	88C	87H	-	-	*06/60*
5503	TN	83B	83B	83B	-	-	*05/61*	5528	BRD	82A	82A	82A	-	-	*11/59*
5504	TN	83B	83B	83B	-	-	*10/60*	5529	YEO	82E	88C	82A	-	-	*08/60*
5505	NA	83A	83F	-	-	-	*05/57*	5530	NA	85B	85B	82A	-	-	*01/60*
5506	BRD	82A	82A	-	-	-	*05/58*	5531	SBZ	83D	83D	83D	83E	-	*12/64*
5507	MCH	89C	89C	-	-	-	*08/58*	5532	PPRD	86G	82A	82A	-	-	*07/62*
5508	WES	82D	82D	82D	87H	-	*12/64*	5533	TN	83B	83B	83A	-	-	*12/59*
5509	WEY	82C	82C	82C	-	-	*12/61*	5534	SDN	82C	88A	86G	-	-	*09/60*
5510	SDN	82C	82C	82C	-	-	*10/60*	5535	BRD	82A	82A	-	-	-	*06/57*
5511	BRD	82A	88A	83D	-	-	*21/61*	5536	BRD	82C	82C	82A	-	-	*12/60*
5512	BRD	82A	82A	-	-	-	*02/57*	5537	TR	83F	83F	83F	-	-	*08/62*
5513	WTD	87H	87H	-	-	-	*06/57*	5538	CHEL	85B	85B	85B	-	-	*10/61*
5514	BRD	82A	82A	85B	-	-	*11/60*	5539	BRD	82A	83A	83E	-	-	*04/62*
5515	CHEL	83F	83F	83F	-	-	*11/61*	5540	LA	82C	82C	82C	-	-	*08/60*
5516	NPT	86G	86G	86H	-	-	*08/61*	5541	MCH	89C	89C	89C	-	-	*07/62*
5517	MCH	89C	89C	89C	-	-	*12/58*	5542	TN	83B	83A	82D	-	-	*12/61*
5518	KDR	85D	85B	85D	83E	-	*05/64*	5543	TN	83B	83A	83B	-	-	*07/60*
5519	SBZ	83E	83E	83E	-	-	*06/60*	5544	WOS	83A	83A	86H	-	-	*09/62*
5520	ABDR	86H	86H	87H	-	-	*09/62*	5545	NPT	86G	86F	86F	87H	-	*11/64*
5521	TN	83E	83E	83B	-	-	*04/62*	5546	BRD	82A	82A	83C	-	-	*09/60*
5522	TN	83B	83B	83B	-	-	*03/59*	5547	BRD	82A	82A	82C	-	-	*02/62*
5523	BRD	82A	82A	83E	-	-	*06/60*	5548	BRD	82A	82A	71H	72C	-	*05/63*
5524	MCH	89C	86F	83C	-	-	*06/60*	5549	WTD	87H	87H	87H	-	-	*01/62*

No.	1948	1952	1955	1959	1963	1965	w/dwn
5550	NPT	86A	87H	87H	-	-	09/62
5551	NA	83A	83A	83E	-	-	01/60
5552	NA	83A	83A	83F	-	-	10/60
5553	BRD	82A	82A	82A	-	-	11/61
5554	WES	82D	82D	82D	87H	-	08/63
5555	BRD	82A	86F	86F	83C	-	07/63
5556	TDU	86F	89C	89C	-	-	12/59
5557	NA	83A	83A	83E	-	-	10/60
5558	BRD	83B	83B	83A	-	-	10/60
5559	BRD	82A	82A	83F	-	-	01/60
5560	ABH	89C	86F	87H	-	-	04/62
5561	BRD	82A	82A	82A	-	-	07/60
5562	TR	83F	83F	83F	-	-	09/62

No.	1948	1952	1955	1959	1963	1965	w/dwn
5563	SDN	82C	82E	71H	72C	-	09/64
5564	BRD	82C	82C	86G	82C	-	12/64
5565	YEO	82E	82A	89C	-	-	09/60
5566	SDN	82C	82C	82C	-	-	01/59
5567	LA	83D	83D	83D	-	-	01/60
5568	WTD	87H	88A	86H	-	-	01/63
5569	LA	83D	83D	83D	82C	-	12/64
5570	ABH	89C	89C	89C	82C	-	12/63 NS
5571	TN	83B	83B	83B	87H	-	10/64
5572	BRD	82A	88A	83D	-	-	04/62
5573	KDR	85A	86G	83A	87H	-	01/64
5574	CHEL	85B	86F	86F	-	-	12/58

TOTAL 100

56xx   Collett   0-6-2T

Introduced in 1924 by Collett for service in the Welsh Valleys.
Loco Weight : 68t 12c - 69t 6c   *Driving Wheels :* 4' 7½"   *Cylinders :* (I) 18" x 26"
Valve Gear : Stephenson (piston valves)

No.	1948	1952	1955	1959	1963	1965	w/dwn
5600	FDL	88F	88A	88F	-	-	07/62
5601	THT	88A	88A	88E	88E	-	01/65
5602	NPT	86H	86C	86C	87F	-	09/64
5603	NPT	88D	88D	88D	88D	-	09/64
5604	LDR	87E	87E	87B	-	-	12/62
5605	CHYS	88D	88D	88D	88D	2A	05/66
5606	OXY	84F	84F	84E	84B	-	11/65
5607	THT	88F	88F	88F	88B	-	12/63
5608	THT	88F	88A	88F	88B	-	08/63
5609	BRY	88C	88C	88C	87D	-	10/64
5610	FDL	88F	88A	88F	88D	-	12/63
5611	THT	88F	88F	88F	-	-	01/63
5612	DYD	87K	87F	87F	87F	-	04/63
5613	THT	88F	88F	88F	88B	-	05/65
5614	CHYS	88C	88C	88C	88E	-	08/63
5615	THT	88F	88D	88A	88E	-	07/63
5616	OXF	87D	87D	87D	87D	-	09/63
5617	CHYS	88D	88E	88E	-	-	09/62
5618	AYN	88E	88E	88E	88D	-	03/65
5619	AYN	88C	88C	88C	88C	-	06/64
5620	STJ	86G	86C	86E	86G	-	07/63
5621	BRY	88C	88C	88C	88C	-	06/65
5622	BRY	88D	88D	88C	88D	-	06/63
5623	CHYS	88E	88E	88E	87D	-	02/64
5624	CHYS	84B	86F	86J	88J	-	06/64
5625	STJ	86E	86G	86G	88B	-	10/63
5626	STJ	86E	87B	88D	88D	-	12/63
5627	BRY	88C	88C	88E	88E	-	04/63
5628	CDF	87D	87D	87D	-	-	02/63
5629	DYD	87B	81E	86F	88B	-	05/64
5630	AYN	88A	88A	88D	-	-	12/62
5631	LDR	87E	87E	87E	-	-	09/62
5632	BRY	88C	88C	88F	88B	-	09/64
5633	TDU	86C	86C	86J	88J	-	05/65
5634	TYS	84G	84A	84G	87H	-	07/64
5635	RHY	88D	88D	88D	88B	-	07/64
5636	THT	88A	88A	88A	-	-	05/62
5637	AYN	88E	88E	88F	88C	-	06/64

No.	1948	1952	1955	1959	1963	1965	w/dwn
5638	NPT	86G	86G	86G	86G	-	02/64
5639	DYD	87F	81E	81E	-	-	05/62
5640	RYR	88D	88D	88D	84D	-	07/63
5641	AYN	88E	88E	88E	88E	-	09/64
5642	SALOP	84G	88B	82B	-	-	09/62
5643	AYN	88E	88E	88E	88C	-	07/63
5644	AYN	88E	86J	88E	88E	-	06/63
5645	STJ	86E	86H	86G	88D	-	04/63
5646	CHYS	87H	87H	88F	-	-	09/62
5647	CHR	84K	84K	81E	88J	-	03/64
5648	BRY	88C	88C	88A	88B	-	09/64
5649	PPRD	86J	86J	86J	88J	-	03/63
5650	THT	88E	88A	88D	88D	-	06/63
5651	CHYS	84F	84F	84G	88B	-	12/64
5652	CH	88D	88D	88D	-	-	09/62
5653	CH	88A	88A	88F	-	-	01/63
5654	MTHR	88A	88A	88F	88B	-	12/63
5655	RYR	88D	88D	88D	88D	-	06/65
5656	DYD	87E	87E	87E	87D	-	02/64
5657	OXY	87H	87F	86A	-	-	07/62
5658	CHYS	84F	84F	84E	84E	-	11/65
5659	CHYS	88A	88A	86G	86G	-	11/65
5660	RHY	88D	88D	88D	88D	-	10/64
5661	CHYS	88D	88D	88D	-	-	07/62
5662	BRY	88D	88D	88D	88D	-	11/64
5663	THT	88F	88A	88F	-	-	08/62
5664	BRY	88C	88C	88C	-	-	08/62
5665	BRY	88C	88C	88F	88F	-	06/65
5666	CH	88D	88D	88D	-	-	07/63
5667	BRY	88C	88C	88C	87A	-	07/65
5668	FDL	88F	88F	88F	88C	-	09/64
5669	AYN	88A	88A	88A	88F	-	09/64
5670	OXY	88A	88A	88D	87B	-	10/64
5671	CH	88D	88D	88D	88D	-	01/64
5672	CHYS	88D	88D	88D	88D	-	09/63
5673	SALOP	87H	87E	87E	87A	-	03/65
5674	CH	88D	88D	88D	88F	-	04/63
5675	LLY	87F	82B	81D	87D	-	12/64

No.	1948	1952	1955	1959	1963	1965	w/dwn	No.	1948	1952	1955	1959	1963	1965	w/dwn
5676	THT	88F	88F	88F	88F	-	11/65	5688	THT	88F	88F	87B	88F	-	06/65
5677	MTHR	88D	88A	88D	88D	-	11/65	5689	WES	82D	82D	82D	88C	-	05/65
5678	MTHR	88A	88A	88F	88F	-	01/64	5690	CHR	84K	84G	84G	88H	-	08/63
5679	CDF	86C	86C	86C	89B	-	07/63	5691	THT	88F	88F	88F	88E	-	06/65
5680	THT	88E	88E	88E	88J	-	12/63	5692	RHY	88A	88A	88F	87F	-	07/65
5681	CHYS	88A	88D	88D	88D	-	05/65	5693	BRY	88F	88F	88F	-	-	01/63
5682	AYN	88E	88E	88E	-	-	05/62	5694	CH	88D	88D	88F	88F	-	11/64
5683	RHY	88A	88A	88A	88B	-	03/64	5695	THT	88F	88F	88F	-	-	12/62
5684	OXY	84B	84B	88F	88F	-	07/65	5696	RHY	88D	88D	88D	88D	-	05/65
5685	CDF	86C	86C	86C	88E	-	02/64	5697	GLO	88A	81E	81E	88B	-	04/63
5686	AYN	88E	88E	88E	88E	-	03/65	5698	CH	88D	86J	86J	-	-	09/62
5687	CHYS	88A	88A	88F	88D	-	12/63	5699	BRY	88E	88E	88E	88E	-	11/64

Continued with Number 6600

57xx

0-6-0PT

Continued from Number 4699.

No.	1948	1952	1955	1959	1963	1965	w/dwn	No.	1948	1952	1955	1959	1963	1965	w/dwn
5700	TYS	89A	89A	-	-	-	03/56	5741	NPT	86A	86J	-	-	-	06/57
5701	TYS	84A	82D	-	-	-	01/58	5742	TYS	84J	84J	-	-	-	09/58
5702	LLY	87F	87F	87F	-	-	05/60	5743	SED	87D	87D	87C	-	-	01/59
5703	NEA	87C	87C	87F	-	-	02/59	5744	DID	81E	81E	81E	-	-	04/62
5704	SED	87D	87D	87C	-	-	05/60	5745	TYS	84E	84H	84E	-	-	11/59
5705	LLY	87F	87F	87F	-	-	08/59	5746	NEA	87A	87A	81E	-	-	09/62
5706	STJ	86B	86B	86B	-	-	09/61	5747	PILL	86B	86B	86B	-	-	09/59
5707	TDU	86F	86F	86F	-	-	03/59	5748	OXY	84B	87H	87H	-	-	09/60
5708	LTS	86D	86D	86D	-	-	04/59	5749	CDF	86C	86C	86C	88L	-	07/63
5709	NPT	86A	86A	86A	-	-	03/60	5750	SHL	86H	86H	86G	-	-	05/60
5710	DID	88B	88B	-	-	-	08/57	5751	RDG	88C	83B	-	-	-	04/58
5711	MTHR	88D	88D	-	-	-	01/58	5752	DID	81E	81E	-	-	-	03/57
5712	TYS	84E	84H	-	-	-	10/57	5753	SHL	81C	81C	81C	-	-	09/59
5713	DYD	87B	87B	87J	-	-	01/60	5754	STB	84F	84F	84F	-	-	06/60
5714	STJ	86B	86B	-	-	-	01/58	5755	SHL	81C	81C	81B	-	-	07/60
5715	SLO	81B	81B	-	-	-	08/58	5756	TDU	86G	86G	86G	-	-	09/61
5716	FGD	87J	87J	-	-	-	03/58	5757	WES	82D	82D	82D	-	-	12/60
5717	PDN	81A	81A	81A	-	-	05/60	5758	WLN	84H	84H	86B	-	-	05/62
5718	WES	82D	82D	-	-	-	07/58	5759	LDR	87E	87E	86G	-	-	09/60
5719	STB	84F	84F	-	-	-	11/58	5760	EXE	83C	83B	-	-	-	10/57
5720	NEA	87A	87A	87A	-	-	01/62	5761	RDG	87K	87K	87K	-	-	05/62
5721	MTHR	88D	83B	83B	-	-	08/59	5762	RDG	81D	81D	-	-	-	03/56
5722	LLY	87F	87F	-	-	-	09/58	5763	RDG	81D	81D	81D	-	-	05/60
5723	CHR	84K	84K	-	-	-	11/57	5764	PDN	81A	81A	81A	-	-	05/60
5724	BAN	84C	84C	-	-	-	08/57	5765	HFD	85C	85C	85C	-	-	03/59
5725	CHR	84K	84K	-	-	-	08/58	5766	RDG	81D	81D	81B	-	-	05/62
5726	STB	84F	89A	89A	-	-	10/59	5767	YEO	82E	82D	-	-	-	09/58
5727	SHL	81C	81C	86C	-	-	05/60	5768	PPRD	86G	86G	86B	-	-	03/61
5728	PPRD	86G	86G	87K	-	-	05/62	5769	MTHR	88D	88D	82B	-	-	05/60
5729	STJ	86E	86E	-	-	-	10/57	5770	ABDR	86J	87B	87B	-	-	12/61
5730	DG	87C	87C	-	-	-	03/58	5771	WES	82D	82D	82D	-	-	03/61
5731	DYD	87B	87D	87C	-	-	05/60	5772	RDG	81D	81D	-	-	-	06/58
5732	NPT	86A	86A	-	-	-	01/58	5773	DYD	87K	87K	87K	-	-	09/62
5733	ABEEG	86H	86B	-	-	-	08/58	5774	SALOP	84J	84J	84J	-	-	10/62
5734	DYD	87B	87B	86B	-	-	05/59	5775	DG	87C	87G	86G	86G	-	08/63
5735	DYD	81E	81E	-	-	-	11/57	5776	PILL	86C	86C	86C	-	-	05/60
5736	BAN	84E	84E	-	-	-	01/58	5777	LTS	86H	86B	-	-	-	06/58
5737	SLO	81D	81E	81E	-	-	10/59	5778	NEA	87A	87A	87A	-	-	07/62
5738	TYS	84E	84E	87B	-	-	09/59	5779	TR	83B	83B	83B	-	-	05/62
5739	SRD	84A	84K	-	-	-	08/58	5780	OXY	84A	84A	83B	-	-	10/61
5740	PILL	86B	86B	86B	-	-	06/59	5781	WES	82D	82F	-	-	-	09/58

No.	1948	1952	1955	1959	1963	1965	w/dwn	No.	1948	1952	1955	1959	1963	1965	w/dwn
5782	LLY	87F	87F	-	-	-	11/58	5791	CHR	84K	84K	84G	-	-	04/61
5783	SLO	81B	81E	81E	-	-	03/62	5792	PPRD	86G	86G	-	-	-	10/56
5784	SPM	82B	82C	71G	-	-	06/59	5793	GLO	88D	88A	87K	-	-	04/62
5785	WES	82D	82H	86H	-	-	12/58	5794	STB	84F	86C	86H	-	-	12/59
5786	ABEEG	86C	86C	-	-	-	04/58	5795	STB	84F	84F	84F	-	-	04/60
5787	ABDR	86J	87B	87B	87B	-	10/63	5796	ABDR	86J	86A	81E	-	-	03/59
5788	ABEEG	86D	86D	86D	-	-	10/59	5797	TDU	86F	86J	-	-	-	09/58
5789	ABEEG	86H	87B	86G	-	-	05/62	5798	NA	83B	83B	83B	-	-	09/62
5790	TYS	84E	84E	86K	-	-	03/59	5799	SHL	81C	81C	81C	-	-	07/59

Continued with Number 6700

58xx   Collett   0-4-2T

Introduced in 1932 by Collett. Non motor fitted version of '14xx' Class.

Loco Weight : 41t 6c *Driving Wheels :* 5' 2" *Cylinders :* (I) 16" x 24" *Valve Gear :* Stephenson (Slide Valves)

No.	1948	1952	1955	1959	1963	1965	w/dwn	No.	1948	1952	1955	1959	1963	1965	w/dwn
5800	SDN	82C	82C	-	-	-	07/58	5810	CNYD	84J	84J	84J	-	-	01/59
5801	BCN	89B	89B	-	-	-	09/58	5811	CNYD	84J	84J	-	-	-	05/57
5802	SDN	82C	82C	82C	-	-	12/58	5812	TN	89A	89A	-	-	-	06/57
5803	BRD	89A	81F	-	-	-	07/57	5813	BRD	82A	82A	-	-	-	11/57
5804	SDN	82C	82C	82C	-	-	06/59	5814	HFD	85C	85C	-	-	-	06/57
5805	SDN	82C	82C	-	-	-	03/58	5815	WOS	85A	85A	82C	-	-	04/61
5806	OSW	89A	89A	-	-	-	06/57	5816	WOS	85A	85A	-	-	-	07/57
5807	HFD	85C	85C	-	-	-	06/57	5817	HFD	85C	85C	-	-	-	06/57
5808	HFD	85C	81F	-	-	-	02/57	5818	PPRD	86G	85C	81F	-	-	09/59
5809	BRD	82A	82A	89C	-	-	08/59	5819	CARM	87G	87G	-	-	-	06/57

TOTAL 20

49xx   'Hall'   4-6-0

Continued from Number 4999.

Number & Name	1948	1952	1955	1959	1963	1965	w/dwn	Notes
5900 Hinderton Hall	WES	82D	84E	84A	82B	-	12/63	
5901 Hazel Hall	RDG	81D	81D	81D	81D	-	06/64	
5902 Howick Hall	EXE	86E	87F	87F	-	-	12/62	
5903 Keele Hall	DID	81E	87H	87H	87F	-	09/63	
5904 Kelham Hall	OXF	82A	82A	82B	82B	-	11/63	
5905 Knowsley Hall	FGD	87J	87J	87J	87J	-	07/63	
5906 Lawton Hall	NPT	81A	81D	81D	-	-	05/62	
5907 Marble Hall	TYS	84E	85B	85B	-	-	11/61	
5908 Moreton Hall	LLY	87J	87J	87J	82B	-	07/63	
5909 Newton Hall	SRD	84E	83D	87E	-	-	07/62	
5910 Park Hall	CDF	86C	86C	82A	-	-	09/62	
5911 Preston Hall	NPT	86C	86C	86C	-	-	09/62	
5912 Queens Hall	CHR	84E	84E	84E	-	-	12/62	
5913 Rushton Hall	LDR	86C	87F	87E	-	-	05/62	
5914 Ripon Hall	WOS	85B	85A	85B	81D	-	01/64	
5915 Trentham Hall	PZ	83G	83G	81D	-	-	01/60	
5916 Trinity Hall	OXY	84E	86G	84B	-	-	07/62	
5917 Westminster Hall	WOS	85A	85A	85A	-	-	09/62	
5918 Walton Hall	OXY	81C	81C	81C	-	-	09/62	
5919 Worsley Hall	SRD	82A	82A	82A	81A	-	08/63	
5920 Wycliffe Hall	OXY	83A	83A	83A	-	-	01/62	
5921 Bingley Hall	OXY	86B	86A	84C	-	-	01/62	
5922 Caxton Hall	PDN	82C	82C	82C	81F	-	01/64	
5923 Colston Hall	CHR	86E	86C	81A	81F	-	12/63	
5924 Dinton Hall	WES	82B	82B	82B	82B	-	12/63	
5925 Eastcote Hall	WES	86C	86C	81C	-	-	10/62	

Number & Name	1948	1952	1955	1959	1963	1965	w/dwn	Notes
5926 Grotrian Hall	SBZ	83D	83E	84A	-	-	09/62	
5927 Guild Hall	SRD	84E	84E	84E	84F	-	10/64	
5928 Haddon Hall	FGD	87J	87J	87J	-	-	05/62	
5929 Hanham Hall	NEY	87E	87E	81A	81C	-	10/63	
5930 Hannington Hall	BAN	84C	84C	84C	-	-	09/62	
5931 Hatherley Hall	PDN	81A	81A	81A	-	-	09/62	
5932 Haydon Hall	PDN	81A	81A	81A	81C	-	10/65	
5933 Kingsway Hall	RDG	81D	81D	81C	81F	-	08/65	
5934 Knellor Hall	SDN	82C	83D	83G	82B	-	05/64	
5935 Norton Hall	DID	81E	81E	82B	-	-	05/62	
5936 Oakley Hall	PDN	81A	81A	81A	81D	-	01/65	
5937 Stanford Hall	PDN	81A	87G	87G	88L	-	11/63	
5938 Stanley Hall	PDN	81A	87G	87G	86A	-	05/63	
5939 Tangley Hall	PDN	81A	81A	81A	86A	-	10/64	
5940 Whitbourne Hall	PDN	81A	81A	81A	-	-	09/62	
5941 Campion Hall	PDN	81A	81A	81A	-	-	07/62	
5942 Doldowlod Hall	SRD	81D	81D	81D	89A	-	12/63	
5943 Elmdon Hall	SDN	85A	85A	81E	82C	-	06/63	
5944 Ickenham Hall	SRD	84B	84B	84B	85B	-	04/63	
5945 Leckhampton Hall	OXY	84B	84B	82D	81F	-	04/63	
5946 Marwell Hall	CDF	86C	86C	86C	-	-	07/62	
5947 Saint Benet's Hall	OXY	81A	84C	84C	-	-	07/62	
5948 Siddington Hall	RDG	86G	86G	86G	86G	-	08/63	
5949 Trematon Hall	BRD	82B	82B	82A	-	-	05/61	
5950 Wardley Hall	TYS	84E	84C	82A	-	-	11/61	
5951 Cliffe Hall	GLO	85A	85B	85B	85B	-	04/64	
5952 Cogan Hall	PDN	81C	83G	85A	86C	-	06/64	
5953 Dunley Hall	CDF	86C	81C	87F	-	-	10/62	
5954 Faendre Hall	BAN	84C	84C	81A	82B	-	10/63	
5955 Garth Hall	BRD	87E	87E	87E	81F	-	04/65	Renumbered from 3950, 10/48
5956 Horsley Hall	RDG	81D	81D	85A	81F	-	03/63	
5957 Hutton Hall	OXY	81D	81D	81D	81F	-	07/64	
5958 Knolton Hall	CDF	86C	87E	81A	82B	-	03/64	
5959 Mawley Hall	RDG	81D	83G	83C	-	-	09/62	
5960 Saint Edmund Hall	OXF	81F	81F	81F	-	-	09/62	
5961 Toynbee Hall	WES	82D	87F	87F	87A	-	08/65	
5962 Wantage Hall	PDN	81A	84K	86C	88L	-	11/64	
5963 Wimpole Hall	CARM	87G	87G	82D	82B	-	06/64	
5964 Wolseley Hall	SPM	83D	83D	82C	-	-	09/62	
5965 Woollas Hall	GLO	81F	81F	81F	-	-	07/62	
5966 Ashford Hall	CHR	84D	84B	81F	-	-	09/62	
5967 Bickmarsh Hall	BAN	84C	84C	83A	81A	-	06/64	
5968 Cory Hall	WEY	84K	84K	84G	-	-	09/62	
5969 Honington Hall	WEY	83G	83G	82B	-	-	08/62	
5970 Hengrave Hall	CDF	86C	86C	86C	86C	-	11/65	
5971 Merevale Hall	WES	85A	85A	85A	81C	82E	12/65	
5972 Olton Hall	CARM	84E	83F	83G	81A	-	12/63	
5973 Rolleston Hall	RDG	81D	81D	81D	-	-	09/62	
5974 Wallsworth Hall	WES	82D	82D	82D	82D	-	12/64	
5975 Winslow Hall	PPRD	82D	82C	82D	82B	-	07/64	
5976 Ashwick Hall	SPM	83C	83C	83C	87F	-	07/64	Renumbered from 3951, 11/48
5977 Beckford Hall	CDF	86C	86C	81A	81D	-	08/63	
5978 Bodinnick Hall	SDN	82F	82F	82C	82B	-	10/63	
5979 Cruckton Hall	OXY	81D	81D	81D	81D	-	11/64	
5980 Dingley Hall	GLO	85B	85B	85B	-	-	09/62	
5981 Frensham Hall	SALOP	84G	84G	82C	-	-	09/62	
5982 Harrington Hall	TN	82B	82B	82D	-	-	09/62	
5983 Henley Hall	WOS	81C	81C	82C	84E	-	04/65	
5984 Linden Hall	SPM	87G	87G	85A	81A	-	01/65	
5985 Mostyn Hall	WES	82D	83F	84B	81C	-	09/63	

Number & Name	1948	1952	1955	1959	1963	1965	w/dwn	Notes
5986 Arbury Hall	PDN	81A	84G	82C	82D	–	09/63	Renumbered from 3954, 02/50
5987 Brocket Hall	PDN	81A	81A	81A	81E	–	01/64	
5988 Bostock Hall	GLO	85A	87E	87E	81A	–	10/65	
5989 Cransley Hall	OXY	81C	81C	84C	–	–	07/62	
5990 Dorford Hall	GLO	85B	85B	87E	84C	–	01/65	
5991 Gresham Hall	BAN	84B	84B	84B	89A	–	07/64	
5992 Horton Hall	BAN	82B	83B	83B	83B	–	08/65	
5993 Kirby Hall	TYS	81D	81D	81D	81D	–	05/63	
5994 Roydon Hall	SALOP	84K	82C	85A	89A	–	03/63	
5995 Wick Hall	SRD	84A	84B	84B	84B	–	04/63	
5996 Mytton Hall	PDN	81A	81A	81C	–	–	08/62	
5997 Sparkford Hall	TYS	83D	82F	82C	–	–	07/62	
5998 Trevor Hall	LA	83D	83D	85C	86C	–	03/64	
5999 Wollaton Hall	TN	83B	83B	83B	–	–	09/62	

Continued with Number 6900

60xx   'King'   4-6-0

The largest of the G.W.R. four cylinder 4-6-0s, the 'King' Class were introduced by Collett in 1927, but because of their weight were restricted to the London to Plymouth & London to Wolverhampton main lines. They carried a special 'Double Red Circle' route restriction on their cab sides.

6029 'King Stephen' was renamed 'King Edward VIII' in May 1936, and 6028 'King Henry II' was renamed 'King George VI', during January 1937, after the former king abdicated and his younger brother came to the throne late in 1936.

Very powerful and successful locomotives, they were fitted with four row superheaters from 1947 onwards, and double chimneys (DC) from 1955.

Loco Weight : 89t 0c   *Driving Wheels :* 6' 6"   *Cylinders :* (4) 16¼" x 28"   *Valve Gear :* Walschaerts (piston valves)

Number & Name	1948	1952	1955	1959	1963	1965	w/dwn	Notes
6000 King George V	LA	82A	81A	81A	–	–	12/62	DC 12/56
6001 King Edward VII	PDN	81A	84A	84A	–	–	09/62	DC 02/56
6002 King William IV	LA	81A	81A	81A	–	–	09/62	DC 03/56
6003 King George IV	PDN	81A	81A	81A	–	–	06/62	DC 04/57
6004 King George III	LA	84A	83D	83D	–	–	06/62	DC 11/56
6005 King George II	SRD	84A	84A	84A	–	–	11/62	DC 07/56
6006 King George I	SRD	84A	84A	84A	–	–	02/62	DC 06/56
6007 King William III	PDN	81A	81A	81A	–	–	09/62	DC 09/56
6008 King James II	SRD	83D	83D	83D	–	–	06/62	DC 07/57
6009 King Charles II	PDN	81A	81A	81A	–	–	09/62	DC 05/56
6010 King Charles I	LA	83D	83D	83D	–	–	06/62	DC 03/56
6011 King James I	SRD	84A	84A	84A	–	–	12/62	DC 03/56
6012 King Edward VI	LA	83D	81A	81A	–	–	09/62	DC 02/58
6013 King Henry VIII	PDN	81A	81A	81A	–	–	06/62	DC 06/56
6014 King Henry VII	PDN	81A	84A	84A	–	–	09/62	DC 09/57
6015 King Richard III	PDN	81A	81A	81A	–	–	09/62	DC 09/55
6016 King Edward V	LA	84A	81A	81A	–	–	09/62	DC 01/58
6017 King Edward IV	LA	83D	83D	83D	–	–	07/62	DC 12/55
6018 King Henry VI	NA	81A	81A	81A	–	–	12/62	DC 03/58
6019 King Henry V	LA	81A	81A	81A	–	–	09/62	DC 04/57
6020 King Henry IV	LA	84A	84A	84A	–	–	07/62	DC 08/56
6021 King Richard II	PDN	81A	81A	83D	–	–	09/62	DC 03/57
6022 King Edward III	LA	83D	83D	81A	–	–	09/62	DC 05/56
6023 King Edward II	NA	83D	83D	81A	–	–	06/62	DC 06/57
6024 King Edward I	NA	83D	81A	81A	–	–	06/62	DC 03/57
6025 King Henry III	PDN	83D	83D	83D	–	–	12/62	DC 03/57
6026 King John	LA	83D	83D	83D	–	–	09/62	DC 03/58
6027 King Richard I	NA	83D	83D	83D	–	–	09/62	DC 08/56
6028 King George VI	NA	81A	81A	81A	–	–	11/62	DC 01/57
6029 King Edward VIII	LA	83D	83D	83D	–	–	07/62	DC 12/57

    TOTAL 30

Introduced 1931 by Collett for London suburban services.

Loco Weight : 78t 9c *Driving Wheels :* 5' 8" *Cylinders :* (O) 18" x 30" *Valve Gear :* Stephenson (Piston Valves)

No.	1948	1952	1955	1959	1963	1965	w/dwn	No.	1948	1952	1955	1959	1963	1965	w/dwn
6100	SLO	81D	81D	-	-	-	09/58	6135	PDN	81A	81A	81A	81A	81F	12/65
6101	SLO	81D	81D	81D	-	-	03/62	6136	RDG	81B	81B	81B	81E	81F	12/65
6102	SHL	82A	86A	81D	-	-	08/59	6137	PDN	81A	81A	85B	85B	-	11/64
6103	OXF	81D	81D	81D	81D	-	12/64	6138	OXF	81F	81F	81F	81D	-	09/63
6104	SLO	81D	81D	81D	-	-	06/60	6139	SHL	81C	84E	84E	81E	-	11/64
6105	SLO	81D	84E	87H	-	-	03/60	6140	RDG	81B	81B	81D	86E	-	07/64
6106	SLO	81B	81F	81F	81D	81F	12/65	6141	PDN	81A	81A	81A	81A	82F	12/65
6107	SLO	82A	82A	82A	81D	-	11/64	6142	PDN	81A	81A	81A	81A	-	09/64
6108	SLO	81B	81B	81B	81C	-	08/65	6143	SLO	81B	81B	81B	81B	-	11/65
6109	RDG	82A	81A	81B	-	-	08/62	6144	PDN	81A	81A	81A	81F	-	09/64
6110	SHL	81C	81A	81A	81C	-	06/65	6145	SLO	81D	81D	81A	81E	81F	12/65
6111	SLO	81F	81F	81F	81F	81F	12/65	6146	SLO	81B	81B	81B	-	-	09/62
6112	PDN	81F	81F	81F	81E	-	09/65	6147	SHL	81C	81C	81C	82E	85A	12/65
6113	SLO	81B	81F	81A	83B	-	11/65	6148	SHL	81C	81C	81C	82B	-	09/64
6114	SLO	82A	86A	81D	86E	-	10/64	6149	PDN	81A	81A	81A	81F	-	06/64
6115	RDG	81B	81B	81B	86G	-	11/64	6150	SLO	81B	81B	81B	81F	-	03/65
6116	SLO	81E	84E	84E	87J	-	06/65	6151	SLO	81B	81B	81B	87G	-	11/63
6117	RDG	81D	81D	81B	81B	-	09/65	6152	SLO	81B	81B	81B	-	-	01/62
6118	SHL	81E	84E	86E	87H	-	11/63	6153	SLO	81B	81B	81D	-	-	01/62
6119	SLO	81B	81B	86E	81D	-	03/63	6154	RDG	81B	81B	81B	81F	-	06/65
6120	PDN	81A	81A	81A	-	-	04/62	6155	PDN	81A	81A	86E	85A	-	10/65
6121	RDG	81A	81A	81A	-	-	07/60	6156	SHL	81C	81C	81C	81F	81F	12/65
6122	OXF	81F	81F	81B	81C	-	09/64	6157	SLO	81B	81B	81C	-	-	05/62
6123	SLO	81B	81B	81B	-	-	04/62	6158	PDN	81A	81A	81A	86E	-	06/64
6124	SLO	81B	81B	81B	81F	-	06/64	6159	PDN	81A	81A	81A	81E	-	06/65
6125	SHL	81C	81C	81C	81A	-	01/65	6160	SLO	81B	81B	84E	81B	85B	12/65
6126	SLO	81C	81D	81B	81E	81F	12/65	6161	SLO	81D	81D	81D	81D	-	10/65
6127	SLO	81B	81B	81B	-	-	03/62	6162	RDG	81D	81D	81D	-	-	03/62
6128	SHL	81C	81C	81C	81B	-	03/65	6163	RDG	81D	81D	81F	81A	-	10/65
6129	PDN	81D	81D	81D	84C	-	09/65	6164	SLO	81B	81B	81B	81D	-	11/63
6130	RDG	81D	81D	81D	81E	-	07/64	6165	SHL	81C	81C	81C	81C	85A	12/65
6131	RDG	81B	81B	81D	81D	-	09/64	6166	PDN	81E	84E	86E	-	-	01/62
6132	PDN	81B	81B	81A	81C	-	10/65	6167	SLO	81E	81B	81B	81B	-	10/65
6133	SLO	81B	81B	81B	81C	-	12/63	6168	PDN	81A	81A	81A	-	-	03/62
6134	PDN	81E	84E	81D	81D	81F	12/65	6169	SHL	81C	81C	81C	81A	-	11/65

TOTAL 70

43xx   **2-6-0**

Continued from Number 5399.

No.	1948	1952	1955	1959	1963	1965	w/dwn	No.	1948	1952	1955	1959	1963	1965	w/dwn
6300	OXF	81C	83E	83F	-	-	06/60	6314	WES	82D	85C	85D	84G	-	07/63
6301	EXE	83C	83C	83D	-	-	10/62	6316	CNYD	84J	84J	84J	-	-	07/62
6302	RDG	81D	81D	81D	-	-	03/62	6317	TN	83B	84G	84F	84C	-	11/63
6303	CNYD	84J	84J	84G	-	-	04/59	6318	PZ	83G	86A	86G	-	-	01/59
6304	LDR	87G	81E	82B	85B	-	01/64	6319	LA	83D	83D	83D	82D	-	08/63
6305	TN	83B	83E	87G	-	-	09/59	6320	SDN	82C	82C	82D	86E	-	11/63
6306	WOS	85A	82B	87H	-	-	11/61	6321	SRD	84A	84E	-	-	-	03/56
6307	SALOP	84G	84E	82C	-	-	07/60	6322	SDN	82A	83C	83A	-	-	01/59
6308	CHR	84K	85C	86C	-	-	08/59	6323	TN	83B	83B	83B	-	-	07/60
6309	GLO	85B	82C	82C	81E	-	09/64	6324	WOS	85A	84B	81D	-	-	04/62
6310	CARM	87G	87G	87F	-	-	07/62	6325	SHL	87E	87F	86E	-	-	11/59
6311	CHR	84J	84J	84B	-	-	01/60	6326	CHEL	85C	85C	86C	88L	-	09/64
6312	RDG	81D	81D	82B	-	-	09/62	6327	CNYD	84F	84E	82B	83B	-	09/63
6313	RDG	81F	81E	81D	-	-	11/61	6328	TN	83B	83B	87F	-	-	01/59

'King' Class 4-6-0 No. 6004 'King George III' at Shrewsbury. The double chimneys fitted to these locos transformed both the steaming, and the appearance, of the Great Western's most powerful and prestigious locomotives.

photo courtesy Steve Davies

64xx 0-6-0PT No. 6419. Designed by Collett for passenger trains, they were motor fitted for working with push pull trailers.

photo courtesy Steve Davies

No.	1948	1952	1955	1959	1963	1965	w/dwn	No.	1948	1952	1955	1959	1963	1965	w/dwn
6329	DID	81E	87G	87G	-	-	10/61	6365	WES	82D	85B	85B	85B	-	10/63
6330	SBZ	83A	85B	85B	-	-	09/62	6366	RDG	81D	81D	82C	-	-	09/62
6331	CARM	87G	84K	84C	-	-	04/59	6367	CARM	87G	84K	85A	84C	-	11/64
6332	OXY	84F	84F	84F	-	-	09/60	6368	WES	82D	85B	86G	89C	-	12/63
6333	PPRD	86C	86C	86C	-	-	10/60	6369	WES	82D	86E	86E	-	-	01/63
6334	RDG	85A	85A	82C	-	-	04/59	6370	PPRD	86C	86A	86A	-	-	01/63
6335	OXY	84B	84B	89C	86G	-	07/63	6371	NEY	89C	89C	89C	-	-	09/60
6336	TYS	84E	81F	82C	-	-	04/62	6372	TN	83B	83B	83B	83B	-	12/63
6337	CHR	84K	84K	83B	81D	-	07/64	6373	TR	83D	85B	85B	86E	-	12/63
6338	SALOP	81D	84J	86F	86F	-	06/64	6374	SDN	82A	82B	82B	-	-	08/62
6339	CHR	84K	84J	84J	-	-	07/62	6375	WES	82F	86E	83B	89A	-	09/63
6340	SDN	81E	81E	84F	-	-	07/62	6376	BHD	6C	6C	6E	-	-	05/62
6341	CHEL	85B	85B	82B	-	-	11/61	6377	TN	83B	83B	87G	-	-	10/60
6342	OXY	84C	84E	89A	-	-	09/62	6378	WOS	85A	85A	89C	89C	-	06/64
6343	TN	83B	83B	83B	-	-	09/60	6379	DID	81D	81F	81E	81D	-	08/63
6344	CARM	87G	84K	71G	85B	-	11/63	6380	CHR	84K	84K	6E	89A	-	12/63
6345	NA	82B	84K	6E	88L	-	09/64	6381	GLO	85B	85B	85B	85B	-	11/63
6346	BHD	6C	6C	6C	83C	-	09/64	6382	WOS	85D	85A	85D	-	-	11/60
6347	NEY	87H	87H	87J	87F	-	12/63	6383	RDG	81D	89C	-	-	-	05/56
6348	SALOP	84G	85A	86A	-	-	02/62	6384	SDN	82C	82C	86E	86E	-	06/63
6349	HFD	85C	85B	84F	87F	-	07/64	6385	WOS	85B	83C	83C	81D	-	11/63
6350	BHD	6C	6C	6C	81E	-	01/64	6386	STJ	86A	86E	86E	-	-	09/62
6351	WES	82A	82B	82B	-	-	11/60	6387	SDN	82C	82C	84C	-	-	06/62
6352	HFD	85C	86C	86C	-	-	11/60	6388	SHL	81C	85A	81E	-	-	09/62
6353	CDF	86C	86C	85B	82D	-	05/63	6389	NEY	87H	85A	87H	-	-	09/60
6354	PZ	84F	85A	82C	-	-	02/59	6390	BAN	84C	83B	83B	-	-	05/62
6355	NEY	87D	84B	87H	-	-	03/59	6391	SRD	84F	84F	82B	-	-	09/62
6356	SBZ	83A	83A	82B	-	-	01/63	6392	CHR	84K	84K	89C	-	-	10/61
6357	SDN	82C	85A	84E	87F	-	07/64	6393	RDG	81D	86G	87G	-	-	01/60
6358	SDN	82C	82D	82D	-	-	10/59	6394	TN	83B	84E	85B	85B	-	06/64
6359	DID	81E	85A	85C	-	-	09/59	6395	HFD	85C	85C	84G	87F	-	11/64
6360	SDN	82C	82C	82B	-	-	11/60	6396	WOS	85A	85A	-	-	-	03/58
6361	OXY	84B	86G	86J	88J	-	05/64	6397	EXE	83C	83E	83E	-	-	09/59
6362	OXY	84K	84J	86E	-	-	09/62	6398	TN	83B	83B	83B	-	-	10/60
6363	RDG	84B	82B	82B	81E	-	09/64	6399	WES	82D	82D	82D	-	-	11/59
6364	TN	83B	83B	83B	84G	-	11/64								

Continued with Number 7300

64xx   Collett   0-6-0PT

Introduced 1932 by Collett, this class was fitted with push - pull equipment for branch passenger work.

Loco Weight : 45t 12c   *Driving Wheels :* 4' 7½"   *Cylinders :* (I) 16½" x 24"   *Valve Gear :* Stephenson (Slide Valves)

No.	1948	1952	1955	1959	1963	1965	w/dwn	No.	1948	1952	1955	1959	1963	1965	w/dwn
6400	PPRD	86G	86G	86G	88H	-	04/64	6414	LA	83D	83D	83D	-	-	06/59
6401	AYN	88E	88E	86A	-	-	06/60	6415	NPT	86A	86A	85B	-	-	11/61
6402	CHYS	88A	88A	83D	-	-	06/59	6416	CHYS	88A	88A	88D	88D	-	09/63
6403	PPRD	86G	86G	84F	84F	-	12/63	6417	LA	83D	86J	86A	-	-	06/59
6404	BHD	84J	84A	84J	-	-	06/59	6418	SRD	84A	84A	84A	-	-	11/62
6405	BHD	84J	84J	84J	-	-	06/59	6419	LA	83D	83D	83D	88H	-	12/64
6406	LA	83D	83D	83D	-	-	06/60	6420	SBZ	83D	83D	83D	-	-	11/59
6407	SHL	83D	83D	-	-	-	08/58	6421	LA	83D	83D	83D	-	-	01/63
6408	MTHR	88D	88D	82D	-	-	02/62	6422	SRD	84J	84A	84A	-	-	09/62
6409	NPT	86B	86A	86A	-	-	03/59	6423	CHYS	88A	88A	-	-	-	08/58
6410	ABDR	86J	86J	86J	-	-	11/62	6424	PPRD	86G	86G	86G	84F	-	09/64
6411	AYN	88E	88E	88A	-	-	03/61	6425	LDR	87E	87E	86A	-	-	01/61
6412	LDR	87E	87E	86A	86A	-	11/64	6426	NPT	86A	86A	86A	-	-	03/61
6413	ABDR	86J	86J	86J	-	-	11/61	6427	MTHR	88D	88D	-	-	-	08/58

No.	1948	1952	1955	1959	1963	1965	w/dwn	No.	1948	1952	1955	1959	1963	1965	w/dwn
6428	NPT	86A	86A	84F	-	-	03/59	6434	MTHR	88D	88D	88A	86A	-	09/64
6429	PPRD	86G	86G	86G	-	-	03/62	6435	CHYS	88A	88D	88E	88H	-	10/64
6430	PPRD	86G	86A	86A	88H	-	10/64	6436	CHYS	88A	88D	88D	-	-	09/62
6431	LDR	87E	87E	86J	-	-	01/63	6437	ABDR	86J	86J	86J	85B	-	07/63
6432	PPRD	86G	86G	86G	-	-	03/59	6438	AYN	88E	88E	88E	-	-	11/62
6433	CHYS	88A	88D	88D	-	-	01/63	6439	NPT	86A	86A	86K	-	-	05/60

TOTAL 40

56xx
0-6-2T

Continued from Number 4179.

No.	1948	1952	1955	1959	1963	1965	w/dwn	No.	1948	1952	1955	1959	1963	1965	w/dwn
6600	OXY	86C	86C	86C	-	-	08/62	6647	BRY	88A	88A	88A	-	-	09/62
6601	SPM	82B	82B	82B	-	-	12/62	6648	CHYS	88F	88F	88A	88B	-	05/65
6602	BRY	86C	86C	87B	87D	-	10/64	6649	NPT	86F	86J	87E	87A	-	02/65
6603	RYR	88A	88A	88A	88B	-	03/64	6650	LMTN	87B	87B	87A	88C	-	05/65
6604	LDR	87E	87E	85A	89B	-	10/65	6651	PPRD	86J	86J	86J	86G	-	10/65
6605	ABDR	86J	86J	86J	88J	-	01/64	6652	ABDR	86J	86J	86J	87F	-	12/63
6606	SALOP	84G	84G	88A	88B	-	01/65	6653	BRY	86G	86G	86H	87F	-	12/63
6607	RYR	88A	88A	88A	88B	-	03/63	6654	NPT	86C	81C	81D	88F	-	06/65
6608	RYR	88A	88A	88A	88B	-	06/64	6655	CHYS	88F	81C	81D	88L	-	03/65
6609	OXY	84F	84F	84F	84E	-	09/63	6656	SPM	82B	82B	82B	88B	-	09/65
6610	OXY	84B	84B	84B	-	-	01/63	6657	LMTN	84D	84D	84D	88B	-	06/65
6611	TYS	84J	84J	84J	89B	-	11/65	6658	BRY	88C	88C	88C	88D	-	04/65
6612	NPT	88A	88A	88A	88B	-	05/65	6659	CHYS	88A	88A	88A	88B	-	10/63
6613	NEA	87D	87D	87A	88D	-	10/65	6660	CHYS	88A	88A	88A	88B	-	06/64
6614	BRY	88C	84E	88A	88B	-	06/65	6661	CHYS	88E	86J	86J	88J	-	06/65
6615	CHYS	88C	88C	88C	89B	-	05/63	6662	BRY	87D	87D	87D	87D	-	04/63
6616	DYD	87B	87B	87B	-	-	09/62	6663	NPT	86H	86H	86H	84D	-	06/63
6617	STB	84J	84J	84J	-	-	09/62	6664	RYR	88A	81B	81F	88J	-	12/63
6618	RYR	88A	88A	88A	84E	-	11/63	6665	STB	88A	88A	88A	88B	-	10/65
6619	BRY	88C	88C	88F	88C	-	03/63	6666	STJ	86E	86E	86E	86E	-	07/63
6620	BRY	88C	84E	87B	87B	-	12/63	6667	STB	84F	84F	84F	84F	-	11/65
6621	ABEEG	86C	86H	86H	88B	-	12/64	6668	BRY	88C	84E	84E	84E	6C	12/65
6622	CDF	86J	86J	86J	88J	-	12/64	6669	BRY	88C	84E	85B	-	-	12/62
6623	GLO	87B	87B	87B	87H	-	06/63	6670	SPM	82B	82B	82B	88G	-	10/63
6624	CHR	84G	84D	88A	88B	-	06/64	6671	SPM	82B	82B	82B	84D	-	10/65
6625	LMTN	84C	82D	82D	89B	-	11/65	6672	NPT	86A	86E	86E	86E	-	07/65
6626	CHYS	88A	88A	88A	88B	-	11/65	6673	STJ	86E	86E	86F	88J	-	03/63
6627	CHYS	88D	81D	81D	87H	-	11/63	6674	STB	84F	84F	84F	89B	-	07/63
6628	ABDR	86J	86J	86J	88J	-	05/65	6675	TDU	86G	86G	86G	86G	-	06/63
6629	DYD	87B	87B	86H	-	-	10/62	6676	STJ	86E	86F	86F	88H	-	04/63
6630	TYS	84E	81E	82B	-	-	09/62	6677	STB	84F	84F	84F	-	-	01/63
6631	HFD	85B	85B	84E	84B	-	09/63	6678	STB	84F	84F	84F	84F	-	11/64
6632	LMTN	84J	84J	84J	89B	-	09/63	6679	LDR	86F	86F	85D	84G	-	09/65
6633	SALOP	84G	84G	88A	86E	-	06/65	6680	LDR	87E	87E	87E	87D	-	04/64
6634	PPRD	86G	86G	86G	86G	-	04/64	6681	GLO	85C	84F	85A	88L	-	10/65
6635	CHYS	88A	88A	88A	88B	-	06/64	6682	OXF	88A	88A	88A	88B	-	02/65
6636	PPRD	86G	86G	86G	86G	-	06/63	6683	SALOP	84K	84F	84F	84F	-	10/65
6637	BRY	88C	88C	88C	88B	-	06/64	6684	STB	88A	88A	88A	88B	-	11/64
6638	OXY	84B	88A	88A	88B	-	06/64	6685	TDU	86G	86G	86G	86G	-	09/64
6639	STJ	86E	86E	82C	88G	-	10/63	6686	DYD	87B	87B	87B	87B	-	04/64
6640	OXY	84B	84B	84B	-	-	09/62	6687	PPRD	86G	86J	86J	-	-	05/62
6641	BRY	88C	88C	88C	-	-	09/62	6688	DYD	87F	87E	87E	86G	-	04/64
6642	TDU	86H	86A	86E	-	-	01/63	6689	STJ	86E	86E	88A	88B	-	06/65
6643	BRY	88C	88C	88C	88C	-	08/65	6690	WES	82D	85B	85B	88J	-	06/64
6644	LMTN	87K	87D	86H	84B	-	07/65	6691	CDF	87B	87B	87B	87B	-	06/65
6645	OXY	84B	84B	84B	-	-	08/62	6692	ABDR	86J	84F	84F	84F	-	09/65
6646	STB	84F	84F	84F	84F	-	05/64	6693	ABDR	86G	86G	86G	-	-	01/63

No.	1948	1952	1955	1959	1963	1965	w/dwn	No.	1948	1952	1955	1959	1963	1965	w/dwn
6694	CNYD	84J	84J	84J	89B	-	10/63	6697	LMTN	84D	84D	84D	88C	6C	05/66
6695	LDR	87E	87E	87E	87A	-	07/64	6698	CNYD	84J	84F	84F	89B	-	03/63
6696	BAN	84C	84J	84J	88C	-	12/63	6699	WES	82D	82D	88A	88B	-	12/63

TOTAL 200

57xx

0-6-0PT

Continued from Number 5799.   6700 - 6779 were not fitted with vacuum brakes.

No.	1948	1952	1955	1959	1963	1965	w/dwn	No.	1948	1952	1955	1959	1963	1965	w/dwn
6700	CED	88B	88B	87K	-	-	06/61	6740	BRY	88C	88C	-	-	-	01/58
6701	CED	88B	88B	87B	-	-	06/59	6741	SDN	82C	82C	82C	87D	-	12/63
6702	CED	88B	88B	87K	-	-	07/60	6742	PPRD	86B	86B	86B	87D	-	12/63
6703	CED	88B	88B	-	-	-	01/58	6743	PILL	86B	86B	86B	-	-	04/59
6704	CED	88B	88B	-	-	-	03/58	6744	CED	88B	88B	-	-	-	07/58
6705	CED	88B	88B	-	-	-	01/58	6745	BRY	88C	88C	86B	-	-	06/59
6706	CED	88B	88B	-	-	-	01/58	6746	BRY	88C	88C	-	-	-	08/58
6707	CED	88B	88B	86B	-	-	06/59	6747	BRY	88C	88C	-	-	-	07/58
6708	CED	88B	88B	-	-	-	12/57	6748	BRY	88C	88C	-	-	-	01/58
6709	CED	88B	88B	-	-	-	01/58	6749	DYD	87B	87B	87K	-	-	10/62
6710	PILL	86B	86B	-	-	-	08/57	6750	BRY	88C	88C	86B	-	-	01/60
6711	PILL	86B	86B	86B	-	-	06/59	6751	CED	88B	88B	86B	-	-	08/60
6712	BRY	88C	88C	87K	-	-	07/60	6752	BRY	88C	88C	88C	-	-	01/61
6713	DG	87C	87K	-	-	-	09/57	6753	BRY	88C	88C	88C	-	-	01/61
6714	SED	87D	87C	87K	87D	-	12/63	6754	BRY	88C	88C	88C	-	-	12/62
6715	DYD	87B	87B	-	-	-	05/58	6755	PILL	86B	86B	86B	-	-	06/62
6716	SDN	82C	82C	82C	-	-	02/59	6756	PILL	86B	86B	86B	-	-	07/60
6717	DYD	87B	87B	87K	-	-	02/59	6757	STJ	86B	86B	86B	-	-	12/62
6718	DYD	87B	87B	-	-	-	05/58	6758	BRY	88C	88C	86C	-	-	06/62
6719	DYD	87B	87B	87C	-	-	07/60	6759	PILL	86B	86B	86B	-	-	04/60
6720	DYD	87B	87K	87K	-	-	07/61	6760	11/48	86B	86B	86B	87D	-	12/63
6721	CED	88B	88B	87K	-	-	02/59	6761	11/48	87B	87B	87B	-	-	01/61
6722	BRY	88C	88C	-	-	-	01/58	6762	11/48	87C	87C	87C	87D	-	03/63
6723	BRY	88C	88C	87K	-	-	02/59	6763	11/48	87C	87C	87K	87D	-	12/63
6724	BRY	88C	88C	86B	87D	-	11/63	6764	11/48	86B	86B	86B	87D	-	12/63
6725	PILL	86B	86B	86B	-	-	10/59	6765	12/48	88B	88B	88C	87D	-	05/64
6726	PILL	86B	86B	-	-	-	07/58	6766	01/49	87C	87C	87C	-	-	08/60
6727	PILL	86B	86B	-	-	-	04/58	6767	01/49	88B	88B	88C	-	-	12/62
6728	PILL	86B	86B	86B	-	-	06/60	6768	01/49	87B	87K	87K	87D	-	01/64
6729	PILL	86B	86B	86B	-	-	06/59	6769	01/49	88C	88C	88C	82B	-	12/63
6730	PILL	86B	86B	-	-	-	09/57	6770	10/50	88B	88B	88C	-	-	10/62
6731	PILL	86B	86B	-	-	-	05/58	6771	10/50	88B	88B	-	-	-	03/58
6732	PILL	86B	86B	-	-	-	07/58	6772	11/50	86B	86B	86B	87D	-	12/63
6733	BRY	88C	88C	-	-	-	05/58	6773	11/50	88B	88B	88C	-	-	10/59
6734	DG	87K	87K	87K	-	-	02/59	6774	11/50	88C	88C	87K	-	-	12/59
6735	PILL	86B	86B	88B	-	-	06/59	6775	11/50	88C	88C	88C	-	-	08/60
6736	BRY	88C	88B	82C	-	-	02/59	6776	11/50	87B	87B	87K	-	-	01/61
6737	SDN	82C	82C	-	-	-	07/57	6777	12/50	87B	87B	87K	87D	-	05/64
6738	BRY	88C	88C	88C	-	-	10/62	6778	12/50	88B	88B	87K	-	-	05/62
6739	SDN	82C	82C	86B	-	-	06/62	6779	12/50	88B	88B	87K	-	-	06/59

Continued with Number 7700

68XX

'Grange'

4-6-0

Introduced 1936 by Collett. Variation of 'Hall' with smaller wheels & recycled parts from 43xx 2-6-0s

Loco Weight: 47t 0c   *Driving Wheels:* 5' 8"   *Cylinders:* (O) 18½" x 30"   *Valve Gear:* Stephenson (piston valves)

Number & Name	1948	1952	1955	1959	1963	1965	w/dwn	Notes
6800 Arlington Grange	LDR	83G	83G	83G	86A	-	06/64	
6801 Aylburton Grange	PZ	83G	83G	83G	-	-	10/60	

Number & Name	1948	1952	1955	1959	1963	1965	w/dwn	Notes
6802 Bampton Grange	RDG	81D	83D	86G	-	-	08/61	
6803 Bucklebury Grange	BAN	84F	84F	84F	84B	-	09/65	
6804 Brockington Grange	WES	82B	82B	82B	87F	-	08/64	
6805 Broughton Grange	CDF	82B	82C	83F	-	-	03/61	
6806 Blackwell Grange	LDR	83G	84K	84B	85A	-	10/64	
6807 Birchwood Grange	WOS	85A	85A	85A	85A	-	12/63	
6808 Beenham Grange	PZ	83G	83G	83G	87F	-	08/64	
6809 Burghclere Grange	SHL	83G	83G	82B	81C	-	07/63	
6810 Blakemere Grange	CDF	87F	87F	87F	86G	-	10/64	
6811 Cranbourne Grange	CDF	82B	82B	82B	84F	-	07/64	
6812 Chesford Grange	SRD	86E	86A	86G	81D	-	02/65	
6813 Eastbury Grange	NA	83A	83A	83A	86A	-	09/65	
6814 Enborne Grange	NA	83A	83A	83E	82B	-	12/63	
6815 Frilford Grange	STJ	83B	83B	83B	87F	-	11/65	
6816 Frankton Grange	BAN	84C	83D	83G	82B	-	07/65	
6817 Gwenddwr Grange	CDF	83G	84K	84B	85A	-	04/65	
6818 Hardwick Grange	CARM	87G	87F	87F	87F	-	04/64	
6819 Highnam Grange	BHD	84C	86G	86G	86G	-	11/65	
6820 Kingstone Grange	PPRD	86A	86A	85A	86G	-	07/65	
6821 Leaton Grange	NPT	81A	83D	81F	86G	-	11/64	
6822 Manton Grange	NA	83A	83A	81F	86G	-	09/64	
6823 Oakley Grange	FGD	87J	84F	83F	84B	-	06/65	
6824 Ashley Grange	CARM	83G	83G	83G	81E	-	04/64	
6825 Llanvair Grange	PZ	83G	83G	83G	81D	-	06/64	
6826 Nannerth Grange	SHL	83G	83G	83G	81D	-	05/65	
6827 Llanfrechfa Grange	CDF	82B	82B	82B	84F	-	09/65	
6828 Trellech Grange	LDR	84F	84F	87F	84B	-	07/63	
6829 Burmington Grange	NA	83A	83A	83A	86A	-	11/65	
6830 Buckenhill Grange	SPM	82B	82B	82B	84B	-	10/65	
6831 Bearley Grange	TYS	6C	6C	82B	84B	-	10/65	
6832 Brockton Grange	BAN	82B	82C	83F	87F	-	01/64	
6833 Calcot Grange	TYS	84K	82B	82B	84B	-	10/65	
6834 Dummer Grange	STJ	81A	81D	82B	81C	-	06/64	
6835 Eastham Grange	BAN	84K	82B	82B	82B	-	05/63	
6836 Estervarney Grange	SPM	82B	83G	83A	86G	-	08/65	
6837 Forthampton Grange	NPT	86C	83G	83G	87F	-	07/65	
6838 Goodmoor Grange	PZ	83G	83D	86A	86G	-	11/65	
6839 Hewell Grange	BAN	84C	84B	84B	84B	-	05/64	
6840 Hazeley Grange	PPRD	86G	86G	86G	86G	-	02/65	
6841 Marlas Grange	BAN	6C	6C	82B	81C	-	06/65	
6842 Nunhold Grange	SPM	82B	82B	82B	84F	-	11/64	
6843 Poulton Grange	TYS	84E	84E	87F	87F	-	02/64	
6844 Penhydd Grange	SRD	87F	87F	87F	87F	-	04/64	
6845 Paviland Grange	WES	82B	82B	83G	84E	-	09/64	
6846 Ruckley Grange	SPM	82B	82B	82B	82B	-	09/64	
6847 Tidmarsh Grange	TYS	84E	86A	86A	88L	85A	12/65	
6848 Toddington Grange	SRD	87F	83A	81F	86G	85A	12/65	
6849 Walton Grange	BAN	86G	84K	83D	81E	81F	12/65	
6850 Cleeve Grange	SPM	82B	82C	83D	86A	-	12/64	
6851 Hurst Grange	WOS	85A	85A	85A	84B	-	08/65	
6852 Headbourne Grange	SPM	82B	82B	82B	86A	-	01/64	
6853 Morehampton Grange	TYS	84E	84E	84E	84E	-	10/65	
6854 Roundhill Grange	BAN	84C	84B	81F	84B	-	09/65	
6855 Saighton Grange	TYS	83D	83D	83D	84B	-	10/65	
6856 Stowe Grange	OXY	84C	84B	85A	85A	-	11/65	
6857 Tudor Grange	LDR	84F	84F	84B	84B	-	10/65	
6858 Woolston Grange	TYS	84E	84G	81F	84B	-	10/65	
6859 Yiewsley Grange	CHR	6C	6C	82B	88L	-	11/65	
6860 Aberporth Grange	TYS	84B	83G	83G	82B	-	02/65	
6861 Crynant Grange	SPM	86G	84B	84E	84E	-	10/65	

Number & Name	1948	1952	1955	1959	1963	1965	w/dwn	Notes
6862 Derwent Grange	OXY	84B	84B	84B	84B	-	06/65	
6863 Dolhywel Grange	SPM	82B	82B	83D	81D	-	11/64	
6864 Dymock Grange	RDG	81D	81D	81F	84B	-	10/65	
6865 Hopton Grange	PDN	81D	81D	86A	-	-	05/62	
6866 Morfa Grange	TYS	84E	84E	84E	84E	-	05/65	
6867 Peterston Grange	SPM	82B	82B	86G	86G	-	08/64	
6868 Penrhos Grange	NPT	83B	83B	83B	81E	-	10/65	
6869 Resolven Grange	PDN	83G	83D	82B	81C	-	07/65	
6870 Bodicote Grange	NPT	86A	86A	83G	84B	-	09/65	
6871 Bourton Grange	STJ	86G	86G	83D	84B	-	10/65	
6872 Crawley Grange	LDR	86G	86G	86G	86G	85A	12/65	
6873 Caradoc Grange	STJ	83D	83D	83D	82B	-	06/64	
6874 Haughton Grange	NPT	81A	83B	83B	81E	-	09/65	
6875 Hindford Grange	PPRD	83B	83B	83G	88L	-	03/64	
6876 Kingsland Grange	SPM	82B	82B	82B	86G	-	11/65	
6877 Llanfair Grange	WOS	85A	85A	85A	85A	-	03/65	
6878 Longford Grange	BHD	6C	6C	82B	82B	-	11/64	
6879 Overton Grange	OXY	84C	84B	83D	84E	-	10/65	

TOTAL 80

49xx   'Hall'   4-6-0

Continued from Number 5999.

Number & Name	1948	1952	1955	1959	1963	1965	w/dwn	Notes
6900 Abney Hall	PDN	82A	82A	82A	82C	-	10/64	
6901 Arley Hall	SRD	84K	84K	86C	86G	-	06/64	
6902 Butler Hall	SDN	82F	82F	82C	-	-	05/61	
6903 Belmont Hall	LDR	87E	87E	87E	84B	-	09/65	
6904 Charfield Hall	TYS	84E	84E	84E	84C	-	02/65	
6905 Claughton Hall	HFD	85C	87E	87E	87A	-	06/64	
6906 Chicheley Hall	BAN	84C	84C	84C	84C	-	04/65	
6907 Davenham Hall	LA	83D	83D	84B	84B	-	02/65	
6908 Downham Hall	SRD	82B	82B	82A	82B	-	07/65	
6909 Frewin Hall	SPM	86E	87J	87J	81E	-	06/64	
6910 Gossington Hall	PDN	81E	81E	81E	81F	-	10/65	
6911 Holker Hall	PZ	83G	83G	83F	84C	-	04/65	
6912 Helmster Hall	SPM	83D	83D	87E	88L	-	02/64	
6913 Levens Hall	LA	83D	83D	83D	81D	-	06/64	
6914 Langton Hall	TYS	82B	82D	71G	87H	-	04/64	
6915 Mursley Hall	OXY	82C	82C	81E	89A	-	02/65	
6916 Misterton Hall	WOS	85C	85C	84G	89A	-	08/65	
6917 Oldsland Hall	GLO	85B	85B	85B	84B	-	09/65	
6918 Sandon Hall	LDR	87E	87E	87E	88L	-	09/65	
6919 Tylney Hall	CARM	87G	82F	82A	82B	-	08/63	
6920 Barnigham Hall	HFD	84B	81F	81A	87B	-	12/63	
6921 Borwick Hall	WOS	85B	85B	83D	83D	-	10/65	
6922 Burton Hall	SPM	82B	81F	81F	89A	-	04/65	
6923 Croxteth Hall	DID	81D	81D	81D	81D	81F	12/65	
6924 Grantley Hall	SRD	84D	84B	81F	81D	-	10/65	
6925 Hackness Hall	OXF	82B	82B	84B	84B	-	11/64	
6926 Holkham Hall	NPT	86E	84B	84A	84E	-	06/65	
6927 Lilford Hall	NPT	81A	81D	81F	81F	-	10/65	
6928 Underley Hall	CDF	86C	86C	86G	86G	-	06/65	
6929 Whorlton Hall	BAN	84C	84C	84C	84C	-	10/63	
6930 Aldersley Hall	WOS	85A	85A	84F	84E	-	10/65	
6931 Aldborough Hall	TR	83F	83F	83E	88L	-	10/65	
6932 Burwarton Hall	OXY	81A	86C	86C	88L	81F	12/65	
6933 Birtles Hall	OXF	81F	83A	83A	84B	-	11/64	
6934 Beachamwell Hall	NA	83A	83G	84B	89A	-	10/65	
6935 Browsholme Hall	SDN	82D	82D	87G	88L	-	02/65	
6936 Breccles Hall	WOS	85B	82A	82A	88L	-	11/64	

Number & Name	1948	1952	1955	1959	1963	1965	w/dwn	Notes
6937 Conyngham Hall	OXF	81F	81F	81F	81E	81F	12/65	
6938 Corndean Hall	WOS	85A	83C	83A	81D	-	03/65	
6939 Calveley Hall	OXY	86C	86C	86C	88L	-	10/63	
6940 Didlington Hall	GLO	83D	83D	83D	82C	-	05/64	
6941 Fillongley Hall	CHR	84K	84K	83D	88L	-	04/64	
6942 Eshton Hall	OXY	84B	84B	81A	81A	-	12/64	
6943 Farnley Hall	HFD	86C	86C	86C	85B	-	12/63	
6944 Fledborough Hall	SPM	81A	84G	84G	88L	86E	12/65	
6945 Glasfryn Hall	WEY	82F	82F	82D	88L	-	09/64	
6946 Heatherden hall	CDF	86C	86C	86G	86G	-	06/64	
6947 Helmingham Hall	WOS	85A	85A	85A	85B	-	10/65	
6948 Holbrooke Hall	CDF	86C	86C	85A	85A	-	12/63	
6949 Haberfield Hall	LA	83D	84A	84C	-	-	05/61	Renumbered from 3955, 04/49
6950 Kingsthorpe Hall	WOS	85A	85A	85A	88L	-	06/64	
6951 Impney Hall	WOS	85A	86C	82B	85A	2A	12/65	
6952 Kimberley Hall	DID	81E	81E	81E	84C	2A	12/65	
6953 Leighton Hall	PDN	81F	81F	81D	81D	81F	12/65	Renumbered from 3953, 09/48
6954 Lotherton Hall	SPM	82B	82A	82A	82B	-	05/64	
6955 Lydcott Hall	WES	82D	82D	82D	82D	-	02/65	
6956 Mottram Hall	OXY	84A	84A	84A	85B	81F	12/65	
6957 Norcliffe Hall	PDN	82B	82A	82A	88L	-	10/65	Renumbered from 3952, 03/50
6958 Oxburgh Hall	BRD	82A	82A	86C	86G	-	06/65	

TOTAL 258

6959   'Modified Hall'   4-6-0

1944 Introduction by Hawksworth with one piece frames & modified bogies.

Loco Weight : 75t 16c   *Driving Wheels:* 6' 0"   *Cylinders :* (o) 18½" x 30"   *Valve Gear :* Stephenson (piston valves)

Number & Name	1948	1952	1955	1959	1963	1965	w/dwn	Notes
6959 Peatling Hall	PDN	81A	81A	81A	81A	81F	12/65	
6960 Raveningham Hall	PDN	81A	81D	81D	81D	-	06/64	
6961 Stedham Hall	PDN	81A	81A	81A	81A	-	09/65	
6962 Soughton Hall	PDN	81A	81A	81A	-	-	01/63	
6963 Throwley Hall	SALOP	84K	84K	86C	81A	-	07/65	
6964 Thornbridge Hall	SRD	84A	84A	84G	89A	-	09/65	
6965 Thirlestaine Hall	SDN	83D	83D	83C	86A	-	10/65	
6966 Witchingham Hall	WES	84C	84C	81A	81A	-	09/64	
6967 Willesley Hall	OXY	82A	82C	81C	81C	81F	12/65	
6968 Woodcock Hall	RDG	81D	81D	81D	87J	-	09/63	
6969 Wraysbury Hall	CDF	86C	86C	81E	81E	-	02/65	
6970 Whaddon Hall	OXY	81F	81F	81F	81F	-	06/64	
6971 Athelhampton Hall	BRD	84E	84E	84E	84E	-	10/64	
6972 Beningborough Hall	BRD	82A	82A	82A	82B	-	03/64	
6973 Bricklehampton Hall	PDN	81A	81A	81A	81A	-	08/65	
6974 Bryngwyn Hall	PDN	81A	81A	81A	81C	-	05/65	
6975 Capesthorne Hall	OXY	84B	84A	84A	87A	-	12/63	
6976 Graythwaite Hall	SALOP	84C	84C	84C	84C	-	10/65	
6977 Grundisburgh Hall	PDN	82A	82B	82B	82D	-	12/63	
6978 Haroldstone Hall	WES	82D	83D	81A	81A	-	07/65	
6979 Helperly Hall	BAN	84C	84C	84C	84C	-	02/65	
6980 Llanrumney Hall	SALOP	84G	84G	84G	84B	-	10/65	
6981 Marbury Hall	02/48	82A	82A	82A	82B	-	03/64	
6982 Melmerby Hall	01/48	82A	82B	82A	82B	-	08/64	
6983 Otterington Hall	02/48	81A	81E	81E	81E	-	08/65	
6984 Owsden Hall	02/48	85C	85C	85A	87H	82E	12/65	
6985 Otterington Hall	02/48	85C	85B	85B	85B	-	09/64	
6986 Rydal Hall	03/48	82B	82B	82B	81C	-	04/65	
6987 Shervington Hall	03/48	85A	85A	84F	88L	-	09/64	
6988 Swithland Hall	03/48	82F	83A	83D	83D	-	09/64	
6989 Whightwick Hall	03/48	85C	85C	85C	85B	-	06/64	

Number & Name	1948	1952	1955	1959	1963	1965	w/dwn	Notes
6990 Witherslack Hall	04/48	81A	81A	81A	81A	82E	12/65	
6991 Acton Burnell Hall	11/48	82D	81C	81C	81C	81F	12/65	
6992 Arborfield Hall	11/48	85C	85C	85C	85A	-	06/64	
6993 Arthog Hall	12/48	82F	82F	82C	85B	81F	12/65	
6994 Baggrave Hall	12/48	83C	82D	82D	81C	-	11/64	
6995 Benthall Hall	12/48	83B	83B	83B	88L	-	03/65	
6996 Blackwell Hall	01/49	81A	83B	81E	81E	-	10/64	
6997 Bryn-Ivor Hall	01/49	82A	82A	82A	82B	-	11/64	
6998 Burton Agnes Hall	01/49	86C	86C	84G	81A	81F	12/65	
6999 Capel Dewi Hall	02/49	86C	86C	86C	82D	81F	12/65	

Continued with Number 7900

4073   'Castle'   4-6-0

Continued from Number 5099.

Number & Name	1948	1952	1955	1959	1963	1965	w/dwn	Notes
7000 Viscount Portal	NA	83A	83A	83A	85A	-	12/63	
7001 Denbigh Castle / Sir James Milne	CDF	81A	81A	81A	84A	-	09/63	renamed 01/48 DC 09/60
7002 Devizes Castle	LDR	87E	87E	87E	85A	-	03/64	DC 06/61
7003 Elmley Castle	LDR	87E	87E	87E	85B	-	08/64	DC 06/60
7004 Eastnor Castle	GLO	81A	81A	81A	85A	-	01/64	DC 02/58
7005 Lamphey Castle / Sir Edward Elgar	WOS	85A	85A	85A	85A	-	09/64	renamed 08/57
7006 Lydford Castle	SALOP	85B	85B	83D	81A	-	12/63	DC 05/60
7007 Ogmore Castle / Great Western	SRD	85A	85A	85A	-	-	02/63	renamed 01/48 DC 03/61
7008 Swansea Castle	05/48	81F	81F	81A	81A	-	09/64	DC 06/59
7009 Athelney Castle	05/48	87E	87E	87E	81A	-	03/63	
7010 Avondale Castle	06/48	81F	81A	81A	81A	-	03/64	DC 10/60
7011 Banbury Castle	06/48	82A	82A	82A	81D	-	02/65	
7012 Barry Castle	06/48	87E	87E	87E	84A	-	11/64	
7013 Bristol Castle	07/48	81A	85A	81A	85A	-	02/65	DC 05/58 Became 4082 02/52
7014 Caerhays Castle	07/48	82A	82A	82A	84A	-	02/65	DC 02/59
7015 Carn Brae Castle	07/48	82C	82C	82A	81A	-	04/63	DC 06/59
7016 Chester Castle	08/48	86C	86C	87E	-	-	11/62	
7017 G J Churchward	09/48	86C	81A	81A	-	-	02/63	
7018 Drysllwyn Castle	05/49	87E	87E	82A	81A	-	09/63	DC 05/56
7019 Fowey Castle	05/49	82A	82A	82A	84A	-	02/65	DC 09/58
7020 Gloucester Castle	05/49	86C	86C	81A	81A	-	09/64	DC 02/61
7021 Haverfordwest Castle	06/49	87E	87E	87G	81A	-	09/63	DC 11/61
7022 Hereford Castle	06/49	86C	86C	83D	83D	-	06/65	DC 01/58
7023 Penrice Castle	06/49	86C	86C	86C	85A	-	02/65	DC 05/58
7024 Powis Castle	06/49	81A	81A	81A	84A	-	02/65	DC 03/59
7025 Sudeley Castle	08/49	81A	81A	81A	85A	-	09/64	
7026 Tenby Castle	08/49	84A	84A	84A	84A	-	10/64	
7027 Thornbury Castle	08/49	81A	81A	81A	85A	-	12/63	
7028 Cadbury Castle	05/50	87E	87E	87E	87F	-	12/63	DC 10/61
7029 Clun Castle	05/50	83A	83A	83A	81A	85B	12/65	DC 10/59
7030 Cranbrook Castle	06/50	81A	81A	81A	-	-	02/65	DC 07/59
7031 Cromwell's Castle	06/50	83D	83D	83D	85A	-	07/63	
7032 Denbigh Castle	06/50	81A	81A	81A	81A	-	09/64	DC 09/60
7033 Hartlebury Castle	07/50	81A	81A	81A	-	-	01/63	DC 07/59
7034 Ince Castle	08/50	82A	82A	82A	85B	-	06/65	DC 12/59
7035 Ogmore Castle	08/50	84G	85B	82A	81A	-	06/64	DC 01/60
7036 Taunton Castle	08/50	81A	81A	81A	81A	-	09/63	DC 08/59
7037 Swindon	08/50	82C	82C	82C	81A	-	03/63	

Collett

2-8-2T

1934 Introduction by Collett. Development of Churchward 2-8-0T with trailing bogie and larger bunker.

Loco Weight : 92t 2c *Driving Wheels :* 4' 7½" *Cylinders :* (O) 19" x 30" *Valve Gear :* Stephenson (piston valves)

No.	1948	1952	1955	1959	1963	1965	w/dwn	No.	1948	1952	1955	1959	1963	1965	w/dwn
7200	NA	83A	87E	87E	87F	-	07/63	7227	OXY	84B	86A	86C	86G	-	06/63
7201	CDF	82B	82B	86G	86G	-	04/65	7228	DID	87F	87F	87F	88C	-	07/63
7202	STJ	88A	88A	88A	88C	-	06/64	7229	STJ	86E	86A	86A	87B	-	07/64
7203	NPT	86A	86A	87F	86A	-	12/63	7230	PPRD	86E	86E	88C	86G	-	07/64
7204	DID	87A	85C	86G	87A	-	02/64	7231	NPT	86A	86A	86A	88C	-	10/64
7205	ABDR	88A	88A	88A	88B	-	06/65	7232	PPRD	86A	86A	86A	86A	-	05/65
7206	PPRD	86G	86G	86G	86G	-	07/64	7233	PPRD	86G	86G	86A	86A	-	09/64
7207	OXY	87E	87E	87E	84C	-	11/64	7234	SPM	86G	86G	86A	88J	-	10/63
7208	SPM	84B	86E	86E	88C	-	04/64	7235	PPRD	86G	86G	85A	87F	-	04/64
7209	STJ	83E	87E	87E	88J	-	07/64	7236	OXY	83A	87E	87E	84C	-	11/63
7210	STJ	86A	86A	86G	86G	-	04/65	7237	SPM	83D	86E	86E	87F	-	06/63
7211	SED	87F	87F	87F	87F	-	05/64	7238	OXY	84B	81F	81F	86A	-	04/64
7212	NPT	86E	81F	86A	86F	-	02/64	7239	STJ	86E	81F	81F	87F	-	10/63
7213	ABDR	86J	86J	86G	87F	-	09/64	7240	OXY	83A	87F	86A	86A	-	09/64
7214	DID	86A	86A	86J	88J	-	12/63	7241	NPT	86A	82B	88C	-	-	12/62
7215	SPM	86A	87F	87D	87D	-	06/63	7242	ABDR	88A	88A	88A	88B	-	06/64
7216	STJ	86J	86J	86J	87B	-	10/64	7243	OXY	84B	86A	86A	87B	-	07/64
7217	NPT	87E	87E	87E	86A	-	07/64	7244	LDR	87B	87B	87B	87F	-	02/65
7218	LMTN	84B	86A	86A	84C	-	08/64	7245	NPT	86A	86A	86A	86F	-	09/64
7219	CDF	86C	86A	86A	86A	-	01/64	7246	STJ	86E	81F	86G	86G	-	09/63
7220	NA	83A	86G	86G	86G	-	09/64	7247	NPT	86A	86A	84B	88J	-	03/63
7221	ABDR	86J	86J	86J	88C	-	11/64	7248	OXY	87A	87E	87D	87D	-	06/65
7222	OXY	87F	85C	86A	87B	-	01/65	7249	NPT	86A	88A	87B	86E	-	06/65
7223	STJ	86E	86E	86E	86A	-	11/64	7250	NA	83A	82B	86A	88B	-	09/64
7224	STJ	86E	87D	87F	87F	-	12/62	7251	STJ	86E	86E	86G	86G	-	01/64
7225	LDR	87F	87F	87D	87F	-	05/64	7252	DID	86A	88A	88C	88B	-	06/65
7226	OXY	84B	87D	87D	87D	-	11/64	7253	NPT	86A	86A	86A	86A	-	04/65

TOTAL 54

43xx

2-6-0

Continued from Number 6399.

No.	1948	1952	1955	1959	1963	1965	w/dwn	No.	1948	1952	1955	1959	1963	1965	w/dwn
7300	WES	82D	82D	82D	-	-	09/62	7311	OXY	84B	83B	83C	-	-	09/62
7301	WOS	85C	85C	82B	-	-	09/62	7312	CHEL	85B	85B	85B	87B	-	12/63
7302	WES	82D	82D	82D	-	-	08/62	7313	CHR	84J	84J	84J	-	-	07/62
7303	CHEL	85B	82B	82B	88L	-	09/64	7314	TN	85C	85C	87F	-	-	02/63
7304	TN	83B	83B	83B	83B'	-	11/63	7315	SRD	84A	84C	84C	87F	-	12/63
7305	CNYD	84J	84J	84C	-	-	09/62	7316	EXE	83C	83C	83C	-	-	09/62
7306	NEY	87H	87H	87H	87G	-	09/64	7317	OXY	84E	84E	84E	88L	-	12/63
7307	OXY	85C	85C	87F	87F	-	05/64	7318	RDG	87F	87H	87H	87B	-	11/64
7308	WOS	85C	85C	84C	82D	-	06/64	7319	SALOP	84G	86A	86A	87F	-	10/64
7309	WES	82D	84G	84G	-	-	09/62	7320	RDG	87F	87F	87F	87H	-	11/64
7310	CNYD	84J	84J	84J	89B	-	06/64	7321	SDN	82C	82C	87F	-	-	09/62

No.	1948	1952	1955	1959	1963	1965	w/dwn	Notes
7322	SHL	81C	86C	86E	-	-	11/61	Renumbered from 9300, 04/57
7323	SHL	81C	81C	82B	-	-	08/62	Renumbered from 9301, 09/56
7324	PDN	81C	81F	81E	-	-	10/62	Renumbered from 9302, 02/57
7325	RDG	81D	84E	86G	86E	-	04/64	Renumbered from 9303, 06/58
7326	RDG	81C	86C	85C	83B	-	09/63	Renumbered from 9304, 06/58
7327	RDG	81D	81C	-	81E	-	11/64	Renumbered from 9305, 01/59
7328	PDN	81D	81D	86E	-	-	04/62	Renumbered from 9306, 05/58
7329	RDG	81D	84B	84G	-	-	01/63	Renumbered from 9307, 12/56

No.	1948	1952	1955	1959	1963	1965	w/dwn	Notes
7330	PDN	81D	81D	-	-	-	09/62	Renumbered from *9308, 06/57*
7331	RDG	81C	81C	-	-	-	09/62	Renumbered from *9309, 05/59*
7332	PDN	81C	87G	86C	82D	-	04/64	Renumbered from *9310, 09/58*
7333	SHL	81C	81F	83D	83B	-	10/63	Renumbered from *9311, 06/57*
7334	OXY	84B	84A	-	-	-	04/62	Renumbered from *9312, 01/59*
7335	RDG	81D	81C	83D	85B	-	09/63	Renumbered from *9313, 08/58*
7336	OXY	84B	84B	84B	-	-	09/62	Renumbered from *9314, 06/58*
7337	RDG	81D	81C	-	83B	-	09/64	Renumbered from *9315, 05/59*
7338	OXF	81F	84B	85A	-	-	08/62	Renumbered from *9316, 03/58*
7339	OXF	81F	84B	84B	89B	-	06/64	Renumbered from *9317, 09/56*
7340	RDG	81D	84F	87H	81E	-	06/64	Renumbered from *9318, 12/57*
7341	RDG	81D	84E	84B	-	-	09/62	Renumbered from *9319, 06/57*

Continued with Number 8393

74xx   Collett   0-6-0PT

Introduced 1936 by Collett , this class was designed for light branch passenger work. Unlike the Identical 64xx Class, these locos were not fitted with push - pull control equipment

Loco Weight : 45t 12c   *Driving Wheels :* 4' 7½"   *Cylinders :* (I) 16½" x 24"   *Valve Gear :* Stephenson (Slide Valves)

No.	1948	1952	1955	1959	1963	1965	w/dwn	No.	1948	1952	1955	1959	1963	1965	w/dwn
7400	CARM	87G	87G	87G	-	-	06/60	7425	CARM	87G	87G	87G	-	-	06/62
7401	CARM	87G	87G	87G	-	-	08/59	7426	PPRD	86G	86G	85C	84E	-	07/63
7402	STB	84F	89C	87G	-	-	07/62	7427	NA	-	83A	83A	86E	-	06/64
7403	CNYD	84J	84J	84J	86E	-	01/64	7428	STB	84F	84F	84F	-	-	10/62
7404	OXF	81J	81F	81F	81F	-	06/64	7429	STJ	84F	84F	84F	-	-	02/61
7405	OSW	89A	89A	89A	87G	-	12/63	7430	08/48	84F	84F	84F	84F	-	12/63
7406	ABH	89C	89C	89C	-	-	03/62	7431	08/48	84K	84J	84J	89B	-	09/64
7407	CARM	87G	87G	87G	87G	-	12/63	7432	08/48	84F	84F	84F	84F	-	09/64
7408	WEY	82F	82F	87K	-	-	08/62	7433	08/48	84J	84J	84J	-	-	02/61
7409	CNYD	84J	84J	84J	-	-	08/61	7434	08/48	89A	89A	89A	-	-	10/62
7410	OSW	89A	89A	89A	-	-	01/61	7435	09/48	84F	84F	84F	84F	-	07/64
7411	OXF	81F	81F	81F	-	-	05/59	7436	09/48	81F	81F	83B	83B	-	06/64
7412	OXF	81F	81F	81F	81F	-	07/63	7437	09/48	85A	85C	85C	86C	-	03/65
7413	FGD	87H	82C	82C	86C	-	09/64	7438	10/48	84E	84E	84E	-	-	02/59
7414	CNYD	84J	84J	84J	89B	-	09/64	7439	10/48	87K	87K	87C	87G	-	04/65
7415	SDN	82C	82C	82C	-	-	02/59	7440	01/50	84J	84J	84J	-	-	10/62
7416	WOS	85C	85C	85C	-	-	01/59	7441	01/50	84F	84F	84F	84F	-	12/63
7417	WTD	89C	89C	89C	-	-	09/61	7442	02/50	84J	84J	84J	87G	-	12/63
7418	SDN	82C	82C	82C	89B	-	08/64	7443	02/50	84J	84J	84J	89B	-	09/64
7419	CARM	87G	87G	87G	-	-	07/60	7444	02/50	87G	87G	87G	87G	-	07/64
7420	HFD	85C	85C	84F	-	-	07/59	7445	03/50	88A	88A	83A	87G	-	03/64
7421	TN	83B	82C	82C	-	-	11/61	7446	03/50	83E	83E	83E	89D	-	07/64
7422	TR	83F	83F	87G	-	-	03/62	7447	03/50	84J	84J	84F	-	-	04/59
7423	ABDR	86J	86J	86J	88J	-	07/64	7448	04/50	84F	84F	84F	-	-	04/63
7424	SDN	82C	82C	82C	84E	-	09/64	7449	04/50	84F	84F	84F	84F	-	06/63

TOTAL 50

RAILWAY & BUS PHOTOGRAPHS & NEGATIVES

We are looking to expand our collection of railway and bus photographs for use in future publications.

If you have any photographs or negatives which you can lend, gift, bequeath, or even sell to us, we would be able to make good use of them and are happy to acknowledge the original photographers if they appear in print.

Continued from Number 6779.

No.	1948	1952	1955	1959	1963	1965	w/dwn	No.	1948	1952	1955	1959	1963	1965	w/dwn
7700	KDR	85D	85D	85B	-	-	05/61	7750	WOS	85A	85A	85B	-	-	01/59
7701	NEA	87A	87A	87A	-	-	02/60	7751	CED	88B	88B	88A	-	-	10/59
7702	LMTN	84D	84D	84D	-	-	09/60	7752	TDU	86F	86F	86F	-	-	12/59
7703	ABEEG	86H	86H	86B	-	-	03/60	7753	NPT	86A	86F	86F	-	-	04/62
7704	SED	87D	87D	87D	-	-	12/60	7754	PDN	84H	84H	84H	-	-	01/59
7705	STB	84F	84F	81E	-	-	08/59	7755	LLY	87F	87G	86A	-	-	05/62
7706	DYD	87B	87B	87B	-	-	03/60	7756	SED	87D	87D	87D	-	-	06/61
7707	HFD	85C	85C	85A	-	-	11/60	7757	NEA	87A	87A	87A	-	-	09/60
7708	RDG	81D	81D	81D	-	-	06/60	7758	TYS	84E	84F	87B	-	-	06/60
7709	SBZ	83E	83E	83E	-	-	08/60	7759	OXY	84B	84B	84B	-	-	03/60
7710	DID	81E	81E	-	-	-	09/58	7760	PDN	81F	81F	81F	-	-	12/61
7711	SPM	82B	83E	-	-	-	12/56	7761	EXE	83C	83C	84C	-	-	01/61
7712	NPT	86B	86B	86B	-	-	07/60	7762	LA	83D	83D	6E	-	-	05/62
7713	PDN	84E	84E	84E	-	-	08/62	7763	BAN	84C	84C	84E	-	-	11/59
7714	BHD	6C	6C	6C	-	-	01/59	7764	STJ	86E	86E	86E	-	-	05/62
7715	SBZ	83E	83E	83E	-	-	05/63	7765	LLY	87F	87F	87F	-	-	07/62
7716	EXE	83C	83C	83C	-	-	12/59	7766	MTHR	88D	88D	88A	-	-	11/60
7717	MTHR	88D	88D	88A	-	-	03/60	7767	NEA	87A	87A	87A	-	-	03/60
7718	SPM	82B	87D	87F	-	-	04/62	7768	NPT	86A	86A	86A	-	-	11/59
7719	SPM	82B	82B	82B	-	-	09/60	7769	NEA	87A	87A	87A	-	-	08/59
7720	ABEEG	86J	86J	86J	-	-	05/62	7770	TDU	86F	86F	86F	-	-	04/59
7721	LTS	86B	86B	86B	-	-	07/62	7771	NPT	86A	86A	86A	-	-	11/61
7722	THT	88B	88B	81A	-	-	11/60	7772	MTHR	88D	88D	86B	-	-	11/61
7723	GLO	85B	85B	85B	-	-	08/60	7773	ABDR	86J	86J	86J	-	-	12/59
7724	PPRD	86G	86G	86G	-	-	09/62	7774	PILL	86B	86H	86A	-	-	11/59
7725	TDU	86F	86F	86F	-	-	08/60	7775	TDU	86H	86H	86C	-	-	11/60
7726	SPM	82B	88A	88C	-	-	08/60	7776	LLY	87F	87E	87F	-	-	01/61
7727	WES	82D	82D	82D	-	-	01/60	7777	RDG	81D	81D	85A	-	-	11/60
7728	SPM	82B	82B	82B	-	-	05/60	7778	ABEEG	86F	86F	86F	-	-	12/59
7729	SPM	82B	82B	82B	-	-	07/62	7779	SPM	82B	88A	-	-	-	10/59
7730	SHL	81C	81C	81C	-	-	03/59	7780	SPM	82B	82B	71G	71G	-	07/63
7731	SHL	81C	81C	81C	-	-	04/59	7781	NPT	86A	86A	86A	-	-	07/60
7732	SHL	81C	81C	86F	-	-	10/62	7782	SPM	82B	82A	71G	71G	-	10/64
7733	DYD	87B	87B	88E	-	-	05/60	7783	SPM	82B	82B	82B	-	-	09/62
7734	PDN	81A	81A	81A	-	-	04/59	7784	WES	82D	82D	82D	-	-	03/62
7735	TYS	84E	84E	84E	-	-	05/59	7785	LLY	87F	87F	87F	-	-	05/62
7736	NPT	86A	86A	86A	-	-	05/62	7786	NEA	87A	87A	87A	-	-	05/62
7737	NES	87A	87A	87A	-	-	03/60	7787	LDR	87E	87E	86A	-	-	06/61
7738	PDN	88A	88B	86A	-	-	02/59	7788	RDG	81D	81D	81D	-	-	07/62
7739	NEA	87A	87A	87A	-	-	12/62	7789	ABEEG	86E	86E	86E	-	-	11/59
7740	ABEEG	86G	86G	86G	-	-	12/60	7790	SPM	82B	82B	82B	-	-	12/62
7741	GLO	85B	85B	85B	-	-	12/61	7791	PDN	81A	81A	81A	-	-	12/59
7742	NEA	87A	87A	87A	-	-	07/59	7792	SDN	82C	82C	-	-	-	11/57
7743	NEA	87A	87A	87A	-	-	08/59	7793	SPM	82B	82B	82B	-	-	04/60
7744	DYD	87B	87B	88E	-	-	09/62	7794	SDN	82C	82C	82C	-	-	11/60
7745	LLY	87F	87F	87F	-	-	03/61	7795	SPM	82B	82B	-	-	-	05/58
7746	TDU	86F	86F	86F	-	-	10/59	7796	OXY	84B	86G	86G	-	-	02/62
7747	FGD	87J	87J	87J	-	-	02/61	7797	OXY	84B	84B	84G	-	-	10/59
7748	ABDR	86B	82D	82D	-	-	04/61	7798	TDU	86F	86F	86F	-	-	05/61
7749	SPM	82B	82B	82B	-	-	12/62	7799	NEA	87A	87A	87A	-	-	05/62

Continued with Number 8700

78xx　'Manor'　4-6-0

Introduced in 1938 by Collett, these locos were designed for lighter, secondary lines, and most incorporated parts from 43xx 2-6-0s which had been selectively withdrawn for the purpose.

Loco Weight : 68t 18c　*Driving Wheels:* 5' 8"　*Cylinders :* (o) 18" x 30"　*Valve Gear :* Stephenson (piston valves)

Number & Name	1948	1952	1955	1959	1963	1965	w/dwn	Notes
7800 Torquay Manor	BAN	84E	84K	89A	89A	-	08/64	DEVON
7801 Anthony Manor	SPM	83D	84K	89A	89A	-	07/65	CORN
7802 Bradley Manor	ABH	89C	89C	89C	84E	-	11/65	DEVON
7803 Barcote Manor	ABH	89C	89C	89C	89B	-	04/65	
7804 Baydon Manor	SPM	83D	87G	87G	87F	-	09/64	
7805 Broome Manor	BAN	83A	85C	86C	88L	-	12/64	
7806 Cockington Manor	BAN	83A	83A	89C	84B	-	11/64	DEV
7807 Compton Manor	OSW	89A	84K	89A	89D	-	11/64	
7808 Cookham Manor	OSW	89A	85B	85B	81D	85B	12/65	
7809 Childrey Manor	BRD	83D	83D	86C	89A	-	04/63	
7810 Draycott Manor	LMTN	84G	85B	85B	89D	-	09/64	
7811 Dunley Manor	BAN	84B	84G	84G	87H	-	07/65	
7812 Erlestoke Manor	BRD	83A	83A	83D	89A	-	11/65	WILTS
7813 Freshford Manor	OXY	83A	83A	83D	81D	-	05/65	
7814 Fringford Manor	BRD	83D	83D	86C	87H	-	09/65	
7815 Fritwell Manor	GLO	85B	83D	86C	87G	-	10/64	
7816 Frilsham Manor	NEY	87H	83E	83E	81D	-	11/65	
7817 Garsington Manor	CNYD	84J	84J	84J	81D	-	06/64	
7818 Granville Manor	CHEL	84B	84E	84B	84E	-	01/65	
7819 Hinton Manor	OSW	89A	89A	89A	89A	-	11/65	
7820 Dinmore Manor	11/50	89A	83D	83D	88L	-	11/65	
7821 Ditcheat Manor	11/50	89A	84E	84E	89B	-	11/65	
7822 Foxcote Manor	12/50	89A	84K	89A	89D	-	11/65	
7823 Hook Norton Manor	12/50	84C	84J	83F	84E	-	07/64	
7824 Iford Manor	12/50	85B	83D	87G	84B	-	11/64	
7825 Lechlade Manor	12/50	84J	87G	87G	87H	-	05/64	
7826 Longworth Manor	12/50	84J	87G	87G	87G	-	04/65	
7827 Lydham Manor	12/50	84K	84K	89A	89D	-	10/65	
7828 Odney Manor	12/50	87A	84G	84G	89B	-	10/65	
7829 Ramsbury Manor	12/50	87A	87G	87G	87G	85B	12/65	

TOTAL 30

6959　'Modified Hall'　4-6-0

Continued from Number 6999.

Number & Name	1948	1952	1955	1959	1963	1965	w/dwn	Notes
7900 Saint Peter's Hall	04/49	81F	81F	81F	81F	-	12/64	
7901 Dodington Hall	03/49	82B	82A	82A	82B	-	02/64	
7902 Eaton Mascot Hall	03/49	81A	81A	81A	81A	-	06/64	
7903 Foremarke Hall	04/49	81A	81A	81A	81A	-	06/64	
7904 Fountains Hall	04/49	81A	81A	81A	81A	82E	12/65	
7905 Fowey Hall	04/49	83D	83D	83D	84C	-	05/64	CORN
7906 Fron Hall	12/49	81D	81D	81D	81D	-	03/65	
7907 Hart Hall	01/50	82B	82B	82A	82B	82E	12/65	
7908 Henshall Hall	01/50	82B	82B	84E	84E	-	10/65	
7909 Heveningham Hall	01/50	83D	83D	82D	83B	-	11/65	
7910 Hown Hall	01/50	81C	81C	81C	81C	-	02/65	
7911 Lady Margaret Hall	02/50	81F	81F	81F	81F	-	12/63	
7912 Little Linford Hall	03/50	84E	84E	84E	84C	-	10/65	
7913 Little Wyrly Hall	03/50	84E	84E	82B	88L	-	03/65	
7914 Lleweni Hall	03/50	82C	82C	81D	81D	82E	12/65	
7915 Mere Hall	03/50	84B	84B	84B	84E	-	10/65	
7916 Mobberley Hall	04/50	83E	83A	83A	82B	-	12/64	
7917 North Aston Hall	04/50	82D	82D	82D	87H	-	08/65	

Number & Name		1948	1952	1955	1959	1963	1965	w/dwn	Notes
7918	Rhose Wood Hall	05/50	84E	84E	84E	84E	-	02/65	
7919	Runter Hall	05/50	81D	81D	81D	81D	81F	12/65	
7920	Coney Hall	09/50	85A	85A	85A	85A	-	06/65	
7921	Edstone Hall	09/50	84K	84K	84G	81A	-	12/63	
7922	Salford Hall	09/50	84K	84K	84G	81C	81F	12/65	
7923	Speke Hall	09/50	82C	82C	81C	81C	-	05/65	
7924	Thornycroft Hall	09/50	82D	82D	82D	82B	82E	12/65	
7925	Westol Hall	10/50	83G	83G	83G	88L	81F	12/65	
7926	Willey Hall	10/50	85B	85B	85B	85A	-	12/64	
7927	Willington Hall	10/50	81D	81D	81A	88L	81F	12/65	
7928	Wolf Hall	10/50	85A	85A	85A	85A	-	03/65	
7929	Wyke Hall	11/50	84E	84E	82B	84E	-	08/65	

TOTAL 71

81xx   Collett   2-6-2T

Introduced in 1938 by Collett , this was a rebuild of the 51xx Class with smaller wheels and higher boiler pressure.

Loco Weight: 76t 11c   _Driving Wheels:_ 5' 6"   _Cylinders:_ (O) 18" x 30"   _Valve Gear:_ Stephenson (piston valves)

No.	1948	1952	1955	1959	1963	1965	w/dwn	No.	1948	1952	1955	1959	1963	1965	w/dwn
8100	LMTN	84D	84D	84D	-	-	10/62	8105	SPM	85A	85A	-	85A	-	06/57
8101	KDR	85D	85D	85D	-	-	03/61	8106	WOS	85A	85A	85A	-	-	12/63
8102	WTD	87H	87H	87G	87A	-	05/64	8107	WTD	87H	87H	87H	-	-	05/62
8103	OSW	89A	87G	87G	87F	-	11/63	8108	TYS	84E	84E	84E	-	-	11/60
8104	NEA	87A	87A	87A	85A	-	12/64	8109	LMTN	84D	84D	84D	84E	-	06/65

TOTAL 10

43xx   2-6-0

Continued from Number 7341.

8393   For details see No. 5393

Continued with Number 9300

94xx   0-6-0PT

Continued from Number 3409.

No.	1948	1952	1955	1959	1963	1965	w/dwn	No.	1948	1952	1955	1959	1963	1965	w/dwn
8400	08/49	84C	84C	85F	85D	-	09/64	8420	07/50	88E	88F	88A	81A	-	06/65
8401	08/49	86E	86E	85F	85D	-	09/64	8421	07/50	83C	83F	83F	-	-	12/59
8402	09/49	86H	86C	85F	85D	-	11/64	8422	10/50	83D	83D	83D	-	-	07/62
8403	09/49	83A	83A	85F	85D	-	06/65	8423	10/50	87B	87B	87B	-	-	12/59
8404	09/49	83F	83A	85F	-	-	11/61	8424	12/50	88E	88B	81F	-	-	01/61
8405	12/49	84C	84C	85F	85D	-	09/64	8425	02/51	83D	83D	84A	88L	-	11/63
8406	12/49	86A	86A	85F	-	-	01/61	8426	01/51	83D	83D	84A	81C	-	11/63
8407	12/49	84C	84C	87B	-	-	10/62	8427	02/51	85A	85A	85A	-	-	09/60
8408	01/50	87C	87C	87D	-	-	09/59	8428	02/51	84B	84B	84B	-	-	10/62
8409	01/50	83G	83G	83G	85D	-	08/64	8429	03/51	88B	88B	86H	-	-	01/60
8410	01/50	87B	87B	87B	-	-	01/60	8430	01/53	-	81D	81D	81D	-	05/63
8411	01/50	84A	84A	84A	-	-	06/60	8431	01/53	-	87D	87D	87D	-	08/64
8412	01/50	83F	83F	83F	-	-	07/59	8432	02/53	-	81A	81F	-	-	07/59
8413	01/50	82B	82B	81C	-	-	01/61	8433	03/53	-	81A	82C	81A	-	06/65
8414	01/50	88B	88B	87D	87D	-	04/64	8434	02/53	-	81A	81A	-	-	06/59
8415	03/50	84E	84E	84E	85A	-	06/65	8435	04/53	-	81E	81E	-	-	02/62
8416	03/50	88B	88B	87B	-	-	10/62	8436	05/53	-	86H	86H	81A	-	06/65
8417	03/50	84B	84E	84E	-	-	03/59	8437	05/53	-	84F	88C	86F	-	11/64
8418	03/50	87B	87B	87B	87A	-	08/64	8438	06/53	-	84F	88A	-	-	10/62
8419	04/50	84F	84F	88A	-	-	01/60	8439	06/53	-	86H	86C	-	-	10/62

No.	1948	1952	1955	1959	1963	1965	w/dwn
8440	03/54	-	86A	86A	-	-	07/62
8441	04/54	-	88B	86C	-	-	12/61
8442	03/54	-	87A	87A	-	-	06/59
8443	03/54	-	87D	87D	-	-	06/59
8444	04/54	-	86J	86J	86F	-	07/63
8445	06/54	-	86J	86J	-	-	09/62
8446	06/54	-	86F	88C	88C	-	09/64
8447	06/54	-	86C	86C	-	-	06/59
8448	06/54	-	86F	86F	-	-	08/59
8449	06/54	-	84B	84G	-	-	09/62
8450	08/49	86E	86E	88C	-	-	06/59
8451	09/49	88C	83A	82B	-	-	11/61
8452	10/49	84C	84C	84C	88L	-	04/64
8453	11/49	86A	86A	86A	-	-	10/62
8454	12/49	87B	87B	87B	-	-	01/61
8455	01/50	88B	88C	88A	-	-	01/60
8456	02/50	83C	83C	83C	81C	-	10/63
8457	03/50	88B	88B	86C	-	-	01/61
8458	04/50	88C	85A	81E	81A	-	08/63
8459	05/50	84C	84C	88C	81A	-	06/65
8460	06/50	88C	88F	88A	-	-	01/61
8461	06/50	88C	82C	82C	86G	-	11/63
8462	07/50	84A	84A	84A	-	-	08/59
8463	09/50	84E	87E	87E	-	-	01/60
8464	10/50	88B	88B	86C	84B	-	12/63
8465	11/50	88C	88B	88C	81C	-	11/63
8466	11/50	87B	87B	83A	88B	-	07/64
8467	02/51	87F	87F	87F	-	-	02/62
8468	02/51	84E	84E	84E	-	-	05/60
8469	03/51	88B	88B	88A	88B	-	11/62

No.	1948	1952	1955	1959	1963	1965	w/dwn
8470	05/51	88C	88A	88A	-	-	01/62
8471	05/51	88A	88A	88A	88L	-	06/65
8472	07/51	82C	82C	82C	81A	-	03/63
8473	08/51	83A	83G	83G	-	-	01/61
8474	10/51	87F	87F	87F	87F	-	05/65
8475	11/51	87C	87C	87D	87D	-	09/62
8476	03/52	-	87C	87D	-	-	01/61
8477	03/52	-	87F	87F	-	-	07/62
8478	05/52	-	88A	88A	-	-	01/63
8479	06/52	-	82D	82B	88B	-	10/64
8480	03/52	-	85A	85A	87A	-	07/64
8481	03/52	-	88A	88A	81A	-	06/65
8482	04/52	-	88A	82D	-	-	09/62
8483	05/52	-	87C	87D	-	-	02/62
8484	05/52	-	88A	86C	88L	-	06/65
8485	06/52	-	83F	83F	-	-	06/59
8486	06/52	-	83F	83F	81B	-	06/65
8487	07/52	-	85B	85B	-	-	11/63
8488	07/52	-	85B	85B	87D	-	05/65
8489	07/52	-	88A	86H	-	-	02/62
8490	07/52	-	87B	87B	-	-	10/62
8491	08/52	-	82B	82B	85B	-	07/63
8492	08/52	-	82B	82B	-	-	06/59
8493	09/52	-	86H	86A	86G	-	11/64
8494	09/52	-	86H	86H	-	-	01/62
8495	10/52	-	88A	86A	86G	-	11/64
8496	10/52	-	85A	85A	81D	-	07/63
8497	11/52	-	86F	86F	88B	-	07/64
8498	11/52	-	86F	86F	84A	-	06/65
8499	11/52	-	86A	86A	-	-	06/62

Continued with Number 9400

57xx

Continued from Number 7799.

0-6-0PT

No.	1948	1952	1955	1959	1963	1965	w/dwn
8700	TYS	84E	84E	84E	-	-	02/62
8701	GLO	85B	85C	85C	85B	-	03/63
8702	SPM	82B	82B	83E	86A	-	05/64
8703	SPM	82B	82B	-	-	-	01/58
8704	STB	84F	84F	84F	-	-	02/60
8705	SRD	84A	84A	86H	-	-	04/61
8706	LLY	87F	87K	87K	-	-	07/61
8707	PDN	81A	81A	86G	86G	-	07/64
8708	LLY	87F	87F	87F	-	-	05/60
8709	LA	83D	83D	6E	-	-	09/62
8710	NPT	86A	86A	86A	88H	-	03/63
8711	NPT	86A	86A	86A	-	-	03/62
8712	TDU	86F	86F	86F	-	-	01/63
8713	SPM	82B	82B	84E	-	-	03/62
8714	SPM	82B	82B	82B	87D	-	11/64
8715	NEA	87A	87A	87A	-	-	04/62
8716	PPRD	86G	86G	86G	86G	-	04/64
8717	GLO	85B	85B	85B	88E	-	07/64
8718	KDR	85D	85D	85D	84G	2C	07/66
8719	LA	83D	83D	83B	-	-	05/62
8720	DG	87C	87C	87C	81E	81E	09/64
8721	TDU	86F	86F	86F	-	-	07/61
8722	SPM	81B	88B	85C	-	-	04/61

No.	1948	1952	1955	1959	1963	1965	w/dwn
8723	ABEEG	86C	86C	86C	88D	-	07/64
8724	ABEEG	86H	87C	87C	-	-	07/62
8725	BHD	6C	6C	84E	-	-	10/62
8726	SRD	84A	84A	84A	-	-	04/61
8727	KDR	85D	85D	84J	-	-	04/62
8728	CDF	86C	86C	86C	88L	-	07/63
8729	BAN	84K	84K	6E	-	-	12/62
8730	SPM	82B	82B	6E	-	-	07/62
8731	GLO	85C	85D	85B	-	-	07/62
8732	LLY	87F	87F	87A	87A	-	04/64
8733	SDN	83E	83E	83E	-	-	02/62
8734	SRD	84A	84A	84K	-	-	03/62
8735	PDN	88C	88C	88C	-	-	01/62
8736	MTHR	88D	88D	88D	-	-	03/62
8737	SPM	82B	82B	83A	-	-	12/62
8738	PDN	87F	87H	87H	87H	-	03/63
8739	ABEEG	86D	86D	87H	87H	-	11/64
8740	CDF	86F	86F	86F	-	-	02/61
8741	SPM	82B	82B	82A	-	-	05/62
8742	STB	84F	84F	84F	-	-	09/62
8743	CED	88B	88B	85C	85B	-	06/64
8744	WES	82D	82D	82D	-	-	10/62
8745	WES	82E	82E	71H	72C	-	08/65

'Castle' Class 4-6-0 No. 7007 'Great Western' at Shrewsbury with the CAMBRIAN COAST EXPRESS.

No.	1948	1952	1955	1959	1963	1965	w/dwn	No.	1948	1952	1955	1959	1963	1965	w/dwn
8746	SPM	82B	82B	82B	-	-	12/62	8773	PDN	81A	81A	81A	-	-	10/62
8747	SPM	82B	82B	82B	87A	-	05/64	8774	SHL	81C	81C	81C	-	-	08/61
8748	TDU	86F	86F	86F	-	-	09/62	8775	NEA	87A	87A	87A	-	-	12/61
8749	LLY	87F	87F	87F	87F	-	10/64	8776	ABEEG	86C	86C	86C	-	-	12/62
8750	PDN	81A	81C	81C	-	-	05/62	8777	TDU	86F	86G	87G	-	-	04/61
8751	PDN	81A	81A	81A	-	-	12/60	8778	NPT	86A	86A	86H	-	-	08/60
8752	SHL	81C	81C	81C	-	-	01/63	8779	SDN	82C	82C	82C	-	-	02/62
8753	SHL	81A	81C	81A	-	-	02/62	8780	PDN	88A	88A	88A	-	-	07/62
8754	PDN	81A	81A	81A	-	-	11/60	8781	GLO	85B	85B	85C	-	-	12/62
8755	PPRD	86G	86G	-	-	-	12/57	8782	NEA	87A	87A	87A	-	-	11/61
8756	PDN	81A	81A	81A	-	-	10/62	8783	SBZ	82C	82C	82C	87F	-	06/63
8757	PDN	81A	81A	81A	-	-	09/62	8784	TYS	87A	87A	87A	-	-	04/62
8758	SHL	81C	81C	81C	-	-	01/59	8785	LLY	87F	87F	87F	87F	-	12/63
8759	PDN	81A	81A	81A	-	-	01/63	8786	NPT	86G	86H	86H	86F	-	07/63
8760	PDN	81A	81A	81A	-	-	01/62	8787	BAN	84C	84C	85C	-	-	08/61
8761	PDN	81A	81A	81A	-	-	05/62	8788	PPRD	86G	86G	87E	-	-	05/62
8762	PDN	81A	81A	81A	-	-	08/61	8789	LDR	87E	87E	87E	-	-	06/61
8763	PDN	81A	81A	81A	-	-	08/62	8790	SPM	82B	82B	82B	-	-	05/62
8764	SHL	81A	81A	81A	-	-	05/62	8791	STB	84F	84F	84J	87A	-	03/63
8765	PDN	81A	81A	81A	-	-	09/62	8792	STB	84F	84F	84F	-	-	02/62
8766	SPM	82B	86A	86A	86A	-	07/63	8793	SPM	82C	82C	82C	85A	-	12/64
8767	PDN	81A	81A	81A	81A	2B	07/66	8794	ABEEG	86H	86A	87E	87D	-	07/63
8768	PDN	81A	81A	81A	81A	-	09/64	8795	SPM	82B	82B	82B	82E	-	07/65
8769	PDN	81A	81A	81A	-	-	04/61	8796	NPT	86B	86B	84A	-	-	04/61
8770	PDN	81A	81A	81A	-	-	12/62	8797	STB	84F	84F	84F	-	-	04/62
8771	PDN	81A	81A	81A	-	-	07/62	8798	OXY	84B	84A	84A	-	-	06/61
8772	PDN	81A	81A	81A	-	-	08/61	8799	STJ	86E	86E	71G	-	-	11/62

Continued with Number 9600

90xx   Collett 'Dukedog'   4-4-0

Introduced by Collett in 1936, these locomotives were a combination of 'Duke' class boilers and 'Bulldog' frames, being designed for use on secondary lines.

Loco Weight : 49t 00c   *Driving Wheels :* 5' 8"   *Cylinders :* (I) 18" x 26"   *Valve Gear :* Stephenson (Slide Valves)

No.	1948	1952	1955	1959	1963	1965	w/dwn	No.	1948	1952	1955	1959	1963	1965	w/dwn
9000	MCH	89C	89C	-	-	-	03/55	9015	DID	81E	81F	89C	-	-	06/60
9001	OSW	89A	-	-	-	-	04/54	9016	OSW	89A	89C	-	-	-	07/57
9002	ABH	89C	-	-	-	-	05/54	9017	ABH	89C	89C	89C	-	-	10/60
9003	OSW	89A	89C	-	-	-	10/55	9018	SDN	82C	89C	84J	-	-	06/60
9004	MCH	89C	89C	84J	-	-	06/60	9019	TYS	-	-	-	-	-	11/48
9005	MCH	89C	89C	89A	-	-	07/59	9020	OSW	89A	89C	-	-	-	07/57
9006	DID	84E	-	-	-	-	08/48	9021	ABH	89C	89C	89C	-	-	12/57
9007	TYS	-	-	-	-	-	07/48	9022	OSW	89A	89C	-	-	-	08/57
9008	TYS	89A	89C	-	-	-	07/57	9023	SDN	82C	82C	-	-	-	07/57
9009	MCH	89C	89C	-	-	-	07/57	9024	SALOP	89C	89C	-	-	-	08/57
9010	TYS	89A	89A	-	-	-	07/57	9025	ABH	89C	89C	-	-	-	08/57
9011	SDN	82C	82C	-	-	-	07/57	9026	OSW	89C	89A	-	-	-	08/57
9012	MCH	89C	89C	-	-	-	07/57	9027	MCH	89C	89C	-	-	-	08/57
9013	ABH	89C	89C	89C	-	-	12/58	9028	OSW	89C	84J	-	-	-	08/57
9014	MCH	89C	89C	84J	-	-	10/60								

TOTAL 29

3252   Dean 'Duke'   4-4-0

Dean design from 1895, these locos were previously numbered, until 1946, from 3254 to 3291 in order. The survivors were long lived but anachronistic looking, as were the 'Dukedogs' (see above).

Loco Weight : 47t 6c   *Driving Wheels :* 5' 8"   *Cylinders :* (I) 18" x 26"   *Valve Gear :* Stephenson (Slide Valves)

Number & Name		_1948_	_1952_	_1955_	_1959_	_1963_	_1965_	_w/dwn_	_Notes_
9054	Cornubia	MCH	-	-	-	-	-	06/50	
9064	Trevithick	GLO	-	-	-	-	-	12/49	
9065	Tre Pol and Pen	OSW	-	-	-	-	-	12/49	
9072		MCH	-	-	-	-	-	06/49	
9073	Mounts Bay	SALOP	-	-	-	-	-	12/49	
9076		SALOP	-	-	-	-	-	11/49	
9083	Comet	DID	-	-	-	-	-	12/50	
9084	Isle of Jersey	STB	-	-	-	-	-	04/51	
9087	Mercury	ABH	-	-	-	-	-	07/49	
9089		GLO	-	-	-	-	-	07/51	
9091	Thames	MCH	-	-	-	-	-	02/49	

TOTAL 11

43xx   2-6-0

Continued from Number 7341.

9300 - 9319   _For details see No. 7322 - 7341_

TOTAL 241

94xx   0-6-0PT

Continued from Number 8499.

No.	_1948_	_1952_	_1955_	_1959_	_1963_	_1965_	_w/dwn_	No.	_1948_	_1952_	_1955_	_1959_	_1963_	_1965_	_w/dwn_
9400	SDN	82C	82C	81A	-	-	12/59	9436	01/51	87A	87A	87E	-	-	07/60
9401	PDN	81D	81D	85A	85D	-	07/63	9437	01/51	87B	87B	86C	88L	-	06/65
9402	PDN	81D	81D	81D	-		08/59	9438	02/51	84C	85B	85B	-	-	06/59
9403	PDN	81F	81F	81F	-	-	06/59	9439	02/51	83C	83C	83C	-	-	06/59
9404	PDN	81D	81D	81D	81D	-	06/65	9440	02/51	83A	83A	83A	81A	-	07/63
9405	PDN	81D	81D	81C	81A	-	06/65	9441	03/51	85B	85B	85B	87D	-	11/63
9406	PDN	81B	81B	81B	81B	-	09/64	9442	03/51	87A	87A	87B	87A	-	07/64
9407	PDN	81C	81C	81E	-	-	07/62	9443	03/51	87F	87F	86C	-	-	06/59
9408	OXY	84B	84B	84B	87F	-	05/63	9444	04/51	87B	87B	87B	86F	-	03/63
9409	PDN	81C	81C	81C	-	-	05/62	9445	04/51	85B	85B	85B	-	-	01/60
9410	02/50	81A	81A	81A	-	-	07/62	9446	05/51	87A	87A	87A	87A	-	05/65
9411	02/50	81A	81A	81A	81A	-	06/65	9447	05/51	87B	87B	87B	-	-	01/61
9412	03/50	81A	81A	81A	87A	-	03/63	9448	05/51	87A	87A	87A	-	-	07/62
9413	03/50	81E	81E	81C	81C	-	11/63	9449	06/51	84C	84C	84C	-	-	06/60
9414	04/50	81A	81A	81A	-	-	08/60	9450	06/51	84F	86H	81F	81D	-	06/64
9415	05/50	81B	81B	81B	81C	-	06/65	9451	07/51	87A	87A	86F	-	-	07/62
9416	05/50	81F	81F	81A	-	-	01/62	9452	07/51	87H	87A	87A	87A	-	05/65
9417	05/50	81E	81E	81C	-	-	06/59	9453	07/51	82B	82B	88C	85B	-	11/64
9418	05/50	81A	81A	81A	81A	-	06/65	9454	09/51	87B	87B	87B	-	-	01/62
9419	06/50	81A	81A	81A	81A	-	03/63	9455	09/51	87B	87B	85A	81A	-	04/63
9420	06/50	81A	81A	81A	81A	-	03/64	9456	09/51	87B	87B	87B	87B	-	04/64
9421	07/50	81B	81B	81B	-	-	02/62	9457	10/51	87C	87B	87B	87B	-	07/64
9422	07/50	81A	81A	81A	81B	-	12/63	9458	10/51	86A	86A	86H	-	-	01/61
9423	07/50	81A	81A	81A	81A	-	02/63	9459	11/51	86H	86C	86H	-	-	09/59
9424	08/50	81B	81B	81B	-	-	12/62	9460	11/51	86H	86H	86H	-	-	02/62
9425	09/50	84C	84C	88A	88C	-	11/63	9461	12/51	87B	86C	86C	88L	-	05/65
9426	09/50	84C	84C	86C	88L	-	05/65	9462	12/51	83A	83A	83A	-	-	11/60
9427	09/50	84F	86H	86A	-	-	06/59	9463	01/52	83G	83G	83G	89A	-	06/65
9428	09/50	84A	84A	84A	-	-	06/60	9464	01/52	85B	85B	85B	87B	-	06/65
9429	10/50	85A	85A	85A	87F	-	12/63	9465	01/52	87F	87F	87F	-	-	02/62
9430	10/50	87A	87A	87A	85D	-	06/65	9466	02/52	85A	85A	85A	88H	-	07/64
9431	11/50	87B	87B	87B	87D	-	04/64	9467	02/52	83D	83D	83D	-	-	05/62
9432	11/50	84E	84E	84E	-	-	11/59	9468	02/52	87F	87F	86A	-	-	08/60
9433	12/50	83D	83D	83D	-	-	07/62	9469	03/52	87F	87F	81C	-	-	03/62
9434	01/51	83F	83F	83F	-	-	06/60	9470	03/52	88A	88C	84G	84A	-	09/64
9435	01/51	84A	84A	84A	84A	-	09/64	9471	04/52	85B	85B	85B	85B	-	09/64

No.	1948	1952	1955	1959	1963	1965	w/dwn	No.	1948	1952	1955	1959	1963	1965	w/dwn
9472	04/52	87F	87F	84G	88B	-	05/65	9486	11/52	-	87F	85A	-	-	07/62
9473	05/52	87A	87A	87A	87A	-	07/64	9487	11/52	-	87B	83A	-	-	07/62
9474	05/52	87F	87F	83C	-	-	11/61	9488	12/52	-	82B	82A	86A	-	04/65
9475	06/52	85B	85A	85B	87B	-	05/65	9489	01/53	-	87D	87D	87D	-	04/64
9476	06/52	82C	82C	82C	-	-	06/62	9490	02/54	-	86A	86A	85A	-	12/64
9477	07/52	84F	84F	86C	81A	-	06/65	9491	03/54	-	87C	87D	-	-	06/59
9478	07/52	87A	87A	87A	-	-	07/62	9492	05/54	-	87F	85B	-	-	06/65
9479	07/52	87F	87F	81C	81A	-	07/63	9493	06/54	-	86C	86C	85D	-	09/64
9480	08/52	-	85A	85A	88B	-	04/65	9494	08/54	-	88B	86C	86F	-	11/64
9481	08/52	-	82B	82A	-	-	01/61	9495	10/54	-	82B	82B	81A	-	06/65
9482	09/52	-	86A	86A	86F	-	11/63	9496	10/54	-	84A	84A	-	-	12/59
9483	10/52	-	87B	87B	87B	-	07/63	9497	12/54	-	83C	83C	-	-	05/62
9484	10/52	-	87E	87E	87D	-	04/64	9498	03/55	-	-	84G	89A	-	09/64
9485	10/52	-	87C	87D	87F	-	07/64	9499	07/55	-	-	82B	-	-	09/59

9499 was the shortest lived GWR designed loco, surviving only 4 yrs & 2 months   TOTAL 210

57xx   0-6-0PT

Continued from Number 8799.

No.	1948	1952	1955	1959	1963	1965	w/dwn	No.	1948	1952	1955	1959	1963	1965	w/dwn
9600	SDN	82C	82C	82C	88J	-	09/65	9639	WLN	84H	84H	84H	84H	-	09/65
9601	YEO	82E	82E	82B	82B	-	12/64	9640	SLO	81F	81F	81F	81A	2B	07/66
9602	FGD	87J	87J	87J	87J	-	03/65	9641	SHL	81C	81C	81C	81C	2C	10/66
9603	FGD	87J	86C	86C	88L	-	12/63	9642	WEY	82F	82F	82B	81C	-	11/64
9604	SPM	82A	82A	82C	-	-	12/62	9643	MTHR	88D	88D	88D	-	-	05/62
9605	SPM	82B	82B	82C	82C	-	09/65	9644	NPT	86A	86A	86A	86A	-	06/65
9606	SPM	82B	87C	87G	87G	-	11/64	9645	SED	87D	87D	87C	87J	-	10/63
9607	ABDR	86J	86J	86J	88J	-	04/64	9646	EXE	83B	83B	83B	84F	-	05/65
9608	TYS	84E	84E	83B	89B	2C	07/66	9647	EXE	83B	83B	83B	83B	-	06/65
9609	ABDR	86J	86J	86F	88H	-	10/65	9648	CDF	86C	86C	86C	88L	-	07/64
9610	TYS	84E	82A	84K	89B	6C	09/66	9649	TDU	86F	86F	86F	88H	-	07/65
9611	OXF	81F	81F	81F	88E	-	04/65	9650	PPRD	86G	86G	86G	86G	-	12/64
9612	WES	82D	82D	82D	82D	-	12/63	9651	BHD	6C	6C	6C	88L	-	07/65
9613	STB	84F	84F	84F	84F	-	10/65	9652	NEY	87H	87H	87H	-	-	01/63
9614	BCN	84E	84E	84E	84F	2C	07/66	9653	SLO	81B	81F	81F	81F	-	07/65
9615	WES	82D	82D	82D	87B	-	07/65	9654	OXF	81F	81F	81F	81F	-	10/64
9616	LTS	86A	86A	86A	86A	-	08/65	9655	SBZ	83E	83E	83E	86G	-	05/64
9617	DYD	87B	87B	87B	87B	-	06/65	9656	CNYD	84G	84G	84G	87B	-	11/65
9618	MTHR	88D	88D	88D	88D	-	12/63	9657	SALOP	84G	84G	84G	89A	6D	04/66
9619	HFD	85C	85C	86E	86E	-	07/65	9658	PDN	81A	81A	81A	81A	2B	10/66
9620	SPM	82F	82F	71G	71G	-	07/64	9659	PDN	81A	81A	81A	81A	-	06/65
9621	SRD	84A	84A	84A	87F	-	10/64	9660	TDU	86F	86F	86F	88H	-	11/64
9622	MTHR	88D	88D	88C	88E	-	07/65	9661	PDN	81A	81A	81A	81A	-	11/64
9623	NA	83A	83A	82A	82E	-	07/65	9662	04/48	86A	86A	86A	86A	-	09/65
9624	WLN	84H	84H	84F	84F	-	01/65	9663	04/48	83B	83B	83B	83B	-	09/64
9625	SED	87D	87D	87D	87A	-	06/65	9664	04/48	86A	86A	86A	86B	-	05/64
9626	SPM	82B	82B	82A	82E	85A	12/65	9665	04/48	82B	85C	85C	-	-	02/63
9627	NEA	87A	87A	87A	-	-	07/62	9666	04/48	87A	87G	87J	87J	-	09/65
9628	WES	82D	82D	82D	82D	-	03/63	9667	05/48	86A	86A	86A	86A	-	05/65
9629	CDF	86C	83C	83C	88L	-	10/64	9668	05/48	83A	83A	82D	88E	-	12/63
9630	WLN	84H	84H	84H	84H	6C	09/66	9669	05/48	84J	84J	84J	89B	6C	01/66
9631	BRY	88C	88C	88D	88D	-	06/65	9670	05/48	83B	83B	83B	83B	-	06/65
9632	NPT	86A	86A	71H	87G	-	11/64	9671	06/48	83D	83D	83B	88J	-	03/65
9633	NA	83A	83A	83A	87B	-	10/63	9672	06/48	84G	84G	82C	82C	82E	12/65
9634	DYD	87B	87B	87B	87B	-	05/64	9673	02/49	83E	83E	83E	-	-	05/60
9635	TYS	84E	84E	84E	83C	-	06/64	9674	03/49	86F	86A	86A	87D	-	04/64
9636	STB	84F	84F	84F	84H	-	10/63	9675	03/49	88D	88D	88D	88D	-	10/65
9637	NPT	86A	86A	87E	87F	-	09/64	9676	03/49	88C	88C	88C	88D	-	06/65
9638	MTHR	88D	88D	88D	88D	-	12/63	9677	03/49	88B	88B	87J	87J	-	11/64

No.	1948	1952	1955	1959	1963	1965	w/dwn
9678	04/49	6C	83A	83A	88H	-	06/65
9679	04/49	88B	88B	88A	88D	-	11/64
9680	04/49	84E	84E	84E	82C	82E	12/65
9681	05/49	86F	86F	89A	88L	-	08/65
9682	05/49	84E	84E	84E	86F	-	08/65
9700	PDN	81A	81A	81A	81A	-	10/63
9701	PDN	81A	81A	81A	-	-	01/61
9702	PDN	81A	81A	81A	-	-	05/62
9703	PDN	81A	81A	81A	-	-	12/61
9704	PDN	81A	81A	81A	81A	-	11/63
9705	PDN	81A	81A	81A	-	-	10/61
9706	PDN	81A	81A	81A	81A	-	11/64
9707	PDN	81A	81A	81A	81A	-	09/64
9708	PDN	81A	81A	81A	-	-	01/59
9709	PDN	81A	81A	81A	-	-	05/62
9710	PDN	81A	81A	81A	81A	-	10/64
9711	LA	83D	83D	83D	88J	-	07/65
9712	ABDR	86J	86J	86J	-	-	09/62
9713	CDF	86C	86C	86C	88L	-	07/63
9714	OXY	84B	87H	87H	-	-	11/61
9715	OXY	84B	84B	87E	87B	-	07/63
9716	LA	83D	83D	83D	87A	-	06/65
9717	NA	83G	85C	85C	-	-	12/62
9718	TN	83B	83B	83B	-	-	05/62
9719	SALOP	84G	84F	84F	-	-	07/62
9720	SDN	82C	82C	82C	-	-	11/61
9721	SDN	82C	82C	82C	-	-	06/62
9722	RDG	81D	81B	81B	-	-	07/62
9723	ABEEG	86C	86C	86C	-	-	07/62
9724	TYS	84E	84E	84E	84H	2C	01/66
9725	PDN	81A	81A	81A	-	-	12/62
9726	PDN	81C	81C	81C	81C	-	06/65
9727	GLO	85B	85B	84E	-	-	12/62
9728	CHR	84K	84K	6E	-	-	05/62
9729	SPM	82B	82B	82A	82B	-	10/64
9730	OXY	84B	86G	86G	86G	-	05/64
9731	NPT	86A	86J	86J	88J	-	05/63
9732	SPM	83E	82E	71H	72C	-	04/64
9733	TYS	84E	84E	84E	84F	-	09/65
9734	NEA	87A	87A	87A	87A	-	07/64
9735	DYD	87B	87B	87B	-	-	03/61
9736	DYD	87B	87B	87B	-	-	06/61
9737	DYD	87B	87B	87B	-	-	12/60
9738	LDR	87E	87E	87E	-	-	01/62
9739	OXY	84B	84B	84B	-	-	07/61
9740	LMTN	84G	84G	82C	-	-	02/62
9741	STB	84F	84H	84H	-	-	08/62
9742	OXY	84H	84H	87B	87B	-	09/64
9743	LLY	87F	87F	87F	87A	-	05/64
9744	SED	87D	87D	87C	-	-	01/63
9745	STJ	86E	86E	86E	-	-	06/61
9746	LTS	86D	86A	86A	87D	-	04/64
9747	OXY	84B	88D	88D	-	-	01/63

No.	1948	1952	1955	1959	1963	1965	w/dwn
9748	TYS	84E	83G	83G	87A	-	01/64
9749	RDG	81D	81D	81D	-	-	11/60
9750	NEA	87A	87A	87A	-	-	05/62
9751	PDN	81A	81A	81A	-	-	06/61
9752	OXY	84B	84B	84B	87D	-	12/63
9753	TYS	84E	84E	84E	84E	-	05/65
9754	PDN	81A	81A	81A	82D	-	06/65
9755	SHL	83E	83E	83E	81A	-	05/63
9756	NEA	87A	87A	87A	-	-	09/62
9757	TN	83B	83B	83B	-	-	08/62
9758	PDN	81A	81A	81A	-	-	05/62
9759	CDF	86C	86C	86C	-	-	10/62
9760	FGD	87J	87J	87J	87J	-	12/63
9761	LDR	87B	87E	87A	-	-	10/62
9762	WES	82D	82D	82D	-	-	05/61
9763	RDG	81D	81D	81D	81D	-	09/63
9764	SPM	82E	82E	71H	72C	-	08/63
9765	LA	83D	83C	83C	-	-	12/61
9766	DYD	87B	87B	87B	87B	-	07/64
9767	STB	84F	84F	84F	-	-	06/61
9768	OXY	84B	84B	84B	84B	-	12/64
9769	OXY	84B	88B	82B	82D	-	03/63
9770	LA	83D	83D	82D	70A	-	12/63
9771	YEO	82B	82B	82A	-	-	05/61
9772	SDN	82C	82C	82C	-	-	01/59
9773	SDN	82C	82C	82C	82C	81F	12/65
9774	CHR	84K	84H	84H	84H	2A	11/66
9775	LDR	87E	87E	87E	-	-	12/62
9776	GLO	88B	88B	88E	88D	2B	04/66
9777	LDR	87E	87E	87E	87A	-	05/64
9778	CDF	83A	86C	86C	88G	-	11/64
9779	NEA	87A	87A	87A	87A	-	02/64
9780	LTS	86D	86D	86D	88H	-	07/65
9781	SLO	81B	81B	81B	-	-	05/61
9782	BAN	84F	84F	84F	84F	-	11/64
9783	NEA	87A	87A	87A	-	-	05/62
9784	PDN	81A	81A	81A	81A	-	05/63
9785	DYD	87B	87B	87B	-	-	09/62
9786	NEA	87A	87A	87A	87A	-	05/64
9787	LLY	87F	87F	87G	87G	-	09/64
9788	LLY	87F	87F	87F	87B	-	04/64
9789	SLO	81B	81B	81C	81D	81F	12/65
9790	SDN	82C	82C	82C	82C	-	09/65
9791	RDG	81D	81D	81D	81E	-	01/64
9792	NEA	87A	87A	87A	87A	-	04/64
9793	TYS	84J	84J	84J	89B	-	08/63
9794	CHR	84K	84K	6E	88L	-	09/64
9795	SDN	82C	82C	82C	-	-	11/60
9796	CDF	86H	86G	86G	86G	-	02/65
9797	PPRD	86G	86G	86G	-	-	09/62
9798	TYS	84A	84E	84E	85B	-	10/64
9799	DYD	87B	87B	87B	87B	-	10/63

TOTAL 863

LONDON TRANSPORT   0-6-0PT

57xx Pannier Tanks purchased from British Railways between 1959 and 19xx. All were repainted into L.T. lined maroon livery; some were the last _working_ standard gauge steam locos to run regularly on B.R. lines

L.T. No.	B.R. No.	Date to L.T.	Withdrawn	L.T. No.	B.R. No.	Date to L.T.	Withdrawn
L89	5775	08/63	01/70	L94	7752	12/59	06/71
L90 (i)	7711	01/57	09/61	L95	5764	05/60	06/71
L90 (ii)	7760	01/62	06/71	L96	7741	01/62	12/66
L91 (i)	5752	03/57	11/60	L97	7749	12/62	09/68
L91 (ii)	5757	12/60	12/67	L98	7739	12/62	11/68
L92	5786	04/58	09/69	L99	7715	06/63	12/69
L93	7779	10/58	12/67				

TOTAL 13

Ex G.W.R. / B.R. (W.R.) Locos sold into Industrial Service

Class	Wheels	B.R. No.	Sold	New Owner	No.	W/dwn	Notes
TV 'H'	0-6-0T	193	02/52	N.C.B. Caerphilly Tar Plant	193	01/60	
TV 'H'	0-6-0T	195	11/51	N.C.B. Treorchy	195	04/57	
P & M	0-4-0ST	1151	08/63	R.S. Hayes, Bridgend	1151	04/65	
15xx	0-6-0PT	1501	01/61	N.C.B. Coventry Colliery	1501	-	Preserved
15xx	0-6-0PT	1502	01/61	N.C.B. Coventry Colliery	1502	10/70	
15xx	0-6-0PT	1509	08/59	N.C.B. Coventry Colliery	1509	10/70	
16xx	0-6-0PT	1600	03/59	N.C.B. Risca	1600	12/63	
16xx	0-6-0PT	1607	08/65	N.C.B. Cynheidre	1607	09/69	
2021	0-6-0PT	2034	08/55	N.C.B. Hafodyrynys	2034	03/64	
2021	0-6-0PT	2053	04/54	National Smelting, Avonmouth	2053	03/61	
2021	0-6-0PT	2092	08/55	N.C.B. Bargoed	2092	09/64	
2721	0-6-0PT	2794	11/49	Lilleshall Co. Ltd.	12	09/58	
57xx	0-6-0PT	3650	09/63	P.D. Fuels, Gwaum-Cae-Gurwen	3650	-	Preserved
57xx	0-6-0PT	3663	12/62	N.C.B. Nine Mile Point	3663	c. 1970	
57xx	0-6-0PT	7714	01/59	N.C.B. Penallta	7714	-	Preserved
57xx	0-6-0PT	7754	01/59	N.C.B. Mountain Ash	7754	-	Preserved
57xx	0-6-0PT	9424	12/62	A.R. Adams Ltd.	Robert	c. 1966	
57xx	0-6-0PT	9600	09/65	N.C.B. Merthyr Vale	9600	-	Preserved
57xx	0-6-0PT	9642	11/64	R.S. Hayes, Bridgend	9642	-	Preserved
57xx	0-6-0PT	9792	04/64	N.C.B. Maerdy	9792	04/73	

TOTAL 20

Tailpiece

Western Region Autotrain being propelled by Collett 0-4-2T No. 1401

Photo courtesy Steve Davies